Post-Modern Design

RICK WRIGLEY, *CLASSICAL CABINET* FOR FORMICA COLORCORE

00013307

MICHAEL GRAVES, ARMCHAIRS, 1979-81 FOR SUNAR

THOMAS HALL BEEBY, FORMICA SHOWROOM, 1984

TAKEFUMI AIDA, RESTAURANT INTERIOR AND FURNITURE

TERRY FARRELL, LAMP FOR TV-AM

CHARLES JENCKS, *ACADEMY-LIGHT*, 1986 FOR ACADEMY EDITIONS

Post-Modern Design

MICHAEL COLLINS & ANDREAS PAPADAKIS

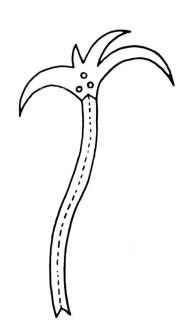

RIZZOLI
NEW YORK

DEDICATED
WITH LOVE
TO BERNARD AND HEDWIG COLLINS

ACKNOWLEDGEMENTS

I should like to thank first and foremost Andreas Papadakis of Academy Editions for his enthusiasm at all times for this book. My appreciation also goes to Charles Jencks for his assistance and encouragement. At Academy Editions my warmest thanks go to Vivian Constantinopoulos, Frank Russell and Stuart Keene. They have been attentive and helpful throughout the editing, preparation and design of this book. In addition to those who very generously provided photographs and whose names will be found in the Photographic Acknowledgements, I wish to express my sincere thanks to all the architects, designers and firms who furnished information and statements regarding their work. Finally, I should like to thank all my students, past and present, for their interest in the subject of Post-Modernism. *Michael Collins*

Jacket front: Michael Graves, kettle with little bird-shaped whistle, 1985 for Alessi. *Jacket back*: Aldo Rossi, tea and coffee pots, 1979-83 for Alessi. *Front flap*: Ettore Sottsass, *Lidia* vase, 1986 for Memphis (detail).

First published in the United States of America in 1989 by
RIZZOLI INTERNATIONAL PUBLICATIONS, INC
300 Park Avenue South, New York, NY 10010

Published in Great Britain in 1989 by
ACADEMY EDITIONS
an imprint of the Academy Group Ltd, 7 Holland Street, London W8 4NA

ISBN 0-8478-1136-0
LC 89-61361

Printed and Bound in Hong Kong

Contents

Introduction 11

CHAPTER I
The Origins of Post-Modernism 15

CHAPTER II
Post-Pop Design 27

CHAPTER III
Post-Modernism 65

CHAPTER IV
Post-Modern Design in America: Robert Venturi 103

CHAPTER V
Charles Jencks Michael Graves Robert Stern
Charles Moore Stanley Tigerman 123
Symbolic Objects by Charles Jencks 139

CHAPTER VI
Deconstruction, Deconstructivism & Late-Modernism 179

CHAPTER VII
Paolo Portoghesi & Aldo Rossi 197
The Sympathy of Things by Paolo Portoghesi 205

CHAPTER VIII
Arata Isozaki & Hans Hollein 221

CHAPTER IX
Secondary Post-Modern Design 241

Conclusion 267

Post-Modernism and Consumer Design 269
by Volker Fischer

Notes 283

Photographic Acknowledgements 285

Selected Bibliography 286

Index 287

CHARLES JENCKS, TEAPOT, 1983 FOR ALESSI

Introduction

ARATA ISOZAKI, CARPET FOR VORWERK, 1988

The ecstasy of communication and choice. In Moscow, most of the few available cars are black. The West celebrates choice; it makes an orgy of over thirty varieties of Mini motor car, for example. And so too with recent design. Ecstasy . . . and orgy . . . the sexual revolution has inseminated design with its hypertrophied sensuality.

As I write this, SKY television has been introduced to Britain, thereby more than doubling the available channels. In the Soviet Union, the hard-won Communist revolution of 1917 is being restructured so that the average Muscovite will be able to buy (and sell) more goods, including cars which aren't necessarily black. Robert Venturi's statement of 1966 that 'I prefer both-and to either-or' is a highly-polished reflection of consumer demand as well as a comment on his own architectural practice.

Post-Modern design is, in part, a development of accelerated 'dynamic obsolescence', Harley Earl's formula for how to beat the competition and sell more. This is the economic imperative behind many Post-Modern objects and it can be traced right back to the mid-1920s when Henry 'you can have any colour so long as it is black' Ford was first outpaced by Earl and General Motors when they introduced colour and greater styling in their automobiles. In 1965, a scientist at Yale University estimated that General Motors easily made available more permutations of cars than there were atoms in the universe. New manufacturers need and encourage design and

style changes, economic 'health' requires it – getting and spending is still the greatest, if not the most defensible of Western drives.

The ecstasy of choice and communication. Language changes, metaphors die. Le Corbusier's ocean liners are no more, and no one could now dare to illustrate a bomber as a design source, as he did in *Towards a New Architecture* in the 1920s. In that and many other ways, 1945 taught us a lesson. So much was lost both in the war itself and in the rash of insensitive rebuilding that was its aftermath, that there arose the deep desire to recoup, repair and restore which has grown, rather than diminished, in the succeeding years. Today there is a longer sense of history. The artistic avant-garde marches no more, and there is instead in the best Post-Modern work, the revelation of a profound need to preserve and rediscover the richness and plenitude of the past. Some of the most rewarding Post-Modern design reinvents past typologies as well as embracing new directions such as Green Party issues, or the visual equivalent of the World Music craze. There are welcome signs that design is becoming less America- and Euro-centric and more international in its embrace of third and fourth worlds, the local and the regional. The International Modern style often spoke a visual form of Esperanto, with its white concrete and shiny tubular steel – a Western-based language, native to no one. The technological achievements of that Modernism still underwrite much in Post-Modern work, but they are turned to new ends such as the mimesis of historical ornament, often in an ironic manner. The objects themselves may be silent, yet they are not dumb – their embodied language is increasingly insistent. Some (Late-Modern and High-Tech) still quietly expound the reasoned language of the scientific text. Others (Neo-Modern) shout the slang of the Italian suburbs, and the lingua franca of television culture, or (Post-Modern) attempt to relearn Greek, Latin and the grammar of ornament. Many create neologisms and portmanteau words, or use oxymoron, irony and metaphor. As with everything daring, the occasional malapropism does appear.

Some recent designs are already academic, bred to the arid environment of the museum. For example, Alessi tea and coffee sets and a chair by Charles Jencks are in the Victoria & Albert Museum; Memphis work can be seen in the British Museum, Metropolitan Museum in New York, Kuntsmuseum in Düsseldorf, or the Musée des Arts Décoratifs in Paris. Inevitably, some recent design will not prove so enduring.

Despite the jargon prefix 'designer' (designer-jeans, clothes, cars) most of the artefacts in this book are in fact by architects. On one level, this is because the much-heralded 'death of the author' is not a commercial reality: quite the contrary. Design is often sold on the name of the author, and no one has a higher profile 'author-ity' than the architect. In addition, the tradition from Adam to Aalto that, in the words of Ernesto Rogers, 'the architect designs everything from the town to the spoon' could not be more sympathetic to expanding architectural practices.

The 'designer' of objects in this book is very often an architect who scales down or miniaturises what are basically architectural forms. There is also a welcome return to the tradition of Karl Friedrich Schinkel or Charles Rennie Mackintosh: the artist-architect whose draughtsmanship is equal to the quality of his architectural ideas.

The age of morality, from AWN Pugin to the Bauhaus, which has been read as a determinist drive towards 'form follows function' and 'good form' has been largely challenged, if not usurped by a new era of gorgeous Pluralism and liberated (or Liberal) Eclecticism. There is a new Free-Style, less restricted and inhibited than in any earlier age, able to range across the whole gamut of the by now widely published history of art, architecture and design.

The constrictive, Minimalist 'black box' of the 1960s surely begat a reaction favouring a less technocratic, more fine arts-based approach to final form and aesthetics. Ornament, recently released after its long incarceration in the jail partly created by Adolf Loos and Le Corbusier, is now out, painting the town red, orange, yellow, green, blue, indigo and violet. This bold, self-confident new epoch may have reached its zenith with these designs. As I write there are signs that the party is winding down and exuberant pluralism begins to be perceived more as disturbing fragmentation. However, Post-Modernism will have left its indelible mark: the house can never again be simply a machine for living in, nor the chair a mere machine for sitting in.   *Michael Collins*

MICHELE DE LUCCHI, *LIDO* SOFA, 1982 FOR MEMPHIS

RICHARD SAPPER, STAINLESS STEEL KETTLE WITH MELODIC WHISTLE, 1983 FOR ALESSI

MICHELE DE LUCCHI, *KIM* CHAIR, 1987 FOR MEMPHIS

CHAPTER I

The Origins of Post-Modernism

ALESSANDRO MENDINI, WATCHES, 1988 FOR TÜRLER OF ZURICH

The Death of Ornament and the Rebirth of Historicism

It is rather frightening to read the words of the new broom architects, Adolf Loos and Le Corbusier, who tried to sweep away ornament. In fact it all sounds rather middle class and literally white. Loos wrote in *Ornament and Crime* (1908) that 'some men and women are sad that we of today, unlike the black men and men of times gone by, are unable to make new ornament. Let them be comforted – that we are unable to make new ornament is a sign of the great qualities of our times – we have gone far past it'.[1] If Loos sees ornament as savage, primitive and, as in the title of his essay, criminal, Le Corbusier associated it with 'peasant art'. He wrote of it thus in *Vers une Architecture* (1923): 'tail pieces and garlands, exquisite ovals where triangular doves preen themselves or one another, boudoirs embellished with "poufs" in gold and black velvet, are now no more than the intolerable witnesses to a dead spirit. These sanctuaries stifling with elegancies, or on the other hand with the follies of "Peasant Art", are an offence'.[2]

Le Corbusier's style is that of the autodidact, assuming the authority of the lawyer, doctor and preacher. He diagnoses that 'if a house is white all over the shape of things stand out without any possible ambiguity . . . you might call it the X-ray of beauty, a permanent court of judgement, the eye of truth'.[3] He turns to legislator when writing in his *Decorative Art of Today* in 1925, 'imagine the effects of the Law of Ripolin. Every citizen is obliged to replace his hangings, his damask, his wallpapers, his stencils, with a pure layer of white Ripolin . . . You are bringing cleanliness to your own house . . . you clean inside yourself '.[4] Not content with his role of lawyer and doctor, in 1935 he takes up that of priest, writing that 'when the cathedrals were white . . . the new world was opening up like a flower among the ruins.' In fact, Le Corbusier was not averse to using paint and colour himself, for example inside the Villa Savoye, and perceptive observers in the midst of the Modern Movement caught on to the fact that he could also be a stylist. Alfred Barr, in his introduction to the *The International Style* by Henry-Russell Hitchcock and Philip Johnson (1931), noted that 'American architects . . . fail to realise that in spite of his slogan, the house as a *machine à habiter*, Le Corbusier is even more concerned with style than with convenient planning or plumbing, and that the most luxurious of modern German architects, Mies van der Rohe, has for over a year been the head of the Bauhaus, having supplanted Hannes Meyer, a fanatical functionalist. "Post-Functionalist" has even been suggested as a name for the new style'.[5] Barr's 'Post-Functional' could be read as seminal for 'Post-Modern' in the sense that he had already discerned a different, luxurious inflection within the Modern Movement. The trail was picked up again by later scholars, notably Reyner Banham, in his *Theory and Design in the First Machine Age* (1960). Writing about Mies van der Rohe's *Barcelona* chairs of 1929, Banham pointed out that 'the movable furniture, and particularly the massive steel-framed chairs flout, consciously one suspects, the canons of economy . . .; they are rhetorically over-size, immensely heavy, and do not use the material in such a way as to exact maximum performance from it'.[6] This is hardly surprising when one learns that they were a type of temporary throne to be used by the King of Spain for the purposes of the exhibition. Banham's point is valid – they are hardly, for example, comparable with the typology for a worker's chair suggested by some of Marcel Breuer's designs.

Banham's line was taken up again by Peter and Alison Smithson in 1965 in *The Heroic Period of Modern Architecture*. They lamented (*pace* Barr and Banham!) that 'no one has properly observed a quite definite special sub-category of modern architecture. An architecture of the enjoyment of luxury materials, of the well-made, of the high finish. It is special to Mies and occasional to Le Corbusier and Gropius. It has a shameless bankers' uxoriousness about materials and a passion for perfection in detail which is obvious in the Barcelona Pavilion . . .'[7]

One suspects therefore that Post-Modernism is as hard and selective about the history of the Modern, as the Modern Movement itself was about other movements. As Barr, Banham, and the Smithsons could see, the Modern Movement was not nearly as single-coded as others have suggested, although it could often promulgate a tunnel view of history. Reyner Banham, in his essay on Bruno Taut ('The Glass Paradise') in *The Anti-Rationalists,* (1973), concluded that 'The official history of the Modern Movement, as laid out in the late twenties and codified in the thirties, is a view through the marrow-hole of a dry bone . . . a skeletal history of the movement with all the Futurists, Romantics, Expressionists, Elementarists and pure aesthetes omitted . . . quite suddenly modern architects decided to cut off half their grandparents without a farthing. In doing so, modern architecture became respectable and gutless; it entered on what Peter Smithson has justifiably called its Academic phase, when it became a style with books of rules, and could be exported to all parts of the Western world'.[8] A similar thing happened with painting and sculpture. The critic John Russell Taylor, writing on The New New Yorkers and the avant-avant garde in 1988 observed a similar hole in Nikos Stangos' *Concepts of Modern Art* (1974) and rightly asked 'what about the whole *rappel à l'ordre* in the early twenties, the Neue Sachlichkeit, Pittura Metafisica, Neo-Classicism (as in Picasso), Populism (as in Léger), American Precisionism and Regionalism, Forces Nouvelles, Socialist Realism, etc?'[9]

Aesthetic as well as political history is often written by the winners, and this can explain the 'marrow-hole' view cited by Banham. The Modern Movement triumphed over Expressionism by the mid-twenties, and easily suppressed the enemies it had, especially in England. It was attacked from the outset by the old guard, exemplified by Sir Reginald Blomfield, who called it 'Modernismus' thereby eliding two British pet-hates at that time – anything advanced and anything German. He prophesied that 'people will tire of what they cannot understand and artists will resume the standpoint that has guided art from time immemorial. If I may venture an opinion, one generation will see the end of this crazy movement'.[10] Direct bluster did not in the end achieve very much, and Blomfield failed to stop the erection of Connell, Ward and Lucas' brave white International Modern house in his beloved Georgian and Neo-Georgian Hampstead of 1936. Satire was another British technique. Heath Robinson and K R G Browne wrote in *How to live in a flat* (1934) that 'whereas formerly the best furniture was made by carpenters . . . the trade is almost entirely in the hands of plumbers, riveters, blow-pipers and metal-workers of all sorts'.[11] Sometimes, good old British common-sense prevailed, as in Osbert Lancaster's *Homes Sweet Homes* (1939), where he wrote that 'the open-plan, the mass-produced steel and plywood furniture . . . are all in theory perfectly logical, but in the home logic has always been at a discount. The vast majority . . . crave their knick-knacks . . . and are perfectly willing to pay the price in prolonged activities with broom and duster'.[12]

It was England that clung on to its sense of history; in fact one of the first books to deal seriously with the *fin de siècle*, Holbrook Jackson's *The Eighteen Nineties*, was published in 1913. Oxford University was a centre for revivalism. It was there that Kenneth Clark wrote *The Gothic Revival* (1928), though in it he admits to the fact that most undergraduates believed William Butterfield's Keble College to have been designed by Ruskin! There too were sown the seeds of Evelyn Waugh's conservatism, his book on Rossetti and his collection of furniture by William Burges. John Betjeman had experimented with Victorian typography whilst an undergraduate, and wrote *Ghastly Good Taste* in 1933. Edward James had also avoided the Modern, though he later became interested in Surrealism, and it was the latter movement that first launched a fully-fledged attack against Modernism. Indeed the very model of Surrealism was taken from the nineteenth-century writing of Isidore Ducasse (Comte de Lautréamont), who in *Chants de Maldoror* wrote: 'as beautiful as the chance meeting on a dissecting table of a sewing machine and an umbrella'. Victorian illustrations and advertisements were transmogrified and appropriated by Max Ernst. Salvador Dali began to revere Gaudí and Art Nouveau, and attack Modern architecture in the pages of the Surrealist-inflected publication *Minotaure*, which ran from 1933 to 1939. Dali could be a rebarbative historicist, writing that 'Possibly – no surely – in the artistic history of France, Ernest Meissonier and Edouard Bataille will take their future place amongst the great French painters, while Paul Cézanne will be seen to be one of the most blundering and evil . . . '[13] Dali was an early lover of Kitsch, long before its appearance in Post-Modernism. He wrote that 'those who have not tasted his [Gaudí's] supremely creative bad taste: they have knowingly committed treason by disregarding the major role it holds in Gaudí's works. The common mistake is to see bad taste as something sterile; it is good taste, and good taste alone,

MICHAEL GRAVES, LAMP FOR YAMIGINA

which holds the power to sterilise and which exists as the prime handicap to any creative function. It is enough to observe the good taste of the French: it has led them into doing nothing at all!'[14]

Dali's fondness for Art Nouveau and for its bad taste made him a precursor of the Italian Neo-Liberty (Neo-Art Nouveau) of the 1950s. Neo-Liberty was one of the first anti-rationalist design gestures after the War. In the post-war *reconstruzione* period, which began optimistically with the democratic republic of 1946, rationalist (Modern) architecture and design was disliked because, paradoxically in Italy, it had been associated with Fascism. In fact one of the purest International Style buildings in Italy had been the Fascist party headquarters in Como, completed by Giuseppe Terragni in 1936, for which he had designed a series of rationalist tubular steel furniture. As Penny Sparke records, 'Italy was committed right from the start of the post-war period, to new materials – among them bent and moulded plywood, sheet metal, steel rod, glass, foam rubber and plastics. The work of Eames and Saarinen appeared in Domus in the late 1940s alongside pieces of sculpture by artists such as Max Bill and Alexander Calder. Together they provided the main visual inspiration for a new generation of designers in search of a modern, expressive, Post-Fascist, Post-Modern Movement furniture aesthetic'.[15] In 1950 Gio Ponti, together with Piero Fornassetti, designed an historicist cabinet, with Fornassetti's *trompe-l'oeil* decoration contrasting Gothic architecture at the base of the cabinet with Renaissance architecture above. The neo-sculptural, free-flow, organic fifties style is exemplified by the work of Carlo Mollino, though he also added anthropomorphic and Surrealist references as well as his own particular brand of bad taste. As Giovanni Klaus Koenig observed in his essay in *Italian Re Evolution,*'his [Mollino's] love for Kitsch – the true Kitsch of Ludwig II of Bavaria, which is a virtue of great rarity – made him the perfect counter-figure for Albini and the Calvinistic functionality of the "Ulm" style fashionable in the sixties. His pupils Roberto Gabetti and Aimaro D'Isola invented Neo-Art Nouveau, followed by Vittorio Gregotti and today Mollino is being rediscovered by young architects'.[16]

Andrea Branzi in *The Hot House* has also credited Mollino with being 'the first person in Italy to penetrate deep into the quagmire of kitsch'.[17] Gregotti, who Koenig mentions as being Mollino's pupil, designed a Neo-Liberty chair in 1958, and a bed for the Milan Triennale of 1960 which resembles simple British Arts and Crafts furniture of the 1900s. The early historicist work of Gae Aulenti is important too; her lamp exhibited at the same Triennale of 1960 has an Art Nouveau outline, and her rocking chair, *Sgarsul,* of 1962 recalls an Art Nouveau bentwood rocker from Vienna at the turn of the century.

Andrea Branzi sums up the intentions of Neo-Liberty very well in writing that 'Neo-Liberty was at one and the same time a critique of anti-historical Rationalism, a rejection of populism and a pointed avoidance of the stylistic tone of those years.

The response to gestural design was to adopt the learned matrices of a historical culture; demagogy was replaced by an openly bourgeois culture, and style by another style. But Neo-Liberty was not just an act of polemical strategy, but also a moment of identity for an intellectual and enlightened middle class that was still too fragile to take on the burden of responsibility for government and for renewal of the country'.[18]

Diehard Moderns outside Italy were quick to attack the Neo-Liberty movement and historicism in general. One such was Sir Nikolaus Pevsner, in his important essay, 'The Return to Historicism', first written in 1961, and published in *Studies in Art, Architecture and Design* (1968). In it he stated that 'the phenomenon which interests me and which I mean by the return to historicism is the imitation of, or inspiration by, much more recent styles, styles which had never previously been revived'.[19] Pevsner, who set great store by originality, then added, 'Of course, all reviving of styles of the past is a sign of weakness, because in revivals independent thinking and feeling matters less than in choice of patterns'.[20] Later in the same article, he coined the first use by an art historian of the word 'post-modern'. He prophetically identified a 'new post-modern anti-rationalism' and ended the article with a last-ditch attempt to defend the Modern by stating that 'the individual building remains rational. If you keep your building square you are not therefore a square'.[21] Design practitioners as well as historians also attacked the fifties style. The more purist, Bauhaus-trained designer Wilhelm Wagenfeld, himself once admonished by his former teacher Laszlo Moholy-Nagy for not being pure enough, wrote in 1954, that 'The kidney table (ie free-form design) is certainly no more attractive than Chippendale reproductions so much favoured by our Philistines, and the Rococo vases adorned with brightly-coloured transfer pictures no more absurd than the asymmetrical knick-knacks of today'.

To some extent the history of twentieth-century historical revival has been peculiarly sequential and ordered. A simple picture would be that Art Nouveau – the style of 1900 – was revived first in the Surrealism of the 1930s, then in Neo-Liberty and in the many exhibitions and books from about 1950 to the 1960s. Landmarks for Victorian and Edwardian revivals were the Festival of Britain of 1951, an obvious centenary of the 1851 Great Exhibition, and then, rather more significantly, Peter Floud's 1952 Victoria & Albert Exhibition, *Victorian and Edwardian Decorative Arts*. Thomas Howarth's *Charles Rennie Mackintosh* was published in the same year. There was a Gaudí exhibition at MOMA, New York, in 1957, and at the same venue, an Art Nouveau exhibition in 1960. Books on Gaudí by G R Collins and then by J J Sweeney and J L Sert came out in 1960. The highpoint of Art Nouveau appreciation was in the mid-1960s, which saw in rapid annual succession Robert Schmutzler's *Art Nouveau* (1964), Maurice Rheims' *L'art 1900* (1965), Mario Amaya's *Art Nouveau* (1966) and S Tschudi Madsen's *Art Nouveau* (1967). Meanwhile Mackintosh was revived in the Victoria & Albert and Edinburgh

ROBERT VENTURI, ART DECO CHAIR, 1984 FOR KNOLL INTERNATIONAL

PETER SHIRE, *PETER* SIDEBOARD, 1987 FOR MEMPHIS

Exhibition of 1968, and in Robert Macleod's monograph of the same year.

In the mid- to late 1960s the searchlight of interest focussed on Art Deco – pioneers of this revival being the exhibition *Les Années '25* at the Musée des Arts Décoratifs in Paris in 1965, and Yvonne Brunhammer's *The Nineteen Twenties Style*, first published in Italy in 1966. Bevis Hillier's *Art Deco* and exhibition entitled *The World of Art Deco* at The Minneapolis Institute of Arts followed in 1968 and 1971 respectively; and Martin Battersby's two books, *The Decorative Twenties* (1969) and *The Decorative Thirties* (1971) were also significant publications.

It has taken until much later for the inevitable 1950s revival, which has informed much recent design. The history of this, the first revival of a style so recently left behind us, will be examined later in this book.

The 1960s – The Continuation of the Modern and its Rupture

The 1950s freeflow style and Neo-Liberty proved to be short-lived alternatives to the continuation of the purer Modern. For a variety of reasons, the 1960s saw a second Modern Movement in art, architecture and design. Rectilinear forms returned to design, partly influenced by the surface functionalism of the German 'second Bauhaus', the Ulm Hochschule für Gestaltung. The results are exemplified by the solid, chaste work of the late 1950s and early 1960s by Hans Gugelot and Dieter Rams for Braun. In *The Waste Makers* (1960), the American writer and critic of consumer society, Vance Packard, saw many of these changes as stylistic or as 'planned obsolescence'. He wrote that ' . . . during the fifties the automobile designers had stumbled upon the streamlined, tear-drop shape as a symbol of modernity. This shape, which came from the discoveries of aircraft designers, had less but some plausible functional relevance in automobile design. But the relevance of the tear-drop look became completely unclear when applied to such things as refrigerators, stoves, meat-grinder handles, electric irons, orange juicers, and radios . . . By the late fifties the tear-drop had run its course. Very shortly after refrigerator makers began talking about the imperative need for planned obsolescence to cope with mounting inventories, refrigerators abruptly received a new shape. Suddenly they no longer seemed designed for flight with rounded corners and oval contours. The new refrigerators were boxes again with sharply squared corners . . . I have before me pictures of seven major brands in 1959. All seven have the severely straight lines of a rectangular slab with sharp, square corners'.[22]

'Sharp square corners' and 'good form' had persisted in Britain as part of the 1960s philosophy of the Design Council, which was set up to promote high standards in design. Such beliefs had contributed to the success of Terence Conran, whose Habitat chain of shops emerged in 1964 as an innovator of 'Bauhaus good form' in Great Britain, albeit forty years after its birth in Germany. Rectilinear high rise buildings, or

what Charles Jencks was later to call 'dumb boxes' continued to mushroom throughout the world, partly inspired by the still-living patriarchs of modernity. (Le Corbusier died in 1965, Gropius and Mies van der Rohe in 1969, and Marcel Breuer in 1981.) The first Modern Movement was studied, and its significance marked by many books. Sir Nikolaus Pevsner's *Pioneers of Modern Design* was a standard work; Reyner Banham's *Theory and Design in the First Machine Age* was published in 1960. Penguin paperbacks by the architect Peter Blake on Le Corbusier, Wright, and Mies van der Rohe were all published between 1960 and 1964. Gillian Naylor's *Bauhaus* appeared in 1968, the year of the major Royal Academy exhibition on the same subject, and Herwin Schaefer's *The Roots of Modern Design* concluded the decade in 1970.

The second Modern Movement was much reinforced by these studies of its ancestor, the 'heroic modern' or International Modern. In Britain for example, post-war reconstruction spawned a thousand clones of the work of Le Corbusier and Mies van der Rohe, but few of them were conceived as the masters would have wished. The economic miracle years, the age of future Prime Minister Harold Wilson's 'white heat of the technological revolution', produced the high-rise Shell building of 1962, the same year that saw the completion of the London Hilton in anticipation of the tourist boom. Ironically, that same year also saw the controversial destruction of Hardwick's Doric Euston Arch, the very type of structure tourists would probably have wished to have seen. It was also the year that Anthony Burgess satirised the council estate high-rise block in *A Clockwork Orange*. The hero, Alex, who speaks 'Nadsat', a teenage slang based in part on Russian, describes his abode thus: 'I lived . . . in Municipal flatblock I8A. I went to the lift, but there was no need to press the electric knopka to see if it was working or not . . . so I had to walk the ten floors up'. Later, Alex passes a 'bolshy flatblock called Victoria Flatblock after some victory or other'. Burgess describes his urban wasteland just one year after the publication in 1961 of Jane Jacobs' sociological account, *The Death and Life of Great American Cities*. 'Lack of defensible space', the cheapness and ugliness of raw concrete, and the fact that very often such buildings had displaced urban housing of an attractive if not always sanitary type, all contributed to sociological and aesthetic dislike of these end products of the Modern Movement. The progressive, ever moving, ever futurist railway train of modernity was about to hit the buffers. Burgess and Jacobs were writing a decade before the event which the influential writer Charles Jencks sees as the death of Modern architecture. In his book *The Language of Post-Modern Architecture* (1977) Jencks wrote: 'Happily we can date the death of Modern architecture to a precise moment in time. Modern architecture died in St Louis, Missouri on July 15th 1972'. The event Jencks refers to, namely the blowing up of the socially undesirable Pruitt-Igoe high-rise blocks built only twenty years earlier, is indicative of the widespread antipathy to this type of architecture. The search for a new idiom, expressed through the word 'Post-Modern', is understandable from two points of view: first, Modern architecture had made a vital contribution during the period when it was revolutionary, when it held that 'less was more'; secondly, it had in some ways failed in its main aim, to realise through social engineering a better quality of life. By the mid-1960s and early 1970s it was seen as stale, outworn and unacceptable by a more individualistic generation.

At the same time, in the 1960s, painting and sculpture seemed to take at least two paths which occasionally converged. The movements of Op Art and Minimalism used strong geometric elements, while the main inflection of Pop Art was a continuation of figurative reference. All three have become absorbed in a collective memory bank, informing Post-Modernism through selected elements or, as in the case of Minimalism, a positive rejection of its poverty.

Op Art took its inspiration from earlier experiments by the Bauhaus artist Josef Albers and also from the work of the painter Victor Vasarély, who had been creating chessboard-like black and white compositions since the mid-1930s. Op Art, especially in its black and white form, dominated graphics, record cover design, painting and the decorative arts in the mid-1960s, especially in the years 1964 and 1965. New exponents of Op Art included the painters Bridget Riley and Jesus Raphael Soto, but the style's influence spread into many other fields. Television was, of course, still black and white, and set designs began to emphasise this heavily. The dress designs of Mary Quant, Ossie Clark, Barbara Hulanicki and Courrèges, and even the heavy black make-up of the period, were all part of this fashion. The Liverpool band, The Beatles, dressed to this style in the mid-1960s. At the same time, the Liverpool poet Adrian Henri captured the spirit of this period of black and white in his suite of poems entitled *Pictures from an Exhibition*, based on paintings shown in the *Painting and Sculpture of a Decade* exhibition at the Tate Gallery in 1964. Henri comments on Albers' *Homage to the Square*, and of Jim Dine's *Black Bathroom* of 1962 he writes:

black splashes on the white walls
interrupting the commercials
TURN ON THE GLEAMING WHITE SINK
AND POEMS COME OUT OF THE TAPS!

Of Vasarély's *Supernovae* of 1959-61, he writes, simply:
Black is White White is Black
while his poem about Louise Nevelson's painting of 1960 ends:

Black Boxes Black Black Black

It was only a short step from this style to Minimalism, with its rectangular emphasis, especially in the 'sculpture' of Don Judd and Carl André. The latter's famous 'pile of bricks' *Equivalent VIII*, made in 1966, remade in 1969, and finally acquired by the Tate Gallery, frightened the so-called 'philistines', but this type of Minimalist statement also prompted artists themselves to inject more flavour into what some considered to be the poverty-stricken, limited diet of formalism.

Pop Art was one current that introduced a greater representational ingredient, as well as an absorption of a Neo-Dada interest in the object and its relationship to consumerism, Kitsch and Camp. Pop Art was, in fact, a child of the 1940s. As early as 1947, Eduardo Paolozzi had produced a collage, *Intimate Confessions*, which mixed mechanical imagery (gun, US warplane) with sexual imagery and a Coca-Cola bottle and logo, together with the word 'Pop'. In that case, the word was treble-coded: the 'pop' of a gun, 'pop' meaning a fizzy drink, and 'pop' for popular. The collage form set a standard typology for presentation which remains in use in much of Post-Modernism. In 1952 Paolozzi became a member of the Independent Group which gathered at the Institute of Contemporary Arts in London. Other members included the writer Lawrence Alloway, the painter Richard Hamilton, the architects Peter and Alison Smithson and the architectural critic Reyner Banham. American cars, consumer goods, advertisements – all these things excited them. Parodying Marinetti's outburst in the first Futurist Manifesto of 1909, that 'a racing car . . . is more beautiful than the Victory of Samothrace', Banham said that a Buick V-8 of 1955 with its 'glitter . . . bulk . . . and deliberate exposure of technical means' was a more practical design model than the Bauhaus. The Smithsons declared that 'today we collect ads', while Alloway was proposing that 'Hollywood, Detroit and Madison Avenue were in terms of our interests producing the best popular culture', thereby anticipating by some years Tom Wolfe's description of Las Vegas as the 'Versailles of America', or Robert Venturi's fascination with the same meretricious city, expressed in his book, *Learning from Las Vegas* (1972).

The British Pop artists were sowing seeds through their work as well as through their statements. Richard Hamilton, shadow-acting the Dadaist interest in sexuality and machinery (especially in the work of Marcel Duchamp), produced images of cars and pin-ups in the 1950s, while Paolozzi's automobile *Head* of 1954 was a strange marriage of car and robot imagery. Hamilton was acquainted with Duchamp, and wrote the catalogue introduction to *The almost complete works of Marcel Duchamp* at the Tate Gallery in 1966, in which he suggested that 'no living artist commands a higher regard among the younger generation than Marcel Duchamp'. Hamilton was fully aware of Neo-Dada, the early work in America of Jasper Johns, Robert Rauschenberg and other artists who emerged in the late 1950s. Pop had some of its roots in Dada, although Duchamp himself could see important distinctions. As Edward Lucie-Smith records in his article on Pop in the anthology *Concepts of Modern Art*:'In his authoritative book on the Dada movement, Hans Richter quotes from a letter written to him by Marcel Duchamp: "This Neo-Dada, which they call New Realism, Pop Art, Assemblage etc, is an easy way out, and lives on what Dada did. When I discovered ready-mades I thought to discourage aesthetics. In Neo-Dada they have taken my ready-mades and found aesthetic beauty in them. I threw the bottlerack and the urinal into their faces as a challenge and

MARIO BOTTA, *SHOGUN TERRA* LAMP, 1987 FOR ARTEMIDE

O M UNGERS, *TOWER CABINET*, 1987

now they admire them for their aesthetic beauty'".[23] Duchamp's proto-deconstructive process regarding the value, authenticity, signature and primacy of an object-based visual culture was probably misread by many Pop artists, but it allowed for an exploration of the artefact in contemporary society. For example, Richard Hamilton's *The Critic Laughs* (1968) is a riposte to Jasper Johns's earlier, ironic relief sculpture, *The Critic Sees* (1964), and further, a Neo-Dadaist juxtaposition of 'good' design (the Braun electric toothbrush) and Kitsch – a seaside-rock denture perches on the Braun base. Hamilton anticipates the subsequent generation's interest in Kitsch as well as anti-design in this image, produced in the year during which there was so much political unrest in universities and art colleges throughout Europe.

'Good taste' was still an issue of debate. As early as 1958, Lawrence Alloway, discussing Clement Greenberg's famous article of 1939, *Avant-Garde and Kitsch*, recorded that he (Alloway) 'objected to his reduction of the mass media to "ersatz culture . . . destined for those who are insensible to the value of genuine culture . . . Kitsch, using for raw material the debased and academic simulacra of genuine culture welcomes and cultivates this insensibility'".[24] American Pop Art should also be seen in the context of both admass culture and post-war society, the values of which had been explored so well in the books of Vance Packard aptly titled, *The Hidden Persuaders* (1957), *The Status Seekers* (1959) and *The Waste Makers* (1960). Andy Warhol's early career began, significantly, as an advertising illustrator and draughtsman, before he became a New York Pop artist. His bright silk screen images often concentrated on popular images, the most famous being *Monroe* of 1962. His famous flowers, for example *Flowers (six together)* (1965) influenced everything from Mary Quant's logo to the shape of some Italian Archizoom *Dream* beds in the mid-sixties, as well as Robert Venturi's 'decorated sheds'. His *Soup Cans* from about 1964 used commonplace imagery or repetition to create icons out of everyday objects. Roy Lichtenstein on the other hand, enobled the comic strip, and the Ben Day dot technique influenced many artists, as well as resurfacing in some work by the 1980s Memphis designers.

Even more significant was the work of Claes Oldenburg, since it was object-based, three-dimensional, and very often quasi-architectural. Between 1960 and 1965 he was involved with other artists in 'happenings' and environmental events. He explored Kitsch in his *Leopard Chair* (1963) and in his seminal *Bedroom Ensemble* of the same year. The furniture was rhomboidal, that is to say, anti-functional, with much use of fake zebra and leopard skin; for example the couch had a fake leopard-skin coat on it. The lamps were painted in a vulgar turquoise to imitate marble, and the work as a whole influenced a generation of Italian anti-design interiors as well as heralding the 1980s interest in marbled effects. In May 1967, Oldenburg wrote about the room and explained : 'to complete the story, I should mention that the *Bedroom* is based on a famous motel along the shore road to Malibu, "Las Tunas

Isles" in which (when I visited it in 1947) each suite was decorated in the skin of a particular animal, ie tiger, leopard, zebra. My imagination exaggerated but I like remembering it that way: each object in the room consistently animal'. Here we have an early example of anti-design as well as an equivalent of Venturi's much later concept of 'Learning from Las Vegas'. Oldenburg's quasi-monumental sculpture did much to explore anthropomorphic form as well as popular culture. His *Swedish Wing Nut* of 1966-7 has 'ears' like those of Mickey Mouse, the cartoon character which became a minor obsession and eventually led to Oldenburg's *Mouse Museum*. His *Building in the form of a British extension plug* of 1967 elides the concept of house and face with the form of an adaptor; the 'sockets' can be read in an obviously punning way as eyes and mouth, or two windows and a door. This heralds the concentration on the house/face analogy set up in some Post-Modern architecture and discussed in the writing of Charles Jencks. His anthropomorphic *Giant Peg* (*Late submission to Chicago Tribune Competition*) of 1967 is an ironic and witty reference to the skyscraper; the 'legs' of the clothes peg make it look human, while its springs extend across its front, like arms.

The relationship between Pop and Kitsch has been touched on, but it is important to stress that Pop also related to 'Camp'. Mark Booth, the author of *Camp* (1983) suggests that 'Unlike kitsch, camp does not even have honourable intentions. Yet although kitsch is never intrinsically camp, it has a certain toe-curling quality that appeals to the camp sense of humour. Kitsch is one of camp's favourite fads and fancies'.[25] Distinctions like these are sometimes slight; for example Susan Sontag's *Notes on Camp,* written in *Partisan Review* in 1964 during the period of Pop Art. Sontag suggested that 'Camp art is often decorative art, emphasising texture, sensuous surface, and style at the expense of content'.[26] Later in her discourse she notes that 'Camp is the consistently aesthetic experience of the world. It incarnates a victory of "style" over "content", "aesthetics" over "morality", of irony over tragedy'.[27] She did however conclude that 'one may compare Camp with much of Pop Art, which – when it is not just Camp – embodies an attitude that is related, but still very different. Pop Art is more flat and more dry, more serious, more detached, ultimately nihilistic'.[28] Mark Booth is more certain of the connection between Pop and Camp, and Andy Warhol is frequently cited as having a Camp sensibility. As Booth writes 'In *Revolt into Style* (1970) George Melly pointed out that in the sixties, Pop was more or less synonymous with Camp. And if we look at Richard Hamilton's famous list of the attributes of Pop, we can draw up a very similar list of attributes of Camp . . .'
POP: Popular (designed for mass audiences), Transient (short term solutions, Expendable, Low-cost, Mass-produced, Young, Witty, Sexy, Gimmicky, Glamorous, Big business. CAMP: Easily accessible, Determinedly facile, Trashy, Mock luxurious, Mass-produced, Youth-worshipping, Witty, Mock sexy, Wilfully hackneyed, Mock glamorous, BIG BUSINESS'.[29]

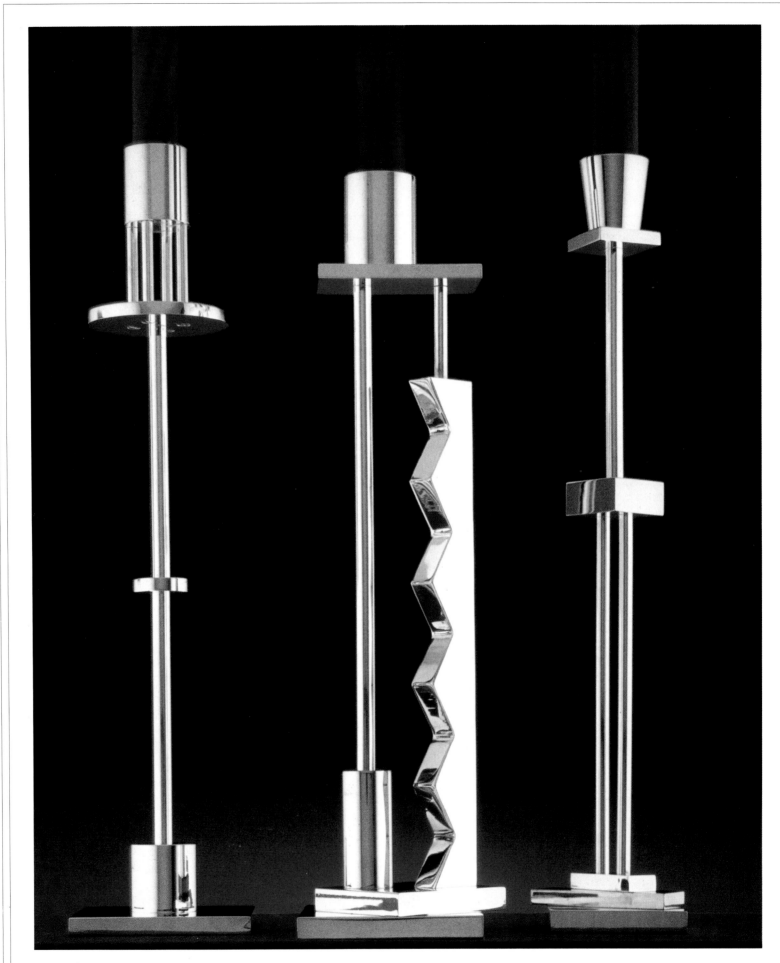

ETTORE SOTTSASS, CANDLESTICKS, 1985 FOR SWID POWELL

CHAPTER II
Post-Pop Design

ETTORE SOTTSASS, *STAIRS* RUG FOR FURNITURE OF THE TWENTIETH CENTURY

Pop Art exerted an enormous influence on the early careers of those designers and architects now associated with Post-Modernism. In this group can be included most of the Italian designers centred around Memphis, and also, for example, Charles Jencks, Robert Venturi, Hans Hollein and Arata Isozaki. As Andrea Branzi recorded in his important book *The Hot House*, 'as far as Rationalism [ie The Modern Movement] was concerned, Pop Art represented an important modification of theory, indeed a complete about-face. Whereas at the beginning of the century nascent modern architecture had adopted the profound logic of the industrial machine, assuming a wholly rational man who would realise his creative potential in production, the model proposed by pop culture in the sixties was that of a man totally taken up by consumption, who would fulfil his highest potential for cultural creativity in the civilisation of prosperity'.[30] It was against this consumerist backdrop that the 'designer' and 'architect-designer' finally emerged. Post-Pop and Post-Modernist developments have extended and accelerated the long-standing tradition of the architect as designer. The accepted brief of C F A Voysey, Charles Rennie Mackintosh or Josef Hoffmann was to design furniture and artefacts as well as buildings, and the desire to design has re-emerged with many Post-Modern architects during the last few years. Though many Post-Modern designs only appeared during the 1980s, their origins are interwoven with Pop Art developments and a 1960s reaction against the idea of 'good form' as preached by the profession from the 1920s onwards.

Charles Jencks, the architect and writer who eventually gave Post-Modernism in architecture its intellectual credibility was, in the 1960s, concerned with both semiotics and his own concept of 'adhocism' exemplified by his two books entitled *Meaning in Architecture* (1969), and *Adhocism* (1972). Semiotics is broadly concerned with the study of communication, which in its spoken and written form constitutes Linguistics; the word is also used for the study of symbols and signs, and is alternatively called Semiology. This area of study was first proposed by the Swiss linguist Ferdinand de Saussure and refined in the 1960s by Roland Barthes, whose *Elements of Semiology* was published in 1967. Barthes also wrote a book about Japan entitled *The Empire of Signs* (1970).

Charles Jencks' actual designs of the late 1960s reveal an intriguing ambivalence between a continuation of Modern formalism and a desire to usurp it. Jencks' youthful admiration for Le Corbusier and the Modern masters is revealed in his tubular steel *George* chair and *The Racing Chair*, both of 1968. In an important internal debate on paper between Jencks the architect and Jencks the critic, which is also perhaps a struggle between the ego and super-ego – his 'speculative dialogue between two characters' – Jencks the architect says of the chairs: 'Yes, they are rather late-sixties, but then this was the period of Late-Modernism which you, after all named and supported'.[31] Jencks' first table design, the *Adhoc* table (1968), is fundamentally different. A marble slab rests on six 'shop window' mannequin legs. As Jencks says, 'It was an idea of the Surrealists crossed with that of the bricoleur . . . The table "legs" revived the oldest metaphor of language and design . . . There was a complete philosophy of Counter-Modern design in this table'.[32]

Since all three designs date from 1968 it is clear that Jencks could be Late-Modern and Anti-Modern at the same time. If you put all three designs together, you get a chance meeting of Le Corbusier and Salvador Dali on a marble slab, to paraphrase the Comte de Lautréamont. Yet more Surreal or Dalinean was Jencks' *Madonna of the Future* (1968). This time a black shop window mannequin, with a working electric heater in place of her head, holds the book *The Madonna of the Future* by Henry James. Jencks acknowledges the connection to the 'similar erotic work of Allen Jones'. Returning to his internal debate, Jencks the architect states that this Madonna 'had less to do with the sensual image than the return of the body to architecture. Think of its presence, from the Egyptians to the nineteenth century, its flowering in Baroque Vienna and Prague so that bridges and doorways and chimneypieces were bedecked with the human figure, a veritable explosion of anthropocentrism onto inanimate architecture . . .'[33]

Jencks' early work exemplifies the dialectic of the 1960s. On the one hand a Late-Modern quotation of Le Corbusier, and on the other, semiotic, adhoc, collaged, anthropomorphic design, full of meaning and reference to Surrealism and Pop Art, Anti-Modern and surely proto Post-Modern. In 1978 Jencks defined Post-Modernism as 'double-coding: the combination of modern techniques with something else (usually traditional building) in order for architecture to communicate with the public and a concerned minority, usually other architects'.[34] Something of this 'double-coding' is already present in his designs of 1968, as well as an eclectic methodology. In 1987, almost twenty years after the *Madonna of the Future*, Jencks wrote in his book *What is Post-Modernism?* (1987) that 'The challenge for a Post-Modern Hamlet, confronted by an *embarras de richesses*, is to choose and combine traditions selectively, to eclect (as the verb of eclecticism would have it) those aspects from the past and present which appear most relevant to the job at hand'.[35]

In the 1960s and early 1970s, two of Post-Modernism's greatest designers and architects, Robert Venturi and Hans Hollein, were doing important pioneering work. Venturi, who was born in Philadelphia in 1925, studied architecture at Princeton University from 1943 to 1950, before working with the architects Eero Saarinen and Louis Kahn. From 1954 to 1956 he was the Rome Prize Fellow at the American Academy in Rome. He taught architectural theory from 1957 to 1965 at the University of Pennsylvania School of Architecture, and his teaching formed the basis for his seminal book, *Complexity and Contradiction in Architecture* (1966). In it he expressed a plea for 'complexity and contradiction . . . elements which are hybrid rather than pure . . . messy vitality over obvious unity

. . . I prefer "both-and" to "either-or"'. During his period as a Professor at Yale, a graduate seminar taught with his future wife Denise Scott Brown and Stephen Izenour in 1968 provided material for his second book, *Learning from Las Vegas* (1972). Both publications did much to undermine International Modern thinking, and searched for eclecticism and variety, especially from within American popular culture. Venturi's ideas were thus formulated at the height of the influence of Pop Art; in *Complexity and Contradiction in Architecture* the work of Jasper Johns, for example, features alongside the eclectic and pluralistic history of architecture. Tom Wolfe wrote in *From Bauhaus to Our House* that Venturi ordered a Ludwig Mies van der Rohe *Barcelona* chair 'in a pretty fabric in the interest of "ironic" reference'. The equally prophetic Hans Hollein used a similar irony in 1966 in his exhibition design for the Vienna Museum of Applied Art, when he hung Marcel Breuer tubular steel chairs from the roof as aerial sculpture. Such undermining of Modern 'classics of design' became commonplace and has continued as a gesture of defiance, as we shall see later in this book. Examples include the *Mies* chair and footstool of chromed steel and rubber by Archizoom in Italy (1969) and extends to Alessandro Mendini's 'redesign' of classic chairs by Gio Ponti and Joe Columbo in 1978. Ponti's chair is given two flags or wings, as if to prepare it for flight, while Columbo's is satirised with a gaudy fake marble effect. Jencks has produced the *Breuer-Jencks* chair which takes the Thonet tubular steel classic and adds a pediment inscribed with the words 'Thonet Stam Breuer Mies Jencks'. As Jencks has written, it 'improves a mass-produced cliché by adding things to it'. He has also written that 'the result is an undeniably ugly body, but an interesting critique of the Breuer chair which has odd proportions due to its thin legs and missing head. The idea of using a temple for a head and piers for legs comes from the skyscraper tradition. Giving a monumental presence to Modernist icons is a task for Post-Modernists, as is pointing out the memory and genealogy of products (viz the pediment)'.[36] This playing with Modern 'classics' suggests not only a realisation that it is difficult to do anything new, but also that designers are linked to the Modern Movement, and find it impossible to escape from the domination of the recent past. Rather more sinister yet, in this continuing ironic vein, is Shiro Kuramata's *Hommage to Hoffmann, Begin the Begin* (1985). The chair is steel rod, the ghost of the outline of a standard Thonet chair which has been burned away from inside the metal wrapping. Of this gesture Emilio Ambasz has written: 'When he wraps steel rods around a Thonet bentwood chair and then burns the chair, he sends smoke signals to the Gods of modern design to assure them that the spirit of ludicrous innovation is still alive'.[37] Given Japan's history, the chair is fully loaded with implications of the relationship between East and West, and Post-Atomic Bomb presence with pre-First World War past. This ironic chair not only swipes at the Modern Movement; its eerie silhouette has a chilling resonance with history.

Japanese architects and designers, most notably Arata Isozaki,

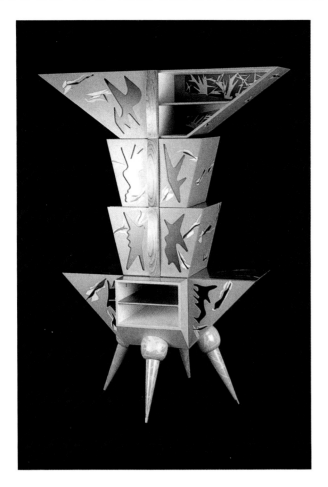
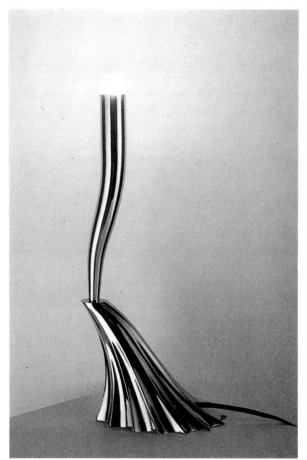
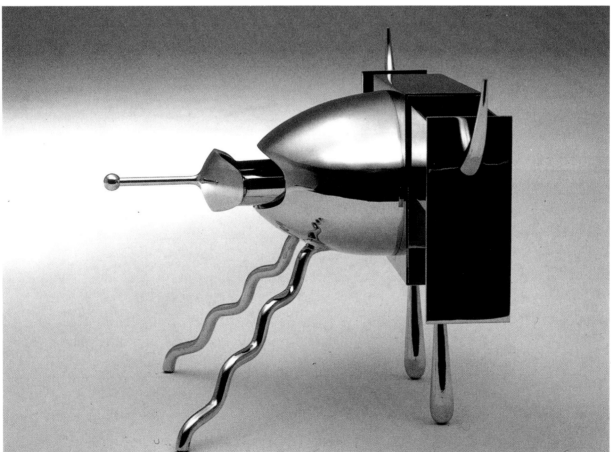

TOP TO BOTTOM, L TO R: ALCHYMIA, *LAMBIS* CUPBOARD, LAMP AND CHEST OF DRAWERS, 1986

ALCHYMIA, *MAJOLICA* PVC FLOORING, 1986

also learned from Pop Art and the political climate of the 1960s. Isozaki, who was born in 1931, worked for Kenzo Tange until 1963, when he set up on his own in Tokyo. He married the artist Aiko Miyawaki, who had been involved with Japanese Neo-Dada, and was aware of such cult figures as Marcel Duchamp and Frederick Kiesler. Isozaki participated in the Japanese protests of 1970, much inspired by the European ones of 1968. Isozaki records in his foreword to Branzi's *The Hot House*, that 'In the mid-1960s, it became apparent that the 'avant-garde' in architecture and design was no longer functioning as it had in the early period of the Modern Movement . . . I consider the course of modern architecture pioneered by the avant-garde to have changed definitively and qualitatively by the confrontation resulting from the occupation of the Triennale exhibition building in 1968, (in Milan), which was in turn part of a cultural revolution whose origins were in Paris . . . After being struck by the coup of confrontation, I turned my attention to the work of architects who were actively engaged in destroying the canon that had supported modern architecture. Among such architects, I found two groups who, breaking off relations with former avant-garde thought, presented an attitude of extreme radicalism. Both groups were based in Florence: Superstudio and Archizoom'.[38]

The 1960s form the background to Isozaki's chair *Marilyn* (1972). In its design, Isozaki has blended a Mackintosh high-backed chair with the sensual curves of Marilyn Monroe; a combination of Pop Art with a tribute to one of the pioneers of twentieth-century furniture design. The chair will be discussed more fully later, but it too can be seen as a Post-Pop Art design.

One aspect of the sixties, and indeed of Pop Art, was the continuing faith in the future shown through technology. That strain led more certainly to Late-Modern and High-Tech developments. Isozaki records that he was 'making full use of technology in assembling a robot, to be displayed at the Milan Triennale of 1968, which abstracted the hidden violent character of technology'.[39] Pop aesthetics lay behind the formation in England in 1961 of Archigram, a think-tank of young architects such as Peter Cook and Dennis Crompton. They used Pop Art graphics and collages of ideas to express fresh and futuristic thoughts, their most famous project being the utopian Plug-in-City. This High-Tech image led finally to the Late-Modern appreciation of such ideas in the architecture of Richard Rogers – his Pompidou Centre of 1971-1977 is, for example, a realisation of such futuristic ideas.

Archigram was the first of three 'A's, the second and third being Archizoom and Alchymia in Italy. Indeed it may well have been an Archigram image of 1964, containing the words 'archigram' and 'zoom', that gave Archizoom its title. Archizoom was formed in Florence in 1966, the year of the flood which damaged so much of that city, and was led by Andrea Branzi, who later worked with both Alchymia and Memphis. He has also written the important survey of Italian new wave design, appropriately entitled *The Hot House*. Archizoom, along with other radical sixties groups, notably

Superstudio and later Gruppo Strum, absorbed elements of Pop into what they called 'anti-design' or 'banal design'. Archizoom's activities were fairly typical of the late 1960s, and were largely prompted by the protests of 1968, especially *les événements* in Paris, when the whole city seemed to take to the streets. Archizoom's Art Deco revival *Dream* beds (1967) and *Mies* chair swipe at 'good form' and use ironic reference to past styles to create contemporary art furniture in the environment of a Pop Art 'happening'. As Andrea Branzi has recalled in *The Hot House*, 'when the Pop artists of America went on show at the 1964 Venice Biennale, the figurative arts in Italy were still obsessed with sophisticated experiments with the non-representational; what was most striking about the American experience was not so much its aspect of Neo-Dada, but that behind the Neo-Dadaism of Rauschenberg or Dine could be made out the disruptive arrival of modern objects and street languages and also of a new affective tolerance for the world "as it is today"'.[40] Thus in the mid- to late sixties, Archizoom learned from Pop culture in a way that, at about the same time, Venturi learned from Las Vegas. Their *Rosa d'Arabia, a dream* bed of 1967, has next to it a 'sculpture' on two wheels clearly inspired by the general form of the American Pop artist Robert Indiana's rather more political sculpture *Cuba* (1961); the *Presagio di rose dream* bed and room, has *faux marbre* walls, and the Art Deco-inspired bed has a 'leopard skin' pattern cover, reminiscent of Claes Oldenburg's seminal *Bedroom Ensemble* (1963). Archizoom's *Safari* couch for Poltronova (1967) also has a Warhol-inspired flower shape in its centre, which is again covered with 'leopard skin'.

The interest in Art Deco at that time has already been discussed, but these *Dream* beds draw more from Pop Art, and indeed the Psychedelic art of the sixties which introduced bizarre colours and tones. Charles Jencks' description of this new Italian work as 'supersensualist' and part of a *dolce vita* tradition is accurate, but to that should be added that there was also a conscious desire to *épater le bourgeois* which formed part of the radical chic of the sixties generation. Even in less overtly intellectual Italian circles, Pop Art had an influence with the group De Pas, D'Urbino, Lomazzi who produced their *Blow* inflatable chair in 1967. Pop Art also inspired their chair of 1970, *Joe*, which was shaped like an American baseball glove. The reference is to the baseball hero Joe DiMaggio, former husband of Marilyn Monroe, whose name had already featured in Simon and Garfunkel's song *Mrs Robinson* for the film *The Graduate* (1967).

The 1970s began to see some definition of Post-Modern architecture, especially in the writings of Charles Jencks, who effectively gave the word 'Post-Modern' currency, even if he did not coin it originally. His *Modern Movements in Architecture* (1973) and *The Language of Post-Modern Architecture* (1977) provide excellent surveys of the emergence of anti-rationalism in the work of the Modern architects. His writing rarely refers to 'design', as opposed to architecture, although, as Robert Stern has written, 'the very best decoration from

Adam to Aalto and beyond has been part of an overall architectural scheme. The rest runs the risk of being so much stuff'. In 1983, *Domus* magazine quoted a statement made thirty years previously by the architect Ernesto Rogers that 'the architect designs everything from towns to spoons', while Alberto Alessi has gone further, in speaking of his firm's silverware, when he proclaimed that 'Architects are much easier to work with than designers'. It is evident that many of Jencks' Post-Modern architects, including himself, are now also Post-Modern designers. It is also clear that Post-Modern design shares a dislike of, or reaction against, the Modern Movement. As with architecture, design emerged from that epoch, with its considerations of 'good form' and 'form follows function' as well as 'less is more'.

Much Italian design shares with rather more ripe Post-Modern design this reaction against canonical, 'classic good form', and yet does not label itself 'Post-Modern'. As we shall see shortly, words such as 'new wave' or 'hot house' are preferred in much of the literature dealing with contemporary Italian work. The best description would probably be Post-Pop, since Post-Modern only applies in the case of a few Italian architect-designers, notably Paolo Portoghesi and to some extent, Aldo Rossi. Any analysis of Post-Pop Italian design must spotlight the oldest 'anti-design' renegade, Ettore Sottsass Jr, who, perhaps significantly, designed a textile called *Schizzo* in 1983. The word means sketch, but suggests schizophrenia. Indeed, Sottsass' career to date seems to have been exactly that, divided between years of 'good form' industrial design for Olivetti, and personal, artistic anti-design gestures, especially from the 1960s onwards. Sottsass was born in Austria in 1917, and set up his office in Milan in 1946 during the years of reconstruction. That city had organised the important Triennales from 1933, and contained the infrastructure which eventually made it the world's foremost design city. Small businesses and workshops flourished, especially in the area of Brianza. Furniture companies such as Cassina were based there, and others such as Artemide became established. Throughout the 1950s and 1960s Sottsass did excellent product design, including important typewriters for Olivetti. In 1961, however, he travelled to India, became interested in Pop culture, and around 1965 began to design ceramics for Poltronova inspired in form by Art Deco ziggurats and in title by Indian mysticism – like Tantra for example. Moreover the decoration of his ceramic vases *Il Sostante* and *Il Sestante* of the same date is Op Art-inspired.

In the late 1970s, Sottsass became part of Studio Alchymia, the Milanese group formed in 1976 by Alessandro Guerriero. The group's activities were underpinned by Alessandro Mendini, who was born in Milan in 1931, and became editor of the influential magazine *Domus* on the death of Gio Ponti in 1979. Alchymia's work continued the irreverent, usurping gestures of the 1960s, and broke the barriers between architecture, design, sculpture and painting by forcing many of these hitherto discrete disciplines together. The group has issued the

work, amongst others, of Mendini, Sottsass, Andrea Branzi, Michele De Lucchi, and the Post-Modernists Trix and Robert Haussmann. Much of Mendini's output was 'banal design' and 'redesign'. The heavily ironic, almost defamatory treatment of Gio Ponti's and Joe Columbo's chairs by Mendini in 1978 has already been discussed in the context of Venturi and Hollein. At the same time, Mendini produced *Proust's Chair*, a redesigned 'Victorian' chair painted in the divisionist style of Seurat, and a salvaged, redecorated second-hand 1940s chest of drawers painted in the manner and colours of a Kandinsky 'Bauhaus' painting. The latter was rendered relatively less functional by having its handles set at 45 degrees to the line of the drawers.

A year later, in 1979, two almost sacrilegious 'redesigns' were produced. The first was a reworking of Rietveld's *Zig-Zag* chair, now with a cross back, making it look like a monument or tombstone to the Modern Movement. Given all the declarations of the 'death of Modernism', this was perhaps a suitable 'Rest in Peace' gesture. The second undermined the standard 'classic' Wassily chair by Marcel Breuer by covering it with asymmetrical, painted decoration which rendered it 'artistic' and disturbed the fineness of its functional metallic lines. Beyond the obvious wit which recognises the fact that the chair was originally designed by the functionalist architect, Breuer, for the 'spiritual' painter, Kandinsky, there is something stereotypically Italian about the gesture. It reminds one of the paradox of, for example, being a Communist and a Catholic, or in an extreme case, going to Mass in the morning, and the whorehouse in the afternoon.

Such anarchic, quasi-Surrealistic gestures came to a head in 1980 with the everyday objects shown at the *Banal Object* Exhibition at the Venice Biennale, which had been 'redesigned' by Mendini, Franco Raggi, Daniela Puppa and Paola Navone. Here, humble product designs such as the Ewbank carpet sweeper were given gaudy arrow-shaped forms at their front, and standard Italian coffee makers were painted red, yellow, orange and green. They set up a resonance with Dada and Surreal objects, reminding one perhaps of Man Ray's *Gift* (1921), when Ray adorned a standard flat iron with menacing carpet tacks on its base, or Meret Oppenheim's fur-lined *Teacup, Saucer and Spoon* (1936), which, beyond its sexual implication, renders a functional ensemble of objects totally useless. However, the 'Banal Objects' were, admittedly, less threatening than Ray's *Gift*.

It is significant that Andrea Branzi, the 'anti-designer' of the 1960s, also worked with Alchymia, and has written that 'redesign emerges out of an attempt to demonstrate that from today and for at least ten years into the future, one can do nothing but redesign'.[41] This somewhat pessimistic statement should be contrasted with Paolo Portoghesi's rather positive exhibition, which was also shown at the 1980 Venice Biennale. Portoghesi's work will be discussed later, but his contribution to Venice, *The Presence of the Past*, was a watershed for Post-Modern architecture, as revealed in the caprice Classicism of

TOP: ALCHYMIA, PAINTING, 1986 FOR THE EXHIBITION 'DESIGN PITTORICO'; *ABOVE*: CYCLING OUTFIT, 1985

PAOLO PORTOGHESI, *LIUTO* ARMCHAIRS AND SOFA, LATE 1970s FOR POLTRONOVA

many of the facade entries for an imaginary street – 'La Strada Novissima'. Excellent Post-Modern designs were submitted by, for example, Leon Krier, Hans Hollein and Robert Venturi. Andrea Branzi has reflected upon the obvious clash of the 'banal' object with Post-Modern work, and writes astutely that 'These two initiatives were marked by profound differences, but both derived from a common fundamental realisation, that of the impracticability of the modern moralistic and methodological project, to which Mendini gave a last farewell ("Goodbye design") and which Paolo Portoghesi wished to supplant by an act of cultural liberation ("The end of prohibitionism"). Both claimed that the historical period marked by the culture of the Modern Movement had come to an end, but whereas banal design postulated the advent of an era which would see the collapse of any possibility of putting design back together again as a culture, and in which it would survive only as a free circulation of superficial signs, the latter proposed a return to the orderly world of historical tradition, styles and the academy'.[42] In fact, somewhat paradoxically to Branzi's argument, Alchymia had produced some Post-Modern Classical work, as if to reconcile the trends. One example is *Colonna*, a fluted column drawer unit in lacquered wood (1979), by the Swiss architects Trix and Robert Haussmann.

The final flowering of all that was Post-Pop in Italy was Memphis, formed upon Sottsass' secession from Alchymia in 1981. As with Alchymia, it too could embrace genuine Post-Modern work by, say, Graves and Hollein, while having at the same time somewhat different intentions. The middle-aged Sottsass surrounded himself with architect-designers, many of whom were under thirty years of age. The name Memphis sounds enigmatic, but is apparently based on the words of a Bob Dylan record entitled 'Stuck inside of Mobile with the Memphis Blues again'. There is a brightly-coloured sculpture of 1966 of the same name by William Tucker, in the Tate Gallery, and even as the name of a city it is ambiguous, referring both to Memphis, Tennessee, and to the ancient Egyptian city of culture.

Memphis has issued new catalogues and designs annually since 1981. The group is like a very large international rock band, its strident visual music played regularly by Italians such as Sottsass and his journalist companion Barbara Radice, Andrea Branzi, Aldo Cibic, Michele De Lucchi and Marco Zanini, and foreign designers resident in Italy, such as the Briton George Sowden and his French-born partner Nathalie du Pasquier, and also the talented Austrian designer, Matteo Thun. Guest appearances have been made by 'new wave' Spanish designers such as Xavier Mariscal, Japanese designers such as Masanori Umeda and Shiro Kuramata, and the American 'funk' ceramics and furniture designer Peter Shire. Finally, occasional pieces have been designed by Post-Modern architects including Michael Graves, Hans Hollein, Arata Isozaki and Arquitectonica. Memphis has of late been backed by Artemide, and relied on many firms to produce its work. Foremost amongst these is Abet Laminates of Bra in North

West Italy, who have been experimenting with high-pressure laminates since 1969 in their important Laboratorio Serigrafico. Memphis have used Up and Up, Massa, near the famous Carrara, to produce their marble furniture. At least three ceramics firms have been pressed into service: Porcellane San Marco, Nove, Bassano, in Northern Italy, Ceramiche Flavia, Montelupo Fiorentino, and Alessio Sarri, Sesto Fiorentino, in Tuscany. The metalwork has been made by Rossi & Arcandi, Monticello Conte Otto, Vicenza, and the glass by Toso Vetri d'Arte, Murano. The result of this is that very little is made in Milan, save for example, fabrics by Studio Rainbow.

In a confused, pluralistic decade when history and popular culture meet, Memphis can be described perhaps as the ultimate 'fruit salad'. The culinary image is not misplaced in an appreciation of the 'style'. Branzi, who has worked for the group, illustrates his own hotly coloured photograph of liquorice allsorts, taken in 1976, in his book *The Hot House*. The title of the book is a good image, a metaphor for growth. Sottsass has said that 'anything that is tamed by culture loses its flavour after a while, it's like eating cardboard. You have to put mustard on it or take little pieces of cardboard and eat them with tomatoes and salad. It's a lot better if you don't eat cardboard at all'.[43] Memphis objects seem to be almost edible, painted in food colours, with reference to many flavours of ice-cream, especially cassata and tutti-frutti. Shiro Kuramata's metal and terrazzo Kyoto table (1983) looks exactly like the latter, as if it had been custom-designed as a table for ice-cream – it also looks like nougat – while Nathalie du Pasquier's fabrics have even been compared to sweet wrappers. Memphis presents many different viewpoints under the parasol of one name, but at its centre remains the work of Sottsass, who, in common with many others, took an interest in suburban materials such as laminates and plastic. Such a veering from 'good taste' was perhaps further legitimised in Italy by the publication of Gillo Dorfles' essays, *Kitsch: The World of Bad Taste* (1969). Many of the Memphis group use Abet Laminates, some of which imitate marble or are highly decorative – *faux* surfaces which would make a Rationalist Modern designer turn in his grave. The cliché of tubular steel has been supplanted by surface plastic, destined to be the most hackneyed embellishment of the 1980s. According to Barbara Radice, 'the idea of patterned plastic laminate furniture came to Sottsass as he was drinking coffee at ten o'clock one morning at the pink-and-blue veined counter of a quasi-suburban milk bar near his house'.[44]

Sottsass' work is often highly zoomorphic or anthropomorphic, so that it 'inhabits' the environment like a living creature. His *Carlton* room divider in plastic laminate (1981) has as its central feature the conventionalised form of a man; some of its shelves slant, setting up an echo of the angled 'anti-design' drawer handles of some Alchymia furniture. The whole room divider has a large, almost living presence. So does Sottsass' *Tahiti* table lamp (1981), which resembles a nodding bird or a duck drawn from the memory bank of all that Walt Disney's cartoons have contributed to popular culture. More arresting, and perhaps self-revealing, is his *Ashoka* table lamp (1981); it seems to be a self-caricature of his own occasionally baleful and bespectacled face. This has not been done since Lutyens' witty self-portrait in a light fitting of about 1930, when the British architect referred to his owl-glasses, Pith helmet and pipe in the structure of the object.

These objects are warm and humorous. By way of sharp contrast, his metalwork can be as cold as ice. The titles, as much as the angular metallic forms of *Alaska* and *Murmansk* (1982), make one shiver. This is an intelligent use of metal, and disproves the often held idea that all Memphis work is over-heated, sensual and highly colourful.

Memphis is to some extent a combination of all the visual arts, with architecture, painting, sculpture, ceramics, glass, metalwork and furniture all blended together and looked at in a new way. Sottsass can be highly ambidextrous in his approach to form. His *Hyatt* briar wood and metal table (1984) is almost a return to a rather restrained Art Deco influence, while some of his ceramics –for example his black and white *Lettuce* of 1985 – seem to get their inspiration from the Ben Day dot technique of Pop artists, notably Lichtenstein. Sottsass' more recent work, such as his glass-topped side table, *Ivory* (1985), crosses the boundary between sculpture and design, in much the same way that Picasso bridged the gap between painting and sculpture during his synthetic Cubist period of 1912-14.

Sottsass' artistry and his *ennui* with 'good form' is expressed through the energy of a new generation of young designers who are Post-Pop – Michele De Lucchi and Nathalie du Pasquier for example, who were born as recently as 1951 and 1957 respectively. Other influences include 'Third World' colours based on flags and textiles, which have particularly inspired Nathalie du Pasquier's fabrics and the titles and colour of some work, for example Peter Shire's *Brazil*. Everything from Hollywood Deco through to 1950s asymmetrical furniture has been part of the Memphis pluralism. Even 1930s rationalism has been revived in Andrea Branzi's work. References to specifically Italian materials such as mosaic and marble are particularly frequent, while in the glass designs of Sottsass and Marco Zanini, a long Venetian tradition can be detected. Sottsass' work in this medium is particularly exciting. His asymmetrical *Sol* fruit dish of blown glass, produced in Murano, has a 1950s feel to it, and is a colourful, hedonistic artefact that in form and title conveys a mood of gastronomic pleasure. Given Memphis' limited production runs, it is also a popular object, 78 having been sold from 1982 to 1986. Sottsass' *Alioth* and *Alcor* glass vases, both of 1983, are an interesting blend of the industrial electrical isolator form with 'traditional' Venetian forms of decoration, coloured trailing and assertive prunts – protruberances which have been used since early times to embellish glass. They work well within the Venetian glass history of which they now form a part. Again, sales from 1983 to 1986 were limited to 23 and 27 respectively, indicating how much some Memphis work really is 'craft',

produced in this case by rather traditional processes.

The concertina form of the porcelain isolator also lies behind some of Marco Zanini's ceramics, especially *Victoria* (1983). This is topped with an ice-cream-like confection of cocks-comb form, which might almost have been taken out of context from a Kandinsky painting. The cocks-comb, rooster's razor shape, is a typical Memphis motif, which also resembles that most borrowed of forms, the outline of one of Andy Warhol's *Flowers*.

The work of Michele De Lucchi has a highly sensuous surface. Like Sottsass, he was a member of Alchymia and, at that stage, in 1979, his ideas included a rethink of product design appliances such as fans, vacuum cleaners and irons, painted somewhat ironically in baby blues, powder pinks and yellows. His Memphis work is often symmetrical, with much use of Op Art black and white, contrasted with hot and cold colours. De Lucchi has revealed that he was inspired in London on New Year's Eve, 1980, by Punks and their bizarre make-up. However, he has also been influenced by the 1950s revival, since working on a 1950s exhibition in Milan in 1977. An example of this tendency is his *First* chair (1983), in metal and wood, with its blue circular backrest and balls for armrests. As it transpired, it was aptly named, turning out to be Memphis' best-selling design. Between 1983 and the end of 1986, 3,065 were sold and generally it is rare for more than 100 of any design in Memphis furniture to be purchased.

A background in the crafts rather than design lies behind much of Peter Shire's work for Memphis. He is very much a Los Angeles artist, with a background not in architecture, but in ceramics. He admires certain pockets of craft and design history, notably Marianne Brandt's work at the Bauhaus and Claes Oldenburg's *Bedroom Ensemble* of 1963. It would be best to describe Shire as part of the 'Funk aesthetic' which began in America, notably in California, in the 1960s. An exhibition on Funk Art was held in 1967, with an introductory essay entitled 'Notes on Funk' by Peter Selz. Part of Funk's contribution was to legitimise the making of non-functional pots and vessels, which were contradictions-in-terms, and transgressed all the rules about 'form following function'. In the liberal 1960s, Selz defined the trend in the following way: 'Funk Art is hot rather than cool; it is sensuous, and frequently it is quite ugly and ungainly'. Without knowing it, and before the event, Selz could be describing Shire's work, or indeed Memphis creations in general. Shire's work is bright, asymmetrical, and very much part of the Californian 'sunbelt' aesthetic which is perhaps why it fits in so well with Italian design. Hot colours and warm climates seem to go well together. Shire uses vast expanses of red in his *Bel Air* fabric-covered armchair for Memphis (1982); it is a true 'hot-house' design which jumps out even further than its competitors from the pages of Memphis' lush, holiday-brochure-coloured catalogues.

Shire is conscious of the difference between his training and that of most of the Memphis group, and has written, 'One of the

ETTORE SOTTSASS, *CASABLANCA* SIDEBOARD, 1981 AND *CARLTON* ROOM DIVIDER, 1981 FOR MEMPHIS, AND *MEDICI* DINNERWARE, 1985
FOR SWID POWELL

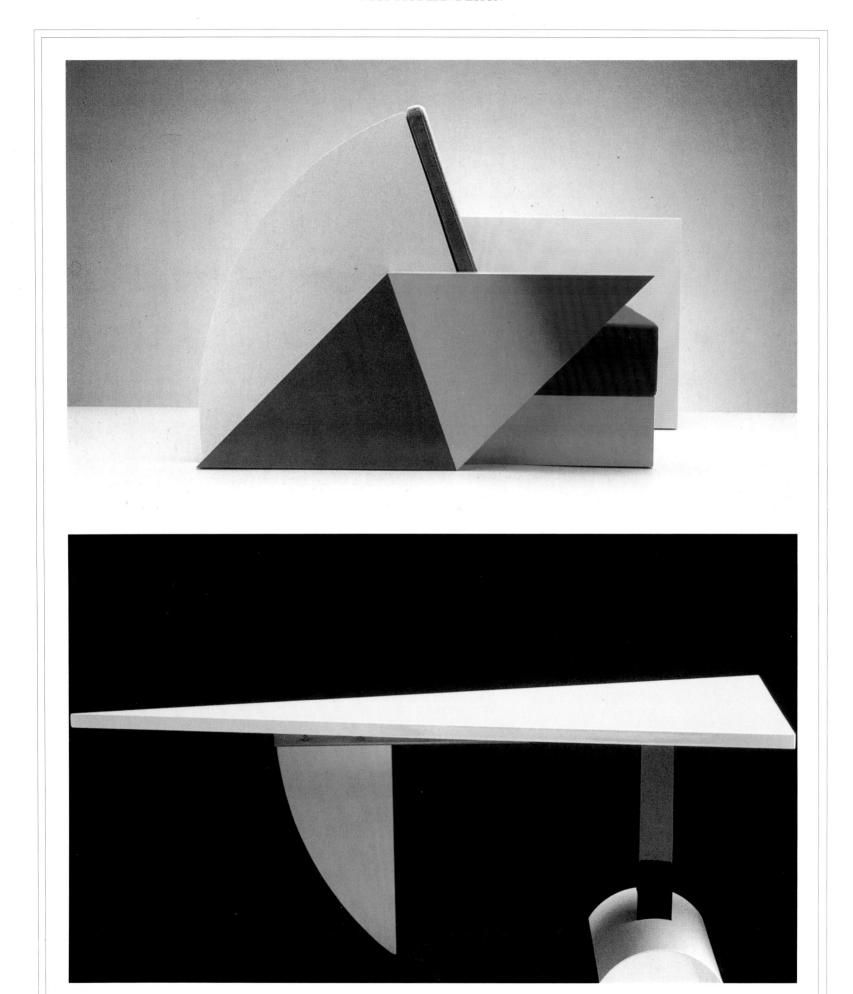

PETER SHIRE, *BONE AIR* CHAIR, 1984 AND *BRAZIL* TABLE, 1981 FOR MEMPHIS

things about Memphis is that they're all architects and I'm the only non-architect but I do have a strong architecture affinity'.[45] Shire, as with some other Memphis designers such as Sottsass, transcends the barrier between painting, sculpture and design. Perhaps his best known object is his table entitled *Brazil*, of 1981, which is predominantly in the yellow and green of the Brazilian flag. It is highly 'sculptural' and with its wedge shape, is more artistic than functional. One wonders whether this genre of furniture could have been achieved without the precedent, say, of the work of David Smith and Anthony Caro in sculpture in the late 1950s or early 1960s. Although it is somewhat more 'controlled' than the work of these sculptors, it penetrates space and uses quasi-sculptural language. The void between the two very different supports – and here one hesitates to call them legs – is as interesting as the solids that delineate it. This Romantic asymmetry can be opposed to the rather 'classic' balance of Modern Movement furniture. Perhaps, even subconsciously, Shire is extending the Gothic tradition of asymmetry as a visual device. Shire was very much a 'guest' designer, admired by the Italians, and has continued to work from California, independently from Memphis. Barbara Radice, in her book *Memphis* has illustrated many of the ceramics which he makes outside the group.

Sottsass has written of his process that 'Peter Shire invented a way of making ceramics that is very special. Using surfaces instead of moulding them on a wheel. He has put together surfaces. I never saw such an approach and we like it very much because we also were interested in not imagining form as a compact whole . . . Peter Shire was doing this independently, but he was following the same process we were, and I thought that this could be the right friend for us'.[46] Arquitectonica's *Madonna* table (1984), for Memphis, should also be seen in the context of 'sunbelt' design, having a blue top with a red edge, and yellow base in lacquered wood. The images set up are those of a swimming pool, blue sky, and the yellow of sun and sand; in short, the images of Miami where Arquitectonica is based. The group, headed by Laurinda Spear and Bernardo Fort-Brescia, have used these primary colours in their architecture, most notably in Atlantis of 1980-82, a twenty-storey condominium building in Miami. As with Shire's work, the table ties in well with the hot colours of Memphis. It is a shaped swimming pool of a design, and conveys all that is luxurious about Florida.

Some of the most strident Memphis and post-Memphis work has been designed by the productive partnership of George Sowden and Nathalie Du Pasquier. Sowden is British and Du Pasquier is French; and it is significant that she travelled in Africa, India and Australia from 1975 to 1978, for her work embraces much interest in the colours and patterns of the Third and Fourth Worlds. Her prowess is in textile and fabric design, whereas Sowden contributes more to the design and three-dimensionality of their work. Her jazzy fabrics for Memphis have exotic names, such as *Mali* of 1981, and *Gabon*, *Zaire*, and *Zambia*, all of 1982. In conjunction with Sowden,

she has designed the bright *Mamounia* armchair in 1985 for Memphis, in lacquered wood, plastic laminate and velvet. Interestingly, the fabric cover has a bird as part of its design, a motif which she has been using quite often of late. It suggests the migrating designer, flying over the globe. Often Sowden and Du Pasquier have designed independently from each other and some recent work has been separate from Memphis, though not from Milan where they work. In 1984 they produced lamps for Arc 74 as *Objects for the electronic age*, and in 1986 a range of brightly-coloured clocks called *Neos*, for Lorenz in Milan. One of the best of these looks like a highly conventionalised form of Mickey Mouse with square black ears – a cartoon character that makes regular appearances in so much recent design. Du Pasquier has done textile and fabric design for Fiorucci, and for Esprit in the United States, and both designers produced exotic carpets for Elio Palmisano in Italy during 1985 and 1986. They have also made one-off ceramics in 1986 – some of which were exhibited at the Galleria Steineman in Lucerne – and in 1987 Sowden designed coffee pots and fruit bowls for Bodum in Switzerland.

Du Pasquier's global village eclecticism is extraordinary, and her approach is sometimes that of the ethnographer or anthropologist of village life. She writes of her interests: 'we have just been taking part in an exhibition in Denmark . . . the exhibition was called: "HOMO DECORANS", the man who decorates. They had presented all kinds of items and images from Japanese tattoos, war paintings of African tribes, Danish jewellery, Italian design furniture and New Yorker's graffiti, to Pakistanese trucks covered in multicolour decorations and lots of other things. I could see us, George and I being part of a tribe just as much as all the other represented groups – we were part of a little tribe in the jungle of North Italian Design . . .'.[47] Barbara Radice has observed that 'Nathalie is a kind of natural decorative genius – anarchic, highly sensitive, wild, abstruse, capable of turning out extraordinary drawings at the frantic pace of a computer. Her visual research is unrestrained, it absorbs everything . . . and nothing in particular . . . her patterns . . . embrace Africa, Cubism, Futurism and Art Deco; India, graffiti, jungles and towns; science fiction, caricature, aborigines, and Japanese comics . . .'.[48]

If only by way of contrast, Nathalie Du Pasquier's work reminds one sharply of the fact that so much Modern and even Post-Modern work has been Eurocentric, or North American, embracing exclusively Old and New World concerns. In drawing inspiration from the Third and Fourth Worlds her work is a salutary intervention, making one aware of how literally white and middle class design has been up to now. At worst, one could accuse her simply of 'going native', but at best her sharp colours draw attention to non-Judeo-Christian traditions. As with true Post-Modernism her prolific output veers away from the Protestant ethos of 'good form' discussed earlier. Few others have taken what Loos called 'tatooing' on board, but she bravely, and sometimes shockingly, counters the Austrian's almost pathological fear of decoration. It may be

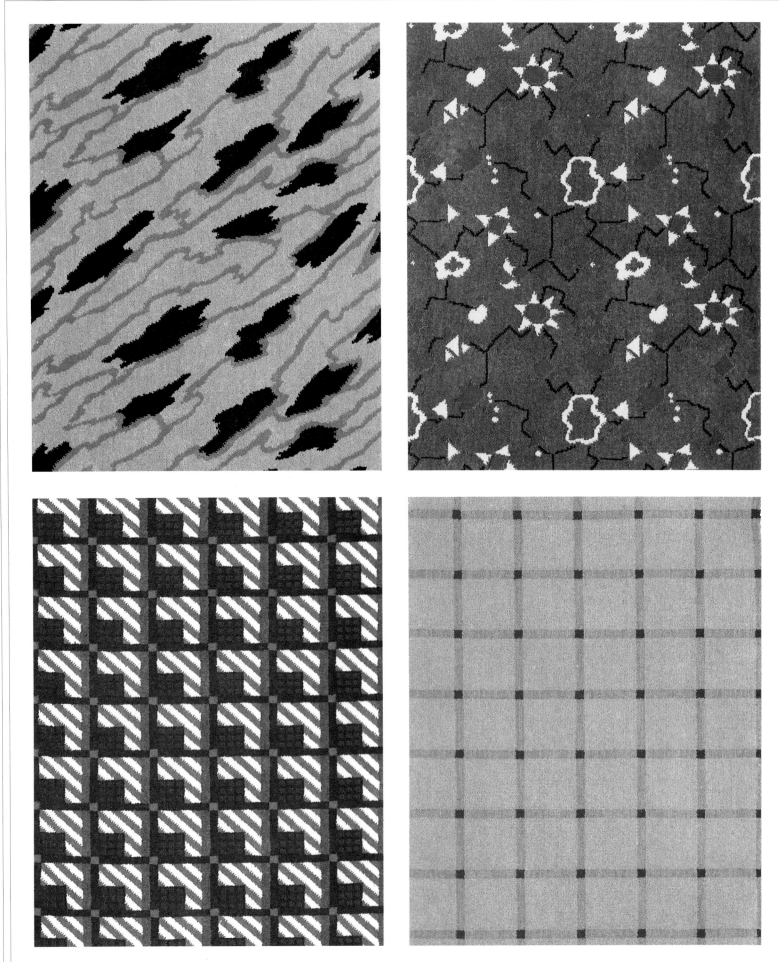

MEMPHIS CARPETS *STREAM*, *TOTEM*, *DOMINO*, *TRESEL*

MEMPHIS CARPET *FLOATING*

relevant to suggest that it took a woman to do this and to break the male reserve, in both senses, that dominated modern design for too long. Loos attacked the art of the tribe; Le Corbusier steered us away from peasant art. Du Pasquier, however, ranges across the gamut of possible inspiration, unfettered by the 'Laws' of design.

One of the most gifted designers attached to Memphis is the Austrian Matteo Thun, whose ceramics often echo Sottsass' interest in zoomorphic forms. Thun's ceramics look like strutting birds. The Hamburg-born couturier Karl Lagerfeld, whose fashion drawings occasionally include a background of Memphis furniture, had an apartment in Monte Carlo filled with some of Thun's best creations. One of Thun's most fascinating designs is a geometrical form, in grey, pink and mauve, aptly called *Pellicanus Bellicosus*, made by Alessio Sarri, Sesto Fiorentino, in 1982. Some of his ceramics pair off, and he sexes them as lovers, such as the 'male' *Passer Passer* and the 'female' *Passer Noctua*, both in 1982. He has said of these that they are 'the couple of the collection "in love". He with his sharp and vulnerable handles protects his "maid"'.[49]

This type of zoomorphic reference has not been seen since the days of Christopher Dresser in the 1880s, when the latter in a design for a claret jug set up visual parallels between the belly, leg, and beak of a bird and the shape of an object designed to pour. Thun also uses the cocks-comb shape extensively in his forms for Memphis, which are generally asymmetrical, and remind us of birds. In his Memphis range, or what might be called a little zoo or aviary, his *Chad* teapot (1982) is a humorous hybrid between a duck and a toy tank. It was made by Porcellane San Marco and, given Memphis' limited runs, it has sold quite well – 112 between its introduction and the end of 1986. Perhaps as a result of his participation in Memphis, Thun has emerged as one of the most adventurous ceramics designers of the 1980s. His strength is that he is a master of form, of what he has called 'affectionate functionality'. His attitude to design is that it should be, among other things, 'experimental', 'metaphorical', and 'post-industrial'. He has coined a most important phrase, the 'Baroque Bauhaus', which describes much of Memphis, and certainly his own work. This oxymoron, as with, for example, Milton's 'burning lake' in *Paradise Lost*, is highly arresting. It sums up one clearly Post-Modern technique, that is, taking what is needed from modernity (eg Bauhaus), and adding more decoration (eg Baroque). The basis of much of Thun's work is 'good form' and as such it relates to the Bauhaus, Ulm and Dieter Rams, but embellishes it further. One cannot be sure yet that such a technique is valid or aesthetically sound, but not withstanding this, Thun can be assessed as a highly competent designer. Thun's important contribution will be examined more fully later in an assessment of new German design. Much of his recent non-Memphis work relies on the use of the oxymoron. His *Rainer Sofa* (1983) forces an Art Deco form into conjunction with some William Morris patterning, a combination of two design languages that is akin to, say, speaking French and English at the same time. Whether or not it is what Evelyn Waugh used to delight in calling 'gibberish', when describing the later writing of James Joyce, has yet to be decided. At best it is design's version of Esperanto and we can all understand the references, and even applaud them. Thun also used the oxymoron in his mass-produced trays for W M F of 1986, which have Morris-inspired surface decoration. This spells out the historical contradiction-in-terms of 'mass-produced Morris'. Thun's storage units for Bieffeplast of 1985 are virtually High-Tech; more Bauhaus than Baroque, more High-Tech than Post-Modern. Like the birds he so evidently draws inspiration from, it is difficult to put him in a cage labelled 'Post-Modern' because he is as likely to fly back and forth to modernity for inspiration. Thun represents quite a lot that is not Post-Modern, and still at heart genuinely admires the Modern Movement.

In the context of this issue, but representing an altogether separate tradition, the Japanese work for Memphis is important. Much still displays what used to be thought of as Japanese restraint. Shiro Kuramata's elegant *Imperial* cabinets (1981), available in tasteful, quasi-oriental silver, black, or aubergine, are exercises in non-supersensualist design. Their quiet presence in the overheated catalogue of Memphis work paradoxically makes them stand out: an inversion of the 'he who shouts loudest strategy' of the 1980s. They have the attraction of the 'shy ones at an orgy', to steal a line from a Leonard Cohen song. Restrained, too, is Kuramata's lacquered and bleached wood *Ritz* writing desk (1981), for Memphis. Though his ironic treatment of *Hommage to Hoffman, Begin the Begin* (1985) has been discussed earlier as a Post-Modern gesture, and his colourful *Kyoto* table (1983) as typical of Memphis, his latest work represents a return to restraint. There is an extraordinary oriental quietness in his anodised metal *Apple Honey* chair (1985) which, with its simple pink metal backrest and evocative title, conjures up the stereotypical image of the Japanese poetic of nature. As a design it is as elementary as Basho's simple seventeenth-century haiku poem which begins: 'A cloud of blossoming cherry trees'. It could be argued that in *Apple Honey*, Minimalism is combined with, say, the simplicity of the haiku tradition. East meets West in Kuramata's steel chair *How high the moon* (1986), with its latticed metal which sets up a dialogue with rather more slick European 'High-Tech' work. Kuramata's work, as a whole, is like Thun's in that it cannot easily be pinned down, categorised or labelled. It transcends 'High Tech' Modernism, Late-Modernism and Post-Modernism.

The simplicity of Japanese 'design' and the distinctness of oriental outlook has been observed by Roland Barthes in the *Empire of Signs* (1970). In it he wrote that '. . . furniture (a paradoxical word in French – meuble – since it generally designates a property anything but mobile, concerning which one does everything so that it will endure: with us furniture has an immobilising vocation, whereas in Japan the house, often deconstructed, is scarcely more than a furnishing-mobile-element) . . . in the ideal Japanese house, stripped of furniture

MICHELE DE LUCCHI, *ANTARES* VASE, 1983, *CAIRO* TABLE, 1986 AND *HORIZON* BED, 1984 FOR MEMPHIS

GEORGE SOWDEN, *MAMOUNIA* ARMCHAIR, 1985 FOR MEMPHIS

GEORGE SOWDEN, *GLOUCESTER*, 1986, CHAIR FOR MEMPHIS, AND *ALHAMBRA*, *CADIZ*, *SARAGOZA*, 1985, CHAIRS FOR PIER-LUIGI GHIANDA

GEORGE SOWDEN, *D'ANTIBES* CABINET, 1981, *BLACK AND WHITE* TABLE, 1986, STEEL AND PLASTIC CLOCK, 1983 FOR ARC 74

(or scantily furnished), there is no site which designates the slightest propriety in the strict sense of the word – ownership: neither seat nor bed nor table out of which the body might constitute itself as the subject (or master) of a space: the centre is rejected (painful frustration for Western man, everywhere "furnished" with his armchair, his bed, proprietor of a domestic location)'.[50] Not all of Kuramata's work is, to echo Barthes' word-play, mobile or light, but it has a greater simplicity than much of the other work by Memphis designers.

Masanori Umeda has also designed for Memphis. His 'boxing ring', *Tawarayi* (1981), constructed of wood and metal with straw mats, sets up a resonance with the rectilinearity of traditional Japanese architecture, and may even suggest a reflection upon the importance of the wrestler. Umeda's somewhat phallic *Orinoco* vase, produced for Memphis by Ceramiche Flavia in 1983, reminds one of penis-emblems at a sexual Shinto shrine. He has written an important statement which sums up his design process: 'Its rhetoric is Japanese in spirit with Western learning . . . What I call "Japanese" is mostly quotation of the traditional sense of aestheticism, which forms a part of our contemporary life, such as the taste of the elegant simplicity and quietness in the Tea Ceremony, the transition of seasons, the subtle and profound beauty of nature, the Oriental cosmos of "Zen", the primitive native religion and folktales, the mind and norm of military arts, the spirit of "haiku" poets which adores nature, the richness and gorgeousness of "Kabuki" plays, the splendid traditional crafts, the sacred rituals, the excitement and fascination of festivals, the eroticism of "Ukiyo-e" prints and the gay quarter, and so on'.[51]

Umeda's eclecticism leads to his Post-Modernism, which relies on quotation from stereotypical Japanese traditions. He writes: 'The products which resulted from the value of modern rationalism in the past are certainly beautiful. However, they recently give me a feeling that there is something lacking, probably because of its excessive stoicism'.[52]

The Japanese Post-Modern architect Arata Isozaki, also designed for Memphis. His work was limited to a pair of sidetables, called *Fuji*, made in 1981. These blend the form of the traditional table tennis bat-shaped Japanese hand mirror with 'new wave' Italian colour. A similar cross-fertilisation took place a century ago when designers such as Christopher Dresser borrowed Japanese devices for their own furniture. Isozaki underlines the old East-West borrowed and borrower tradition, even if he reverses it. Unfortunately, his *Fuji* tables were not highly appreciated, and only two were ever sold, which is almost an all time low for Memphis.

Memphis design has often been presented as a lush, rich departure to be devoured by journalists and lavishly illustrated, not always accompanied by much critical analysis. It also forms part of a growing consumerism; the gaderene rush to produce more, and yet more, artefacts. Isozaki stated that 'the important thing about Memphis is also the way it appeared to the world . . . Memphis appeared suddenly, as fashion does, and it had a very strong impact all over the world . . . things always change rapidly anyhow'.[53] Distinctions have to be made between Italian 'new wave' or 'hot house' design, and 'Post-Modern' design, even if the distinctions are sometimes blurred. The vast majority can be called 'Post-Pop', which covers the pluralistic rather than historicist strain in Memphis.

The difference between Memphis and Post-Modern has been spelled out by both Barbara Radice and Ettore Sottsass. In 1984 Radice wrote that 'Memphis is decidedly different from the Postmodernist mainstream, which is historicist and inclined towards restoration in that it looks backward to classical or vernacular culture. Memphis' efforts and interest are concentrated instead on the present and on that special part of the present which is the hot house of the future'.[54] Her point is important, though it still remains clear that Post-Modern and Italian 'new wave' design have shared roots and interests, and are even tied together like the two tramps in Samuel Beckett's *Waiting for Godot*. Sottsass is more certain that Post-Modernism is American, and he, as with some other writers, almost accuses Post-Modernism of American cultural imperialism. He writes: 'First of all, my point of view concerning Postmodernism is that it is an American movement born in the United States. In some ways I even consider it as a kind of a nationalistic movement which was founded on the will of some young American architects who desired to find the origin of their architecture. They have and are still recouping three possibilities of it. The first is the "peasantry" architecture accompanied with barns, and the second is the "suburbia" or "pop" architecture which is in a word modern anonymous architecture represented by Las Vegas, highways and the hotels along them. The third is the most important one, the "aristocratic" architecture . . . in America . . . related to Palladio . . . I consider Postmodernism as a very academic movement in which there can always be seen a lot of quoting, especially of their own, American history . . . I don't consider our group Memphis to have anything to do with Postmodern at all, for we are quoting from everything, from unlimited time and space. By this means, it may be said that we possibly belong to Neo-Modern, rather than to Postmodern . . . we are much interested in the suburban language; the surroundings of big towns and modern materials, colours and so on. Our method is more actual. We don't quote from historical architectural elements to give identity to the works as the American Postmodernists do'.[55]

Sottsass is correct in seeing the distinctions between 'Neo-Modern' Memphis work and American-inspired Post-Modernism. The latter clearly has a Neo-Classical inflection, which Sottsass associates with the influence of Palladio, yet it is clear that some Memphis work is a return to tradition. The use of marble in itself, and much of the Memphis glass which refers to Venetian glassmaking history, are examples. We have seen that the Japanese designers quote their traditions, and three Post-Modern architects, Arata Isozaki, Michael Graves and Hans Hollein, have produced work for Memphis. Their work will be examined shortly, in the context of Post-Modern design in the 1980s.

MATTEO THUN, TEAPOTS, 1983 FOR MEMPHIS

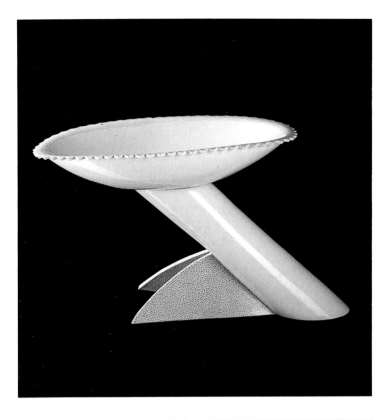

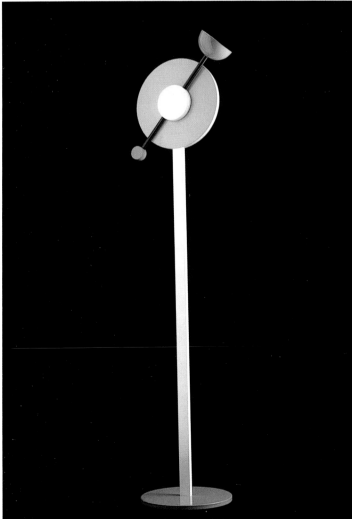
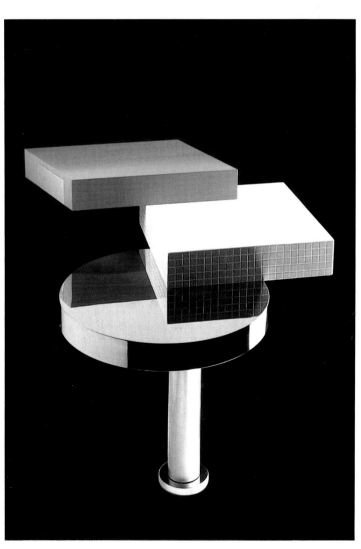

MATTEO THUN, *KARIBA*, 1982, MARCO ZANINI, *ROMA I* ARMCHAIR, 1986, MARTINE BEDIN, LAMP, 1984, JAMES IRVINE, CONSOLE, 1986
FOR MEMPHIS

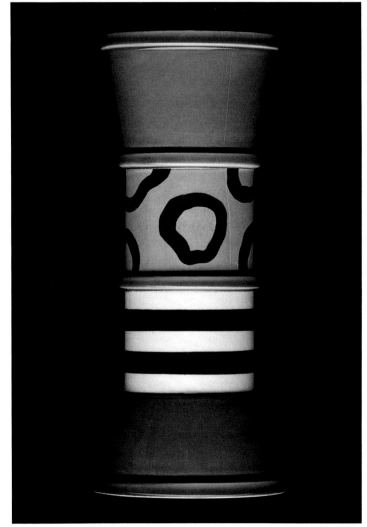

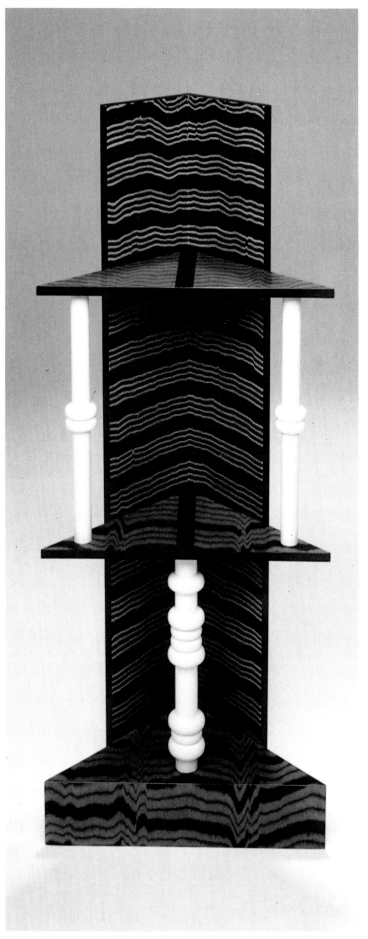

NATHALIE DU PASQUIER, BOX WITH LID, 1983 FOR ARC 74, CORNER UNIT, 1986 FOR PIER-LUIGI GHIANDA, *CARROT* VASE, 1985 FOR MEMPHIS

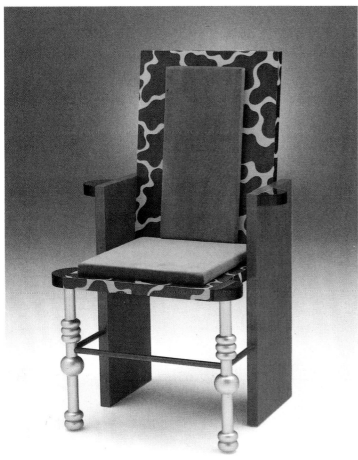

NATHALIE DU PASQUIER, *MERCEDES*, *ESMERELDA*, *PILAR* ARMCHAIRS, 1985 FOR PIER-LUIGI GHIANDA, PROTOTYPE CHAIR, 1986 FOR MEMPHIS

NATHALIE DU PASQUIER, *NATHALIE* CHAIR, 1987 FOR MEMPHIS

NATHALIE DU PASQUIER, *DENISE* CHAIR, 1987 FOR MEMPHIS

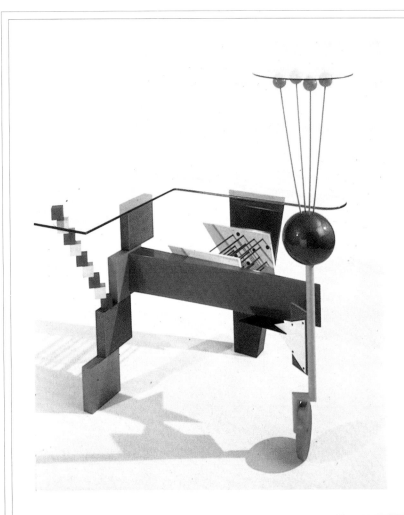

PETER SHIRE, *CHICAGO SERIES* TABLE, 1982, *PHIDIAS* CHAIR, 1984 AND *VARIEGATED HARLEQUIN* TABLE, 1982

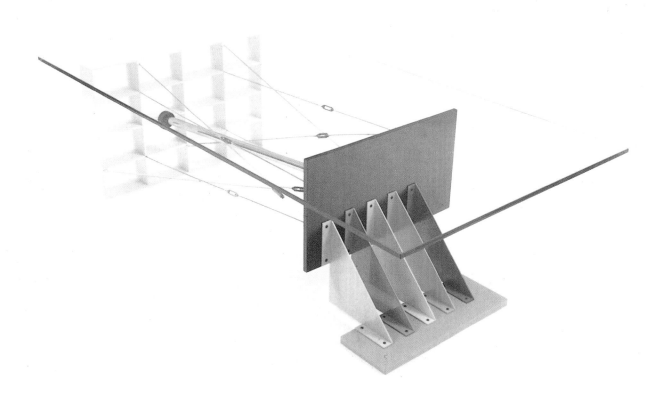

PETER SHIRE AND CHAIR, c1985 AND PETER SHIRE, *STEEL NEEDLE* TABLE, 1984

ETTORE SOTTSASS, *MAX* SIDEBOARD, 1987 FOR MEMPHIS

GEORGE SOWDEN, *GEORGE* SIDEBOARD, 1987 FOR MEMPHIS

MARCO ZANINI, *JUAN* CHAISE LONGUE, 1987 FOR MEMPHIS

ANDREA BRANZI, *ANDREA* CHAISE LONGUE, 1987 AND MASSIMO IOSA-GHINI, *BERTRAND* SIDEBOARD, 1987 FOR MEMPHIS

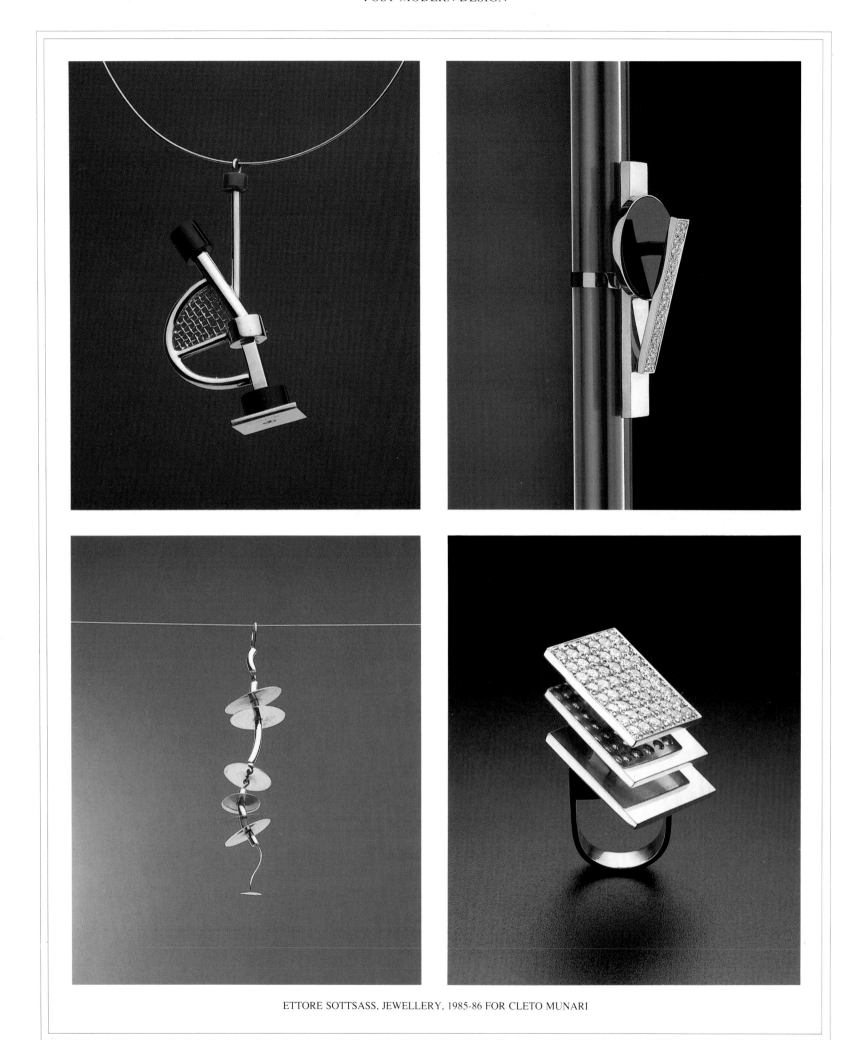

ETTORE SOTTSASS, JEWELLERY, 1985-86 FOR CLETO MUNARI

ETTORE SOTTSASS, *MIZAR*, 1982, AND *ANANKE / NEOBULE*, *ARISTEA*, *CLESITERA*, 1986, GLASSWARE FOR MEMPHIS

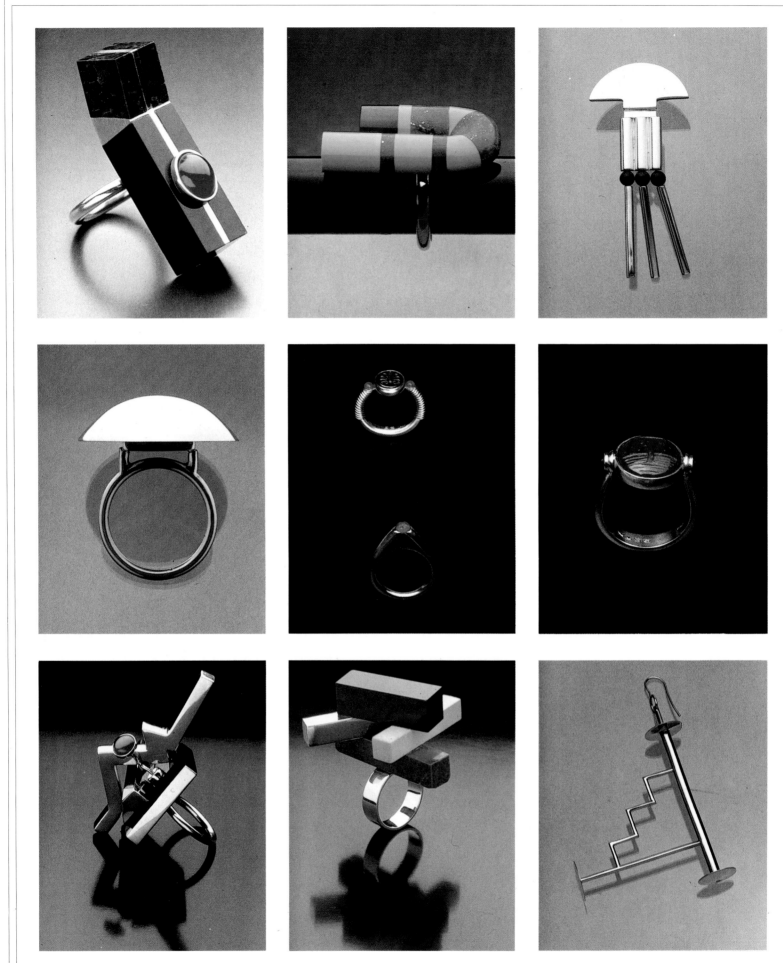

JEWELLERY BY ARATA ISOZAKI, HANS HOLLEIN, MICHAEL GRAVES AND SOTTSASS, 1985-86 FOR CLETO MUNARI

WATCHES BY ARATA ISOZAKI, HANS HOLLEIN, MICHAEL GRAVES AND ETTORE SOTTSASS, 1987 FOR CLETO MUNARI

SITE, DOOR, 1983 FOR FORMICA COLORCORE

CHAPTER III
Post-Modernism

ROBERT VENTURI, MIRROR IN THE GREEK REVIVAL MANNER, 1983 FOR FORMICA COLORCORE

Post-Modernism cannot readily be defined without some prior agreement as to what is meant by 'Modern'. Does the modern age begin with the printing press, the use of vernacular language, the Renaissance, the Enlightenment, the French Revolution, the beginning of the twentieth century, or the International Modern Style? Since no university has ever agreed on when 'modern' begins as an area for study, nor any museum on what constitutes a 'modern' collection, the word is still extraordinarily vague.

For our purposes, the concept of the 'modern' has developed from nineteenth-century French literature and art. Honoré de Balzac, and after him Charles Baudelaire, claimed that beauty existed in modernity, in *la vie moderne*. In painting, this led to an admiration for Courbet, Realism and Impressionism. In architecture, iron was the quintessentially 'modern' material, and it became impossible to ignore its implications – the Neo-Classical architect Karl Friedrich Schinkel and the Gothic revival architect Eugène Viollet-le-Duc both admired it, and the former's sketchbook from his British tour of 1826 is full of references to its use. Yet in the influential English critic John Ruskin the use of such material provoked a hatred and a spirit of anti-modernity. He loathed the 1851 Crystal Palace and resigned in protest at the use of iron for the Oxford Museum of 1855-60, a project with which he had himself been associated.

Ruskin's attitude was far from typical, and the seeds of modernity had been thoroughly sown. Emile Zola's follower,

Joris Karl Huysmans, wrote in *En Ménage* (1881): 'Oh, what insufferable bores they are, the people who sing the praises of the apse of Notre-Dame and the rood-screen at St Etienne-du-Mont! . . . very well, but what about the Gare du Nord and the new Hippodrome?' And Zola himself wrote in *L'Oeuvre* (1886), 'Dubuche . . . turned over to building . . . they were the old theories he had picked up from the revolutionary friends of his youth . . . he went in for tiling and terracotta decorations, vast constructions of glass and iron, especially iron – iron beams, iron staircases, iron roofs'. Zola was writing only a year before the construction of the Eiffel Tower, the prophetic icon of the Modern Movement.

Since that time, a determinist, Whig and progressive view of visual history has been dominant, reaching its peak in the International Modern period of the 1920s and 1930s, and extending into the 1960s. The twentieth century has to a large extent set great store by originality, and revolted against a sense of history. Thus, Alfred Barr of the Museum of Modern Art, New York, could write in 1938: 'Others of us, in architectural schools, were beginning our courses with gigantic renderings of Doric capitals . . . It is no wonder then that young Americans began to turn their eyes towards the Bauhaus as the one school in the world where modern problems of design were approached realistically in a modern atmosphere'. Barr's use of 'modern' implies a rejection of the past, and there was also, in the 1930s, a suggestion of a reductionist trend and a drive towards purity in the International Modern period. George Orwell's simple English reveals this same trend towards linguistic purity, as does the basic English of Raymond McGrath's appendix at the end of his book, *Twentieth Century Houses* (1934). Here, we can see an attempt to strip architectural language of all its flourishes, and reduce its vocabulary to a few key words. This led, in a somewhat determinist way, to the glass 'dumb-box' in architecture, the black box in design, and Minimalism in art in the 1960s. The priests of the International Modern Movement had a pre-Tower of Babel attitude and wanted the world to speak, as in the book of Genesis, 'one language and one speech' – as long as it was their language and speech. Post-Modern design as well as architecture recognises the post-Babel 'confounding of tongues' and the fact that, as Robert Venturi has said, 'less is a bore'.

The architecture and writing of Robert Venturi in the 1960s was an early beginning to Post-Modern architectural developments, and the 1970s brought about the definition of 'Post-Modernism' in architecture in the prolific writings of Charles Jencks. It was he who controversially legitimised the existing term 'Post-Modern' (we have already seen it used by Nikolaus Pevsner in his account of the return of historicism). Jencks' *Modern Movements in Architecture* (1973), *The Language of Post-Modern Architecture* (1977) and *Post-Modern Classicism* (1980), offered excellent surveys of the emergence of anti-Modernism and anti-Rationalism from the work of the Modern architects themselves. Further fillips came from Paolo Portoghesi's *Presence of the Past* exhibition at the 1980 Venice Biennale, with its 'Strada Novissima' by selected Post-Modern architects, including Robert Venturi, Hans Hollein and Leon Krier. Portoghesi also published *Postmodern: the architecture of the post-industrial society* in 1983.

Another key event was the setting up of the German Architectural Museum in Frankfurt, housed in an historic villa adapted by O M Ungers between 1982 and 1984. This has a collection of Post-Modern work organised by Heinrich Klotz, and was followed by the publication of the latter's *Postmodern Visions* (1985) and the *Design Today* exhibition with a catalogue by Volker Fischer, held at the German Architectural Museum between May and August 1988. Key buildings and projects include the following selection, some of which have been especially important to the development of Post-Modern Classicism: Robert Venturi's Chestnut Hill House, Pennsylvania, 1963; Charles Moore's Piazza d'Italia, New Orleans, 1975-80; Ricardo Bofill's Les Arcades du Lac, France, 1975-81; Hans Hollein's Austrian Travel Bureau, Vienna, 1978; Aldo Rossi's Teatro del Mondo, Venice 1979; Charles Jencks' and Terry Farrell's Thematic House, London, 1979-84; Michael Graves's Public Services Building, Portland, Oregon, 1982; Philip Johnson's AT&T building, New York, 1982; Arata Isozaki's Tsukuba Civic Centre, Japan, 1983; James Stirling's Neue Staatsgalerie, Stuttgart, 1984; Gae Aulenti's Musée d'Orsay, Paris 1986. Architects such as those listed above, and others such as Robert Stern and Stanley Tigerman,

have re-established eclecticism, pluralism, decoration, and what in America is called 'ornamentalism'. Ornament is no longer a crime, and strictly speaking, 'Post-Modernism' is an architectural term for the reaction against the International Modern work of architects such as Mies van der Rohe, Walter Gropius, and Le Corbusier.

The term 'postmodern' had also been taken up, usually without the hyphen, by critics and writers in other disciplines. One example is Ihab Hassan's *The Dismemberment of Orpheus; towards a post modern literature* (1971). It was developed in an important collection of essays, edited by Hal Foster in 1983, entitled *The Anti-Aesthetic*, which was published in Britain in 1985 as *Postmodern Culture*. This contained amongst others, important contributions by Jürgen Habermas, Kenneth Frampton, Fredric Jameson and Jean Baudrillard. The French philosopher Jean-François Lyotard's *The Post-Modern Condition* was published in England in 1984. He also curated an exhibition entitled *Les Immatériaux* at the Centre Georges Pompidou in Paris between March and July 1985, which covered philosophy, politics, semiotics, music and literature as well as art and architecture. This has been followed in art by, for example, Victor Burgin's *The end of art theory: criticism and postmodernity* (1986); Brandon Taylor's *Modernism Post-Modernism Realism* (1987), and Charles Jencks' *What is Post-Modernism?* (1987).

Architectural Post-Modernism has been attacked with almost equal vigour by old-guard Modernists and 'without hyphen' postmodernists. In the first group, in 1981, the architect Aldo Van Eyck sniped at 'Rats, posts and pests' while in 1982 the old Modernist architect Berthold Lubetkin came out of retirement to call Post-Modernism 'transvestite architecture, Hepplewhite and Chippendale in drag'. The High-Tech architect Norman Foster has called it 'a game for consenting adults in private only', and in 1986 the critic Deyan Sudjic suggested that it is 'a short time diversion, like art nouveau perhaps, rather than a long-lasting affair'.

The essays, *Postmodern Culture*, edited by Hal Foster, contain some interesting 'without hyphen postmodern' criticisms, especially of Post-Modern architecture. The German writer Jürgen Habermas, when commenting on Portoghesi's *Presence of the Past* exhibition, stated that the architects 'sacrificed the tradition of modernity in order to make room for a new historicism'. He then quoted a German newspaper comment that 'Postmodernity definitely presents itself as Antimodernity'.[56] Although Habermas in general attacks what he sees as neoconservative or reactionary antimodernity, Foster's choice of essays is mainly concerned with what he terms 'oppositional postmodernism' or the 'postmodernism of resistance' rather than the 'postmodernism of reaction'. Another critic selected by Foster, the American Fredric Jameson, agreed with Sottsass in seeing architectural Post-Modernism as American cultural imperialism.

The fact of the matter is that there is a definite geographical inflection towards America in architectural Post-Modernism,

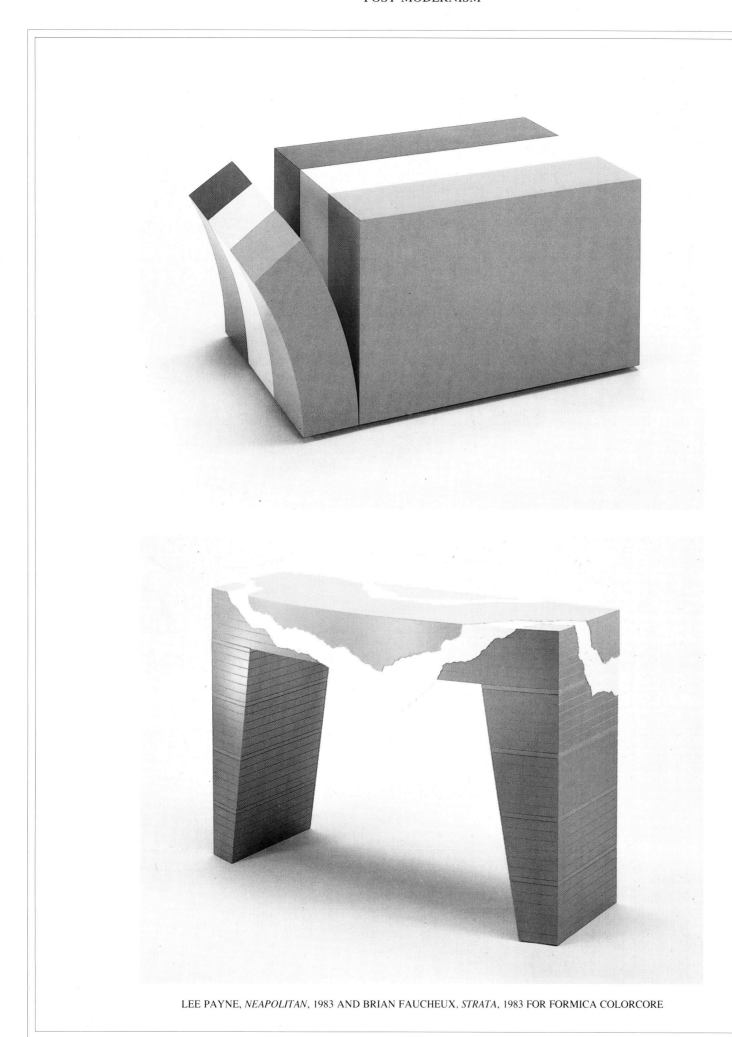

LEE PAYNE, *NEAPOLITAN*, 1983 AND BRIAN FAUCHEUX, *STRATA*, 1983 FOR FORMICA COLORCORE

MASSIMO AND LELLA VIGNELLI, *BROKEN LENGTH*, 1983 AND MILTON GLASER, *MODERN POST- NEO TABLE*, 1983 FOR FORMICA COLORCORE

and non-American Post-Modernists such as Isozaki or Hollein have also worked in America, or studied there. There certainly is a new Classicism, and it is tinged with political problems. The Neo-Classicism of the 1930s has always been seen by most Moderns as the style of totalitarianism, of Stalin and Hitler, and not that of the ideal social order. This ignores the fact that, as we have seen, 'Rationalism' was a Fascist style in Italy, or that, in design at any rate, Moderns such as Wagenfeld kept on working during the Nazi period, with the result that the autobahn, the Volkswagen and the Messerschmitt were all highly 'Modern'.

However, a non Post-Modern Classicism has been embraced by the New-Right critics in England, part of the rearguard that believes that 1930s modernism was an aberration, to be erased forever. The election of Margaret Thatcher in 1979 and Ronald Reagan in 1980 allowed for a return to such a 'silent majority' consensus. As we have seen, this outlook had its adherents even in the 1920s and 1930s with architects such as Reginald Blomfield, and has reappeared in the new right-wing attacks made by David Watkin and Roger Scruton, the latter claiming to speak for 'the common man'. This brand of *rappel à l'ordre* has to be distinguished from others who eagerly accept Classicism for the sake of urban conservation: conservative with a little 'c' is not always the same as that with a big 'C'.

For Americans, on the other hand, it might be logical to see Classicism as one of their founding styles; a point made by Sottsass. It prevailed at the time of the birth of the nation in 1776, of course, and is enshrined in the architecture of parts of Philadelphia and Washington DC. It may thus be seen as a 'national style' in the same way that Pugin thought Gothic was an English national style in the nineteenth century.

For Germans the issue is more complex. It could be seen as part of an uninterrupted tradition stretching from the ideas of the Enlightenment thinkers, Lessing, Winckelmann and Goethe, to the architecture of Schinkel and Semper. Even some great Austrian and German 'Moderns' such as Adolf Loos, Peter Behrens and Ludwig Mies van der Rohe revived Classicism and Neo-Classicism in their architecture. As early as 1910, Adolf Loos said of Schinkel: 'we have forgotten him. May the light of this towering figure shine upon our forthcoming generation of architects'. Loos could not, of course, have predicted that that 'light' shone on Hitler and Albert Speer, and this is where the difficulty begins. Neo-Classicism is too much associated with the darkest period of German history in the 1930s. It is perhaps for that reason (*pace* what has been said about for example the Volkswagen) Late-Modernism is a politically uncontentious style in Germany, while Classicism is bound to set up an awkward resonance with the Nazi period.

If, as Foster, Habermas and others suggest, architectural Post-Modernism is neoconservative, then it is not surprising that on the lips and no doubt in the libraries of such architects are the works of the lions of the eighteenth century, namely Sir John Soane and Karl Friedrich Schinkel, and the visionary paper tigers Etienne-Louis Boullée and Claude Nicolas Ledoux. And the life-support of this neoconservatism is, of course, the column, any column, however it may relate to the Classical Orders.

In 1983, the Scottish artist Ian Hamilton Finlay, whose work expresses a profound interest in the Classical tradition, defined Neo-Classicism in *An Illustrated Dictionary of the Little Spartan War* as a 'rearmament programme for architecture and the arts'. If this is so, then the column is the major weapon. Finlay has also attacked the modern dislike of Classicism in an 'artwork' made in 1981:

'In the back of every dying civilisation
sticks a bloody Doric column,'

Herbert Read, quoted by Charles Jencks

'In the foreground of every revolution
invisible, it seems, to the academics,
stands a perfect classical column.'

Claude Chimérique, quoted by Ian Hamilton Finlay

(Claude Chimérique is a fictitious character, and presumably an invented alter ego of Finlay, bearing a name that suggests the French Revolution).

In fact this admiration for columns and Classicism, like so much else, emerged from Pop Art. As early as the mid-1970s, Gufram in Italy produced a moulded foam chair called *Capitello* in the shape of a fractured Ionic capital, designed by Studio 65. The 'pleasure of ruins' has, historically, inspired many artists and writers from Hubert Robert (nicknamed 'Robert des Ruines'), Henry Fuseli, Shelley in *Ozymandias* (1817) and the writer Rose Macaulay, to mention but a few. That pleasure resurfaced in Pop Art – for example Patrick Caulfield's print entitled *Ruins* (1964), or Roy Lichtenstein's *Temple of Apollo* of the same year. Andy Warhol also moved in that direction in his later years; examples are his acrylic and silkscreen on canvas images of 1982, such as *Monument for 16 soldiers* and *Friedrich Monument* which echo the quiet, noble grandeur of Neo-Classicism, and its disturbing reinterpretation during the Nazi period.

As we have seen, in 1979 Trix and Robert Haussmann designed a fluted column drawer unit called *Colonna* for Studio Alchymia. At the same time, but fundamentally more seriously, Ian Hamilton Finlay erected obelisks, columns and witty tributes to Classical scripts incised in stone in his house and garden, aptly named 'Little Sparta', at Dunsyre, in Lanarkshire. Finlay's artistic interests parallel those of many architects and range from the French Revolution to the troubled period of the 1930s.

Post-Modern Classicism is, however, only one development in the Pluralism of the 1980s. There are as many architects and designers who extend the tradition of the Modern, pay homage to the International Style, or refine it to the level of 'High Tech'. Included in the continuation of the Modern is the production revival of nearly all the famous 'Modern' chair designs of Mies van der Rohe, Le Corbusier and Charlotte Perriand, Eileen Gray, Marcel Breuer, and Guiseppe Terragni,

MITCH RYERSON, *HALL PIECE*, 1984 FOR FORMICA COLORCORE

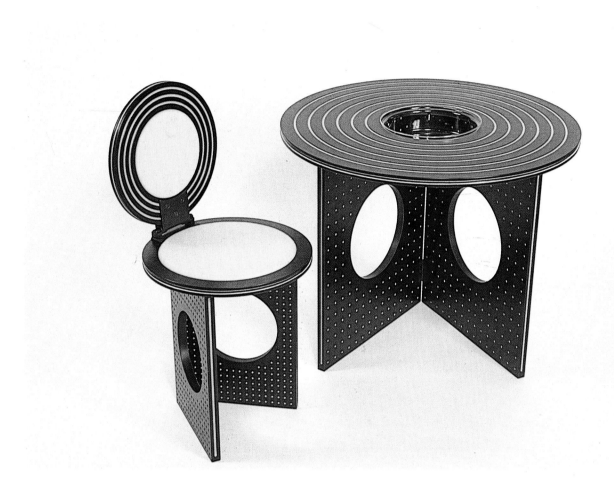

EVA JIRICNA, *FOLDING TABLE AND CHAIR*, 1983 AND ALAIN MARCOT, *TABLE ECHIQUIER*, 1983 FOR FORMICA COLORCORE

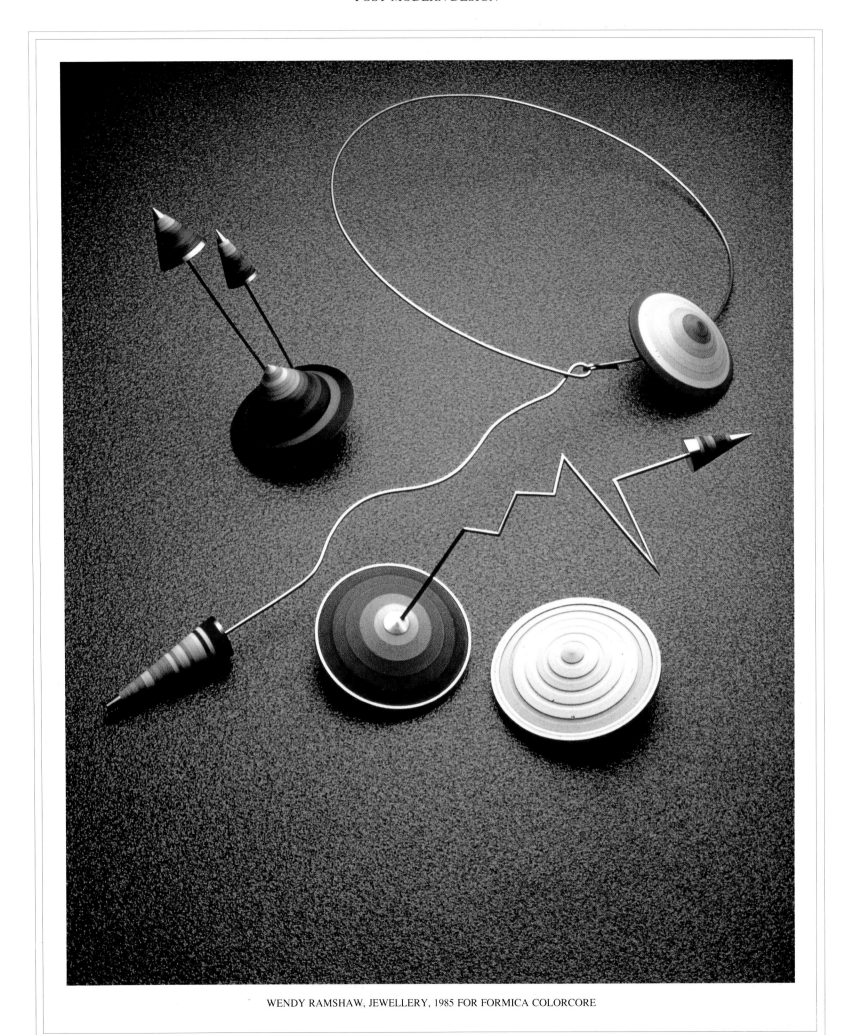

WENDY RAMSHAW, JEWELLERY, 1985 FOR FORMICA COLORCORE

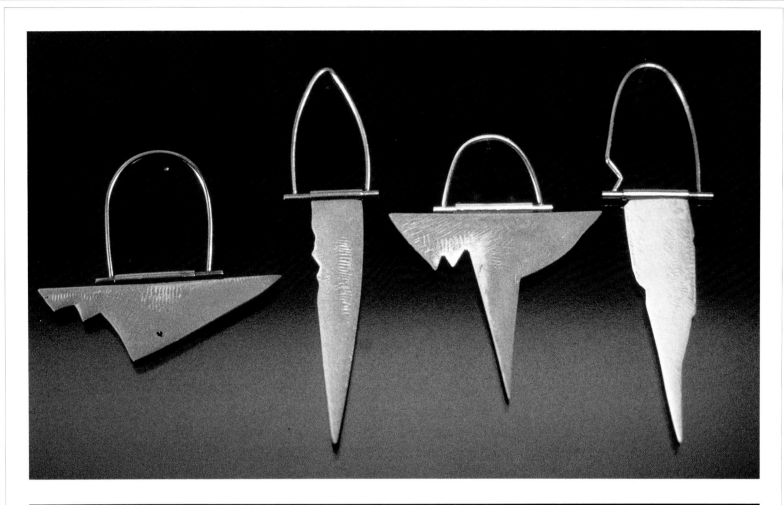

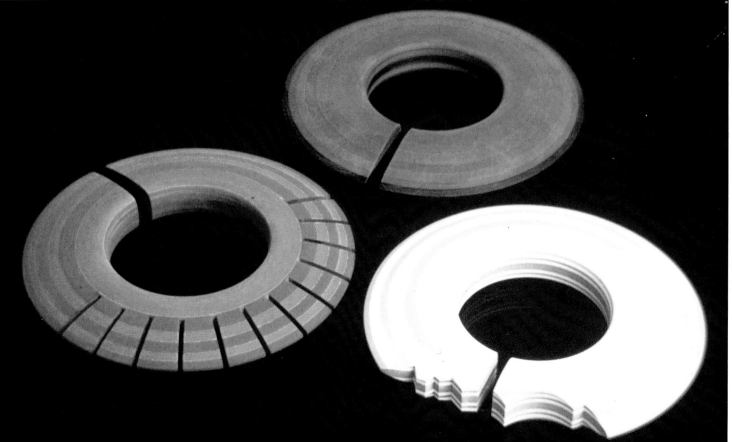

REBEKAH LASKIN (*TOP*) AND DAVID WATKINS (*ABOVE*), JEWELLERY, 1985 FOR FORMICA COLORCORE

to mention only a few. These sell well, and in a way, the more the 'Modern Movement' slips into history, the more these chairs develop a cachet of their own. As with some painters, it takes the death of the author to help raise sales and secure the seal of approval. These 'dead' replicas, often with incorrect screws and plywood that in no way resemble the original, have been exhibited so often as 'classics of modern design' that it is rare for anyone to actually know what the originals looked like. They are as clichéd as reproductions of the *Mona Lisa*, and one supposes that their purchase is a way of buying history rather cheaply – very few American corporations are without their replica *Barcelona* chair and stool. It is not that they are simply good examples of how to design; it is that one buys a 'Mies' or a 'Breuer' in the way that some people collect art. Indeed, they are highly 'academic' pieces now, designed when *gravitas* (applied to the Modern Movement) was held in high esteem. Young designers often admire them, and the larger question here is whether it is now 'historicist' to pay homage to the Modern Movement. It is fairly clear that inspiration drawn from, say Neo-Classicism, is 'historicist' but is not the history of the discourse of the Modern Movement equally revivalist? Included in this category is, for example, the British designer Rodney Kinsman's High-Tech quotation of Hans Coray's aluminium chair with circular holes (1939), in the former's *Omstak* chair (1971). The fact that Kinsman's chair is 'High-Tech' does not necessarily mean that he does not use quotation, in this case from the Modern Movement. In America, some of the New York Five, or 'Whites' as they are known, quote extensively from the 1920s work of Le Corbusier. Richard Meier is an example, although his furniture derives inspiration from Josef Hoffmann, particularly from the latter's 'quadratl' or square phase, when he himself was indebted to Charles Rennie Mackintosh. As we shall see, Meier's metalwork and glass also draws from Hoffmann, while on one occasion referring to Soviet Constructivism. Constructivism has also inspired in varying ways the architecture and design of another 'White', Peter Eisenman, in addition to the architecture of Frank Gehry, and all the work of Zaha Hadid. Indeed, as we shall see, the work of these three has been called 'Deconstructivist' and all essentially draw upon the architectural strategies of early twentieth-century Soviet Constructivism. Other 'New York Five' architects such as Charles Gwathmey produce designs which perpetuate the Modern tradition. Some architects can be read as Post-Modern in their architecture, for example O M Ungers in the pitched roof of his 'house within a house' at the German Architectural Museum; although other elements of his use of grids suggest Josef Hoffmann, Otto Wagner and Peter Eisenman. Much the same is suggested by his grid furniture for the same museum, which on surface reading is not Post-Modern.

A similar surface reading of Mario Botta's furniture, from his steel *Prima* chair for Alias (1982) through to his *Tesi* table (1986) for the same firm would suggest that his design work is 'High-Tech' and we have already noted that Shiro Kuramata's designs have recently developed in the same direction. Philippe Starck's furniture designs are also all 'Slick-Tech' and 'High-Tech', with perhaps one exception, namely *Le Bureau du Théâtre du Monde* which makes a reference in its architectonic form and pyramidal roof to the work of Aldo Rossi. This bureau was created for the Trois Suisses mail-order company to be sold in large numbers, yet was elegant enough to be used by Starck in his design for President Mitterrand's study in the Elysée Palace. It is a strange cross-breed, as, for example, is the Zanussi refrigerator designed by Roberto Pezzetta for that firm's Wizard's Collection. Part Modern, part Post-Modern, this cross-breeding is likely to occur in the decade of Pluralism.

Some architect designers are unequivocally 'High-Tech' Modern. Norman Foster is a case in point in his recent ventures into design with his *Nomos* drawing table and other die-cast aluminium and tubular steel furniture made for Tecno in 1987. Yet more designers, such as Sottsass and Thun, pursue an ambidextrous approach; Neo-Modern in their Memphis output, but in the case of Sottsass, also producing self-effacing 'Modern' metalwork for Alessi. Indeed, this latter firm can only indulge in gestures towards Post-Modern work as a result of the high sales of plain, common or garden trays or condiment sets designed by Sottsass, which sit quietly in their catalogues. They make little noise, but sell well.

What is certain is that none of the above designers refer to 'Classicism'. The Modernism of the twentieth century can be seen to continue as a programme, sometimes challenging Post-Modernism with its sheer technical ability in the 1980s. The Modern Movement has demonstrated its capacity to modify its aims and to progress, and it could be argued that it is only recently that the high degree of technology it requires has become available, in marked contrast to the rather cruder technology of the 1920s. Le Corbusier and the Bauhaus designers had to rely on the aircraft industry for the *tubes d'avion* required for tubular steel. Mart Stam, for his pioneering chair, had to use gas piping, with elbow pieces at the joints. This furniture was only one stage removed from the technology of the bicycle.

In 1978 Joan Kron and Suzanne Slesin wrote *High Tech – the industrial style and source book for the home*. What they illustrated here, for example industrial rubber flooring and Meccano-like shelving, is less in evidence in the home of the 1980s, though High-Tech is still very much part of architecture. Two of High-Tech's greatest British exponents, Richard Rogers and Norman Foster, have shown in their recent buildings – Lloyd's of London, and the headquarters of the Hong-kong and Shanghai Banking Corporation respectively, both completed in 1986 – that the tradition of modern engineering is alive and well. It is a tradition which goes back at least as far as the Crystal Palace of 1851, and Paxton's great structure is 'quoted' by both of them. It is significant that in 1959 both Richard Rogers and James Stirling visited Pierre Chareau's Maison de Verre (1928-32) in Paris. The British architects have taken inspiration from Chareau's work for their own

MARIO BOTTA, *TESI* AND *QUARTA* FURNITURE, 1986 FOR ALIAS

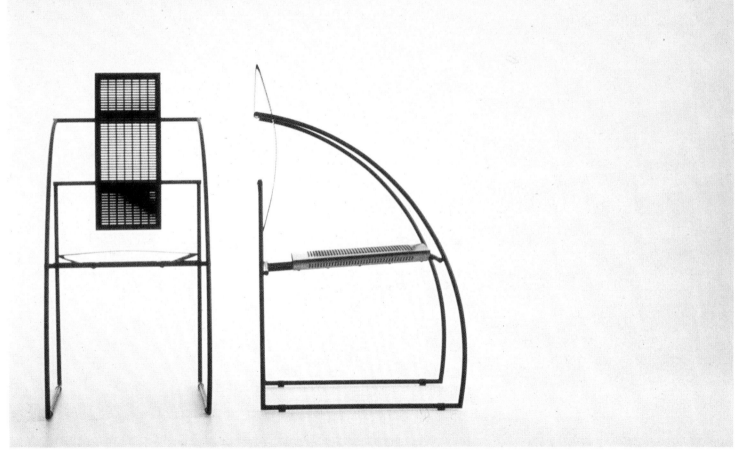

MARIO BOTTA, *PRIMA* 1982 AND *QUINTA* CHAIRS, 1985 FOR ALIAS

MARIO BOTTA, *SESTO* ARMCHAIR AND *TERZO* TABLE, 1985 FOR ALIAS

PAUL CHIASSON, *CLASSICAL CABINET*, 1983 (*DETAIL*) FOR FORMICA COLORCORE

'High-Tech' output, and Rogers' work also realises some of the visionary aspects of Russian Constructivist architecture, interpreted via the futurism of Archigram designs of the 1960s. As with all labels, architects themselves often see their work in other terms. For example, in 1986, Charles Jencks praised James Stirling's Neue Staatsgalerie in Stuttgart as 'the most "real" beauty of Post-Modern architecture to date', though the architect himself wrote in 1981: 'I don't think that our work attempts to be Post-Modernist'. Indeed, Stirling calls some parts of his gallery (which also makes Neo-Classical and neo-International Modern references) 'High-Tech'.

Stirling's pluralism is echoed in the world of design, which he has never entered. He was included in Charles Jencks' survey, *Post-Modern Classicism*, published in 1980, alongside Jencks' own work and that of the Americans Robert Venturi, Robert Stern, Charles Moore and Michael Graves, the Austrian Hans Hollein, and the Italian Aldo Rossi. Stirling is a Modernist, who has learned, so to speak, some words of Greek and Latin. The American Philip Johnson was an arch Modernist, as would be expected from a man who learned from Mies van der Rohe. However, he had already partly converted in 1961 when he stated that 'we cannot today not know history', and by the time of his controversial AT&T skyscraper building in New York (1979-83) his Classicism was ripening. The building has a broken pediment top, in the manner of 'Chippendale', and its base is a stripped version of the Roman triumphal arch. Such a building should be counterposed to the purer revivalist architecture of Quinlan Terry, which continues a tradition. By contrast, Johnson's gesture is 'the dull thunder of approximate words' to appropriate a line from one of Thom Gunn's poems. This is one of the major problems with the aesthetic of Post-Modernism – it steals from the past without having learned its language *ab initio*. As a result it has none of Classicism's *gravitas* or learning. This is a problem which applies to most design as well as to architecture, with one or two notable exceptions, such as the deeply erudite work in Italy of Paolo Portoghesi. One can, however, watch the progress of relearning, in what Portoghesi himself called in the subtitle to his *Presence of the Past* exhibition (1980), the 'end of prohibition'. Classicism is legitimate again, as an alternative, relearned language which forms part of the pluralism of today. Whether or not it is spoken well, and fluently, depends largely on the fact that nearly all Post-Modern designers are apostate Moderns, whose first language was that of the International Style, and, like anyone attempting a new language for the first time, the results are more likely to be perceived as humorous. One of the clichés of the Modern Movement had been the flat roof, which Le Corbusier had suggested was a better use of space than the traditional pitched roof. The responding cliché of Post-Modernism is the return of the pitched roof in architecture, or a reference to it in 'micro-architectural' design. Modernism had mostly relied on one 'solid', the cube; Post-Modernism re-applies others, such as the cone, pyramid and cylinder. Much

Post-Modern design is mimetic of housing typologies which are urban, including the pitched roof house common to many cities before the Modern Movement. The return of the column has been mentioned, but with it has come a *rechauffé* of the aedicule, the gable and the pediment, as well as the pitched roof. Many designs are simulacra in miniature, representations of lost or forgotten typologies in the history of architecture and design. There is little attempt to copy the masters of the past, but a much greater pleasure is taken in merely suggesting them. In that sense architects such as Robert Venturi 'Learn from Lutyens' as much as they 'Learn from Las Vegas'.

It is only quite recently that most Post-Modern architects have ventured into the arena of design, and their excursions into the decorative arts have been very interesting. It is as well to list the major collective design events of Post-Modernism, before concentrating on individual contributions. In 1979, the Italian metalwork company, Alessi of Crusinallo, who had hitherto marketed mass-produced stainless steel flatware and utensils of a modern flavour by such designers as Achille Castiglioni and Ettore Sottsass, invited eleven architects to design a solid silver tea and coffee service. They were the American Post-Modernists Michael Graves, Robert Venturi, Stanley Tigerman and Charles Jencks, the American 'Late-Modernist' Richard Meier, the 'new wave' Spanish designer and architect Oscar Tusquets, the Japanese Kuzumasa Yamashita, well known for his 'Face House' in Kyoto (1974), the Austrian Hans Hollein, and three Italians, Paolo Portoghesi, Aldo Rossi, and Alessandro Mendini. It was the latter who choreographed the scheme, and cited parallels between the resulting 'micro-architecture' with the work of Venturi for Knoll International, the 'Strada Novissima' of the 1980 Biennale, and Memphis. Notwithstanding Mendini's statement, Hollein at least might question the concept of 'micro-architecture' as he does not see his work in those terms. As Mendini records: 'The idea was to offer architects and designers a place where they could work out and put forward experimental methods, forms and styles in the thick of the current debate on Neo- and Post-Modernism'.[57] Mendini concluded that the objects, which he also called 'Domestic Landscapes' are 'a small, though perhaps timely, experiment with the vast issues of today and their purpose is to bring into focus the new reality of possible anthropological objects, set between awareness of tradition and the lure of the unknown'.[58] The results, as we shall see, allowed for a comparison between *rappel à l'ordre* Post-Modern Classicism, Neo-Modernism (in the case of Mendini) and even Neo-Constructivism (in the case of Meier).

The next important event came in 1982 when Formica held a Surface and Ornament Design competition for Colorcore, a new version of their plastic laminate, for which the Post-Modernists Robert Venturi, Charles Moore, Stanley Tigerman and Arata Isozaki designed interesting furniture. The 'Deconstructivist' Frank Gehry produced a 'sculpture', Helmut Jahn designed an elevator cab in 1983, and the Post-Modernist architects SITE designed a door, layered and fractured in the top centre. With the same material, Thomas Hall Beeby designed the Post-Modern Classical Formica Showroom in 1984, using a polychromatic Greek key pattern in terracotta red and sky blue. Here the colour possibilities of Colorcore were used to great effect, although New York designer Paul Chaisson's equally Classical cabinet of 1983 was relatively restrained. Even Charles Jencks' *Sun Chairs*, which will be discussed later, were made in Colorcore in 1985. The material has also been used in an Abet Laminate and Memphis-like manner for Peter Shire's *Mohave* table of 1984. A host of jewellers, including Britain's Wendy Ramshaw, have exploited the possibility of the material; it has even been used by one of Britain's foremost crafts revivalists, John Makepeace, for his *Low Table*.

The greatest fillip for product design, as opposed to furniture, came from Swid Powell Design, which was started in New York in 1984 by Nan Swid and Addie Powell who had both worked with Knoll International, the producers of Venturi's eclectic range of furniture in the same year. Swid Powell have launched ceramics, glass and metalwork by, among others, the Post-Modernists Graves, Hollein, Isozaki, Stern, Venturi, and Tigerman, Robert and Trix Haussmann, Arquitectonica, Late-Modernists Richard Meier and Charles Gwathmey with Robert Siegel, and Neo-Modernists such as Sottsass and Sowden.

Less well known than it should be was the promotion, in 1986, by the Israel Museum in Jerusalem of a religious commission for a design of a *menorah* for the Jewish *Chanukah* festival. The lamps included submissions from the De Pas, D'Urbino, Lomazzi group, Sottsass, Richard Meier, Peter Eisenman, and a host of Israeli and non-Israeli Modernists, Neo-Modernists, Late-Modernists and Post-Modernists. The results reflect the fact that certainly in some areas, Post-Modernism has yet to dominate the design field.

An equally interesting gathering of architect-designers was the launching of new door handles by Franz Schnieder Brakel (FSB) in Germany in 1986 by architects including Hans Hollein, Arata Isozaki, Mario Botta, Peter Eisenman, Dieter Rams, and Alessandro Mendini. Never had so much intellect gone into the design of a mere door handle.

The latest 'collection' to challenge the taxonomy of design has been the launch by Italian entrepreneur Cleto Munari of a vast range of jewellery and watches. Munari, who was born in 1930, studied in Vicenza where he lives and works. He ran a

metalworking firm from 1960 to 1970, and commissioned Gio Ponti and Ettore Sottsass to design for him. From the 1970s, Munari has been more of a promoter; he records: 'My wife Valentina adores jewellery. In 1982, I asked De Lucchi and Sottsass to design a ring for her. From this the idea was born'.[59] In 1985 he asked twenty of the leading architects and designers to design for a collection and in 1987 200 items were presented by Sottsass, Shire, Mendini, Isozaki, Hollein, Graves, Tigerman, Venturi, Eisenman and Meier, among others. Virtually all are very expensive, using gold, precious and semi-precious stones. Some had already been exhibited at the end of 1986 at the Osterreichische Galerie in Vienna. At the same time Munari stated that 'a Roman company asked me to do a wristwatch for their own promotional purposes . . . I asked four architects to design watches choosing professionals from completely different cultural backgrounds: Michael Graves, Hans Hollein, Arata Isozaki, and Ettore Sottsass. Their mechanisms are all made according to Swiss technological traditions, and they are produced in very limited series'.[60] Munari's 'collection' is as catholic as Memphis had been in the early 1980s, embracing as it does the Memphis style of De Lucchi and Sottsass, the 'funk' of Shire, the Post-Modernism of Graves, Venturi, Isozaki, Hollein, and Portoghesi, as well as the 'Deconstructivism' of Eisenman. The 'collection' mirrors perfectly the whole gamut of Pluralism in the 1980s, as well as some of its Post-Pop and 'micro-architectural' concerns. It is also quite unashamedly a return to the order of well made, expensive items which use as their very basis that most hierarchical, traditional material, gold.

All these competitions, events and gatherings of collections have served to demonstrate that in the 1980s a new pluralism reigns and, within that pluralism, almost any gesture is possible. Only the benefit of hindsight will allow us to judge the quality of these contributions and their relative merits, but an examination of the work of the major, or primary Post-Modernists will at least demonstrate differences of approach, as well as the geographical inflection towards America and Italy as the countries of Post-Modern design. More up-to-date, and secondary, Post-Modern work is produced in England, Germany, Spain, Portugal and elsewhere, as well as in Japan. However, since many writers, including Sottsass and Jameson, have identified neoconservative Post-Modernism with America, it is to there that we must now turn.

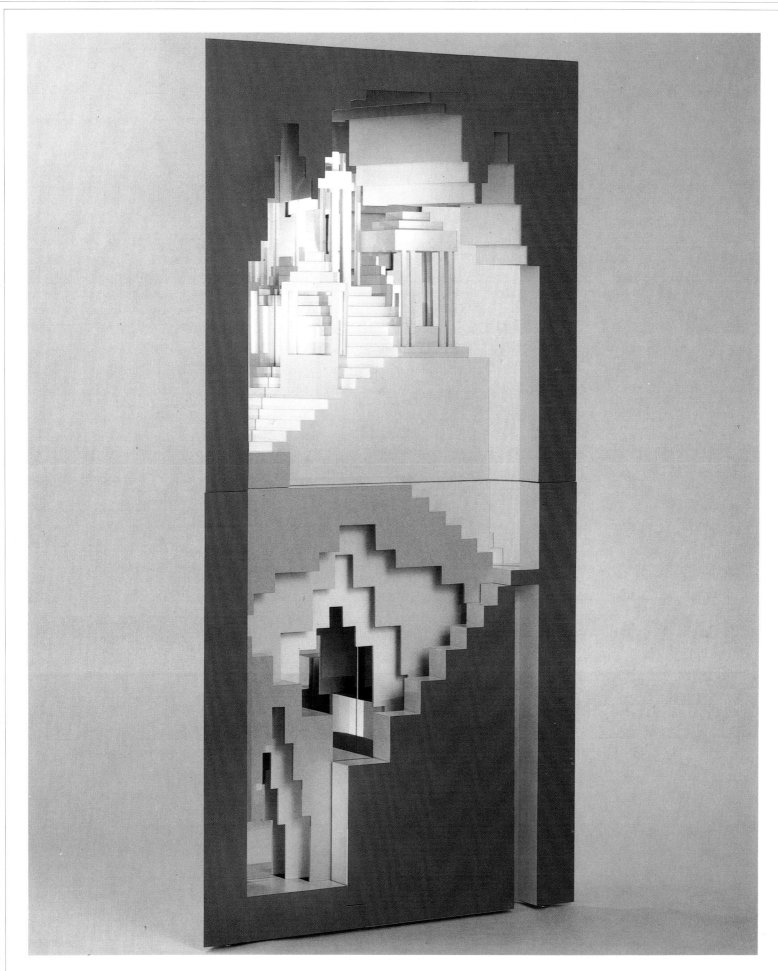

CHARLES MOORE, *CORNER CUPBOARD*, 1983 FOR FORMICA COLORCORE

CHARLES JENCKS, *TEA & COFFEE PIAZZA*, 1979-83 FOR ALESSI

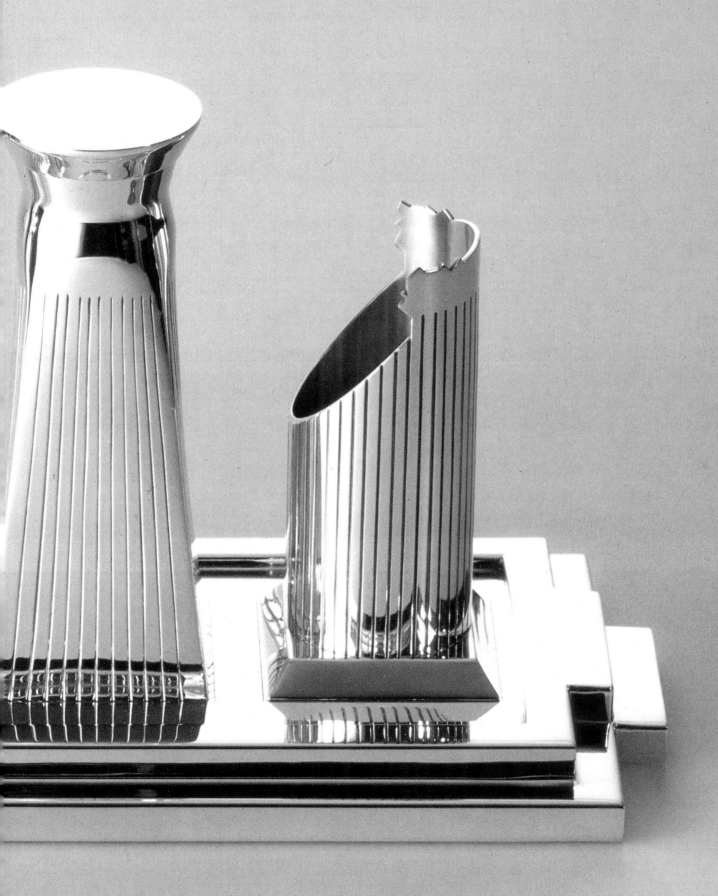

ROBERT VENTURI, *TEA & COFFEE PIAZZA*, 1979-83 FOR ALESSI

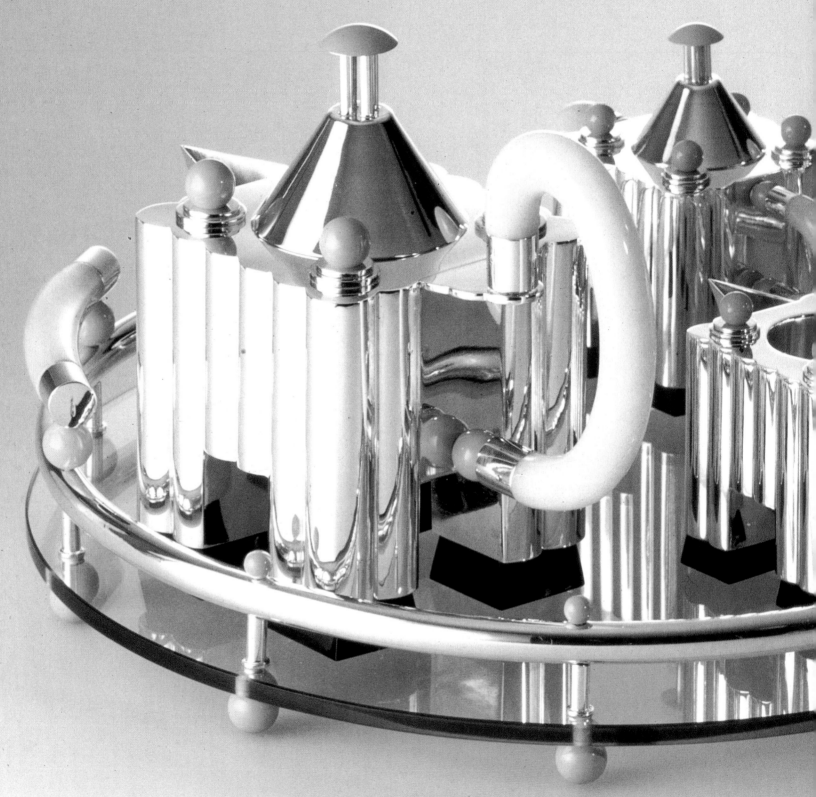

MICHAEL GRAVES, *TEA & COFFEE PIAZZA*, 1979-83 FOR ALESSI

STANLEY TIGERMAN, *TEA & COFFEE PIAZZA*, 1979-83 FOR ALESSI

RICHARD MEIER, *TEA & COFFEE PIAZZA*, 1979-83 FOR ALESSI

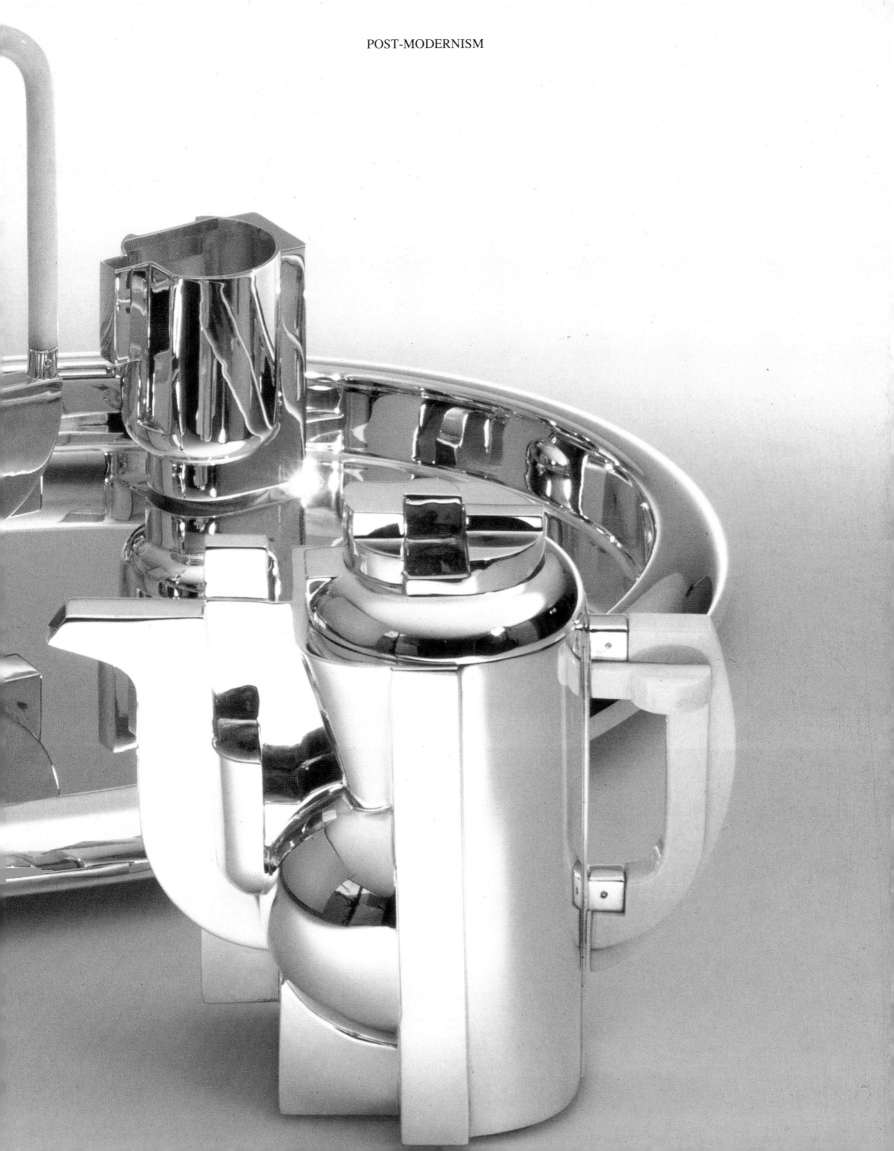

PAOLO PORTOGHESI, *TEA & COFFEE PIAZZA*, 1979-83 FOR ALESSI

KAZUMASA YAMASHITA, *TEA & COFFEE PIAZZA*, 1979-83 FOR ALESSI

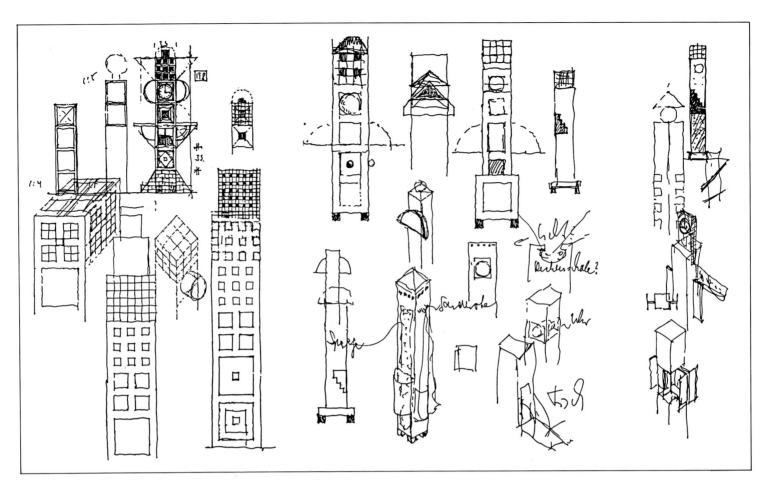

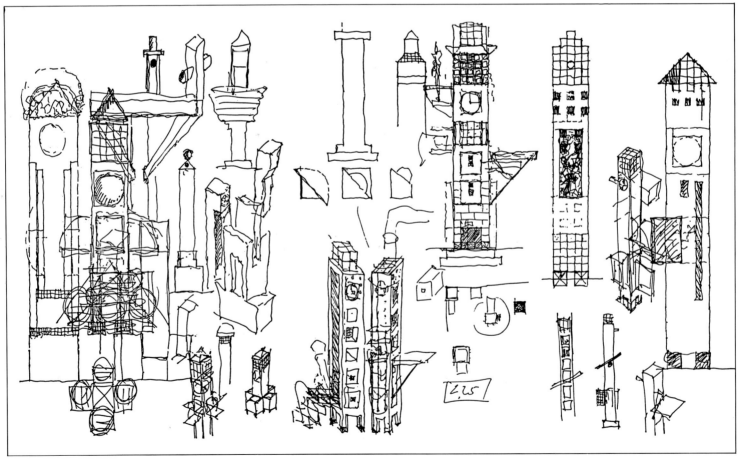

O M UNGERS, STUDIES FOR *TOWER CABINET*

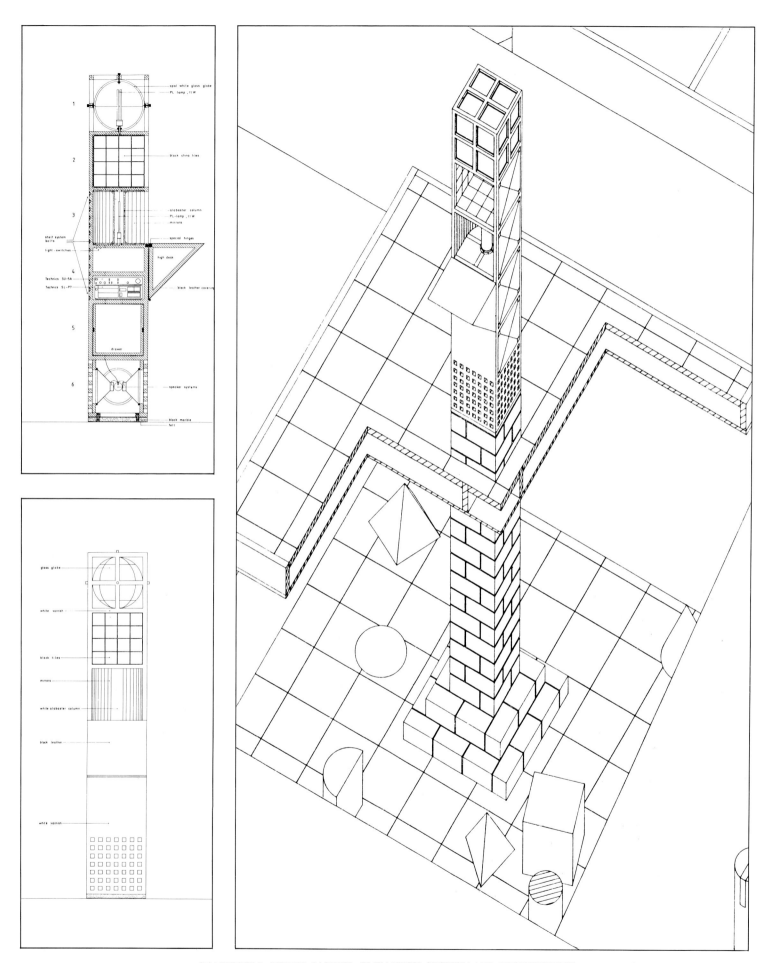

O M UNGERS, *TOWER CABINET* ELEVATION, SECTION AND AXONOMETRIC

O M UNGERS, *TOWER CABINET*

O M UNGERS, *TOWER CABINET*

Stuhl
Sessel

O M UNGERS, ARMCHAIR STUDIES

O M UNGERS, MAHOGANY ARMCHAIR

ROBERT VENTURI WITH HIS COLLECTION OF CHAIRS FOR KNOLL INTERNATIONAL

CHAPTER IV

Post-Modern Design in America:
Robert Venturi

ROBERT VENTURI, *GRANDMOTHER* DINNERWARE, 1984 FOR SWID POWELL

Two of Post-Modernism's founding fathers, Robert Venturi and Charles Jencks, are American, though the latter resides in London. Allowing for all the regional accents that occur within the vastness of such a country, Post-Modern work in America does represent the most complete *rappel à l'ordre* to date. Historicism and eclecticism are used extensively by Venturi and Jencks, as well as by Robert Stern, Charles Moore and Michael Graves, while Stanley Tigerman is more ironic in his approach. Other Americans pursue or extend Modernism, and they include Richard Meier and Charles Gwathmey, and the 'Deconstructivist' Peter Eisenman. In this debate it should be remembered that the 'Modern Movement' was codified by Americans such as Henry-Russell Hitchcock, the youthful Philip Johnson, Alfred Barr, Edgar Kaufmann Jr, and others, mostly from within the Museum of Modern Art in New York. No institution did more for Modern art, architecture and design in the 1930s and 1940s. It even spotlighted Modern architecture in England via an exhibition in 1937, and though much 'Modern' work emanated from Europe, America was, especially in the troubled 1930s, the safest haven for modern thought, backed by MOMA and writers such as Clement Greenberg. MOMA 'collected' Modern design from the period of the International Style, and put its important seal of approval on the furniture of Breuer, Mies van der Rohe and Aalto. Edgar Kauffmann Jr donated an Aalto chair of 1934 and a Mies van der Rohe chair of 1932 among other items; Philip Johnson gave them Rietveld's *Red Blue and Yellow* armchair of 1917 and a transparent glass teapot by Wilhelm Wagenfeld of 1932. The MOMA idea was exported to other countries in spirit, and in body to São Paulo, Brazil where it was almost entirely replicated, complete with catalogue, in 1979. MOMA, in short, made Modernism academic, canonical and fostered the twin concepts of 'classics of modern design' and 'good design'. Such a heavy seal of approval, towards the Modern Movement mainly, was perhaps bound to cause a reaction.

It was, therefore, somewhat ironic that it was MOMA which published Robert Venturi's *Complexity and Contradiction in Architecture* in 1966. This broke the mould of dominant Modernism in his plea for 'complexity and contradiction . . . elements which are hybrid rather than pure . . . messy vitality over obvious unity . . . I prefer "both-and" to "either-or"'. Significantly it was Robert Venturi who hit the International Modern Movement's credo of 'less is more' on the head by countering it with 'less is a bore' in the same publication. Venturi's Philadelphia practice was founded in 1964 with partner John Rauch, and the firm has been known as Venturi, Rauch and Scott Brown since 1967 (Venturi married Denise Scott Brown in 1977). Venturi's better known architecture includes Chestnut Hill House, Pennsylvania, 1962, for his mother, and Guild House Retirement Home, Philadelphia, 1963. Of late his architecture has become Post-Modern Classical, although in the past he has quoted the Shingle Style, the vaulting of eighteenth century Polish synagogues, and split gables based loosely (as in his mother's house) on the facade of Blenheim Palace. Venturi exhibits a positive Neo-Classicism in the stucco and wood house of 1982 at New Castle County, Delaware, which has gables, columns and, significantly, painted stencilled stars in the interior decoration. In 1986 he was chosen as architect for the extension to London's National Gallery, and has furnished Post-Modern Classical plans for that building.

Venturi has put forward the idea of the 'decorated shed', that is a building with applied or surface decoration. One such, his Best Products showroom, Oxford Valley, Pennsylvania, 1979, has a floral pattern decoration, culled from French wallpaper, applied to the enamelled steel panels. The same pattern has been used in Venturi's own home. This latter also has stars on the ceiling, and contains the following in roughly historical, chronological order: Georgian chairs; a French Art Nouveau cabinet; Tiffany lamps; an armchair by Josef Hoffmann; a Wiener Werkstätte ceramic figure; a lithograph by Lichtenstein; and Andy Warhol's *Liz* (Liz Taylor). These eclectic images are mixed together and, if examined according to Susan Sontag's or Mark Booth's defining points of Camp, suggest Camp taste. Pop Art and Art Nouveau, especially Tiffany Lamps, have been seen by both writers as Camp, and one could suggest that the very act of collecting in this way is Camp – witness for example the collecting activities of Liberace, Warhol, or Elton John, to name three exponents of high Camp. Venturi's home contains selections from the history of ornament and design, as well as the Pop Art that so inspired his writing.

Venturi has written extensively about his use of decoration and symbolism. He has stated that 'Our current definition of architecture is shelter with symbols on it. Or, architecture is shelter with decoration on it . . . Definitions of Modern architecture never included ornament, nor did they explicitly refer to shelter . . . Ornament and symbolism – certainly applied ornament and the simple uses of association – have been ignored in architecture, or condemned – ornament equated with crime by Adolf Loos as long ago as 1906, and symbolism associated with discredited historical eclecticism; appliqué on shelter would have been considered superficial by theorists of the Modern Movement and contrary to the industrial techniques integral to Modern architecture . . .'.[61]

Venturi applies ornament to his designs extensively. His contribution to Alessi was a part-gilded silver tea and coffee service with ebony handles, finally produced in 1983, a year before his important Knoll furniture range. The set is typically eclectic in that its circular form could broadly be called Georgian in spirit, and yet the surface decoration of part-gilded tea leaves on the teapot pays homage to the conventionalised patterns of metalwork and fabrics made in the 1920s in Josef Hoffmann's Wiener Werkstätte. Such appropriate ornament to some extent goes back to Sir Henry Cole's design group of the 1840s, which attempted to relate ornament to function. Venturi's

initial drawing for the coffee pot shows it to be coloured, with the spirals picked out in red.

His partnership also produced a *Mirror in the Greek Revival Manner* for Colorcore in 1983. This is quite pure, with all the correct fluting and Neo-Classical form, mimetic of a typology of mirror that existed throughout the nineteenth century. What makes Venturi's mirror Post-Modern is not only its obvious Neo-Classical form, but the fact that it is made of the most modern laminated plastic. Here we have plastic Classicism, as anachronistic as the clocks in Shakespeare's Rome and the cannon in *Macbeth*. In short it is a good taste form in bad taste material; plastics were despised for a long time, and the suggestion of a career in that industry provided a good one-liner laugh in the 1967 film *The Graduate*. The result in Venturi's case is surprisingly attractive.

Venturi's most extreme contribution to design, especially in the context of Knoll as a producer hitherto of 'good form' furniture, is his range designed from 1979 and launched in 1984. Knoll had produced the tubular steel furniture of Mies and Breuer, and the commission given to Venturi is an extraordinary *volte-face* in terms of the furniture company's history. Venturi is clearly aware of that history and has quipped to a writer from *Metropolis* magazine in New York that 'Mies did one chair – I did nine'. One could rephrase that as 'I did none' if one went on the attack, since Venturi's designs are all *réchauffés* of stereotypes from history. However, one could argue that originality is not easy today, and Post-Modernism recognises this problem.

Venturi's chairs are made of moulded and laminated plywood, which brings a degree of economy to the method of production and at the same time brings to mind Alvar Aalto's or Marcel Breuer's experiments with plywood in the 1930s. In this sense they are Modern – the 'Post' comes from their debt to history.

In the main, Venturi's chairs are highly ornamental and run the gamut of Post-Modern revivalism from the Queen Anne style of 1730 through to Hollywood Art Deco of 1930. Although they refer to many styles within these dates, and quote widely from American and European decorative art history, Venturi's approach is not archaeological or pedantic. One can play the game of searching for the precedent, and the *Queen Anne* with its fretted back is probably inspired by the back of the Queen Anne chair of about 1730 by Giles Grendey, now in the Metropolitan Museum, New York. It is largely a trivial pursuit to do this, for Venturi clearly wishes to reinvent the style he quotes. In roughly chronological order of revivalism the nine chairs are *Queen Anne, Chippendale, Gothic(k), Hepplewhite, Sheraton, Empire, Biedermeier, Art Nouveau* and *Art Deco*. Only the jig-sawed and fretted backs make a witty reference to the epoch of furniture history remembered; a reincarnated George Washington would fail to recognise them as accurate versions of the eighteenth-century style, and Thomas Chippendale would disown the one that bears his name, as much as he would the so-called Chippendale top of

ROBERT VENTURI, *QUEEN ANNE* CHAIR WITH *GRANDMOTHER* PATTERN, 1984 FOR KNOLL INTERNATIONAL

ROBERT VENTURI, *GRANDMOTHER* SOFA AND LOW TABLE, 1984 FOR KNOLL INTERNATIONAL

Johnson's AT&T skyscraper. In fact there is something stagey about the flatness of the backs of Venturi's chairs, as if they are pieces of theatre design, mere cut-outs with none of the three-dimensional qualities or roundness of the prototypes for each style. Indeed, Venturi has said that 'their backs are like signs or the false fronts on buildings of the old West, while their side view looks modern'. This has an architectural parallel in Venturi's completely cut-out 'open frame' reconstruction of Benjamin Franklin's house at Franklin Court, Philadelphia, 1972, which uses a modern material, namely steel, to ghost the shape of an eighteenth-century building.

Venturi and Knoll have not neglected colour or surface ornament, and various bright finishes are offered for these chairs, so that one can have, in addition to a blond plywood finish, a red Chippendale or a yellow Art Nouveau. It reminds one a little of the 'penny plain, tuppence coloured' principle of nineteenth-century prints, with the obvious scaling up of today's prices. As a further extra, two chair types, the *Sheraton* and the *Art Deco* are offered with an appropriate polychromatic silkscreen appliqué which suggests the decoration of their 'period'. This is a brave attempt to revive polychromy and a return to ornamentalism which is inspired by Victorian chromolithography and colour in architecture and design. Venturi's may be a humorous and tongue in cheek playing with history, but it does learn from Owen Jones' *Grammar of Ornament*, for example. Venturi's *mélange* of art and design history produces a Post-Modern synthesis. The polychromatic *Sheraton* chair suggests a history of ornament which in its language of swag, column and egg and dart is Neo-Classical, and draws its uses of colour from nineteenth-century colour theory. The most interesting surface decoration of these chairs, and the one used for much of Knoll's publicity, is called 'Grandmother', which relates to but should not be confused with the floral pattern on the couch, part of the Knoll Collection. Venturi has also used the 'Grandmother' pattern for a Swid Powell ceramic. It is based on the favourite tablecloth belonging to the grandmother of Robert Schwartz, an associate of Venturi, Rauch and Scott Brown. It looks a little like Memphis laminate, with the addition of diagonal lines related to those used by Jasper Johns in his paintings. Venturi has written of this that 'it is characteristic of Post-Modernism to use familiar and conventional patterns, but to use them in an unusual way; in the "grandmother" pattern we have juxtaposed two conventional patterns – a floral pattern you might find on a faded tablecloth that belonged to your grandmother, and a typical screen pattern used in commercial art but made much bigger'. Venturi has, in addition to the chairs, designed a whole range of other furniture. This includes two high tables, a low table and a sofa. The high tables include a cabriole leg table which is available in five sizes, and an urn table in three variations. They are made using the same laminated plywood process, available with the same range of finishes as the chairs, and complement them well.

The low table is made of moulded fibreglass and is available in several finishes. It is a capital transformed into that most modern innovation in furniture, namely the coffee table set at a height unknown to much of furniture's history. No particular Classical Order is quoted, and yet Post-Modern Classicism is implied. As we have seen already, such stylophilia, or love of columns, is very much part of 1980s Pluralism.

If the whole Venturi Knoll collection is an *embarras de richesses* of ideas, then his final gesture, the deliberately overstuffed sofa, is a reworking of everything the Moderns loved to hate about Victoriana. As with the other furniture, it suggests another age, but in fact is made of moulded fibreglass. In its brightly-coloured textile version, covered with a Venturi tapestry of large flowers and polka dots, the architect has given us a variation of the 'Grandmother' pattern. It suggests the comfort of late nineteenth-century furniture, the plenitude of a bourgeois life-style. Knoll have, however, produced a plain grey leather version, which does not look out of place next to the Mies chairs marketed by them. Indeed Venturi's furniture is often photographed by Knoll with Mies 'classics', producing an ironic juxtaposition of 'Modern' with 'Post-Modern'. Venturi says of the floral version that 'this fabric juxtaposes soft and hard, representational and geometric, monumentality and grace – again unusual combinations in the context of the recent past'. He is fond of such juxtaposition and of letting the Modern Movement crash into Post-Modernism. Venturi's collection for Knoll is a real 'fruit salad' of styles. With it he has realised many of the aims expressed in his two books. 'Complexity and Contradiction', in addition to 'both-and', rather than 'either-or', are present in his furniture as well as his architecture, and his eclecticism mirrors the desire for wit and the need for historical reference in design that is so much in demand in the 1980s. Venturi has explained that 'this furniture, although it was designed by one firm all at one time, has no motival unity. In its design, historical eclecticism, achieved through the representation of many styles, is paralleled by eclecticism of form and eclecticism of method. We see this furniture as part of the tradition of Modern furniture, as an evolution within the bounds of Modern design'. This statement by Venturi is important, for he clearly implies that this is Modern furniture, and not reproduction in the sense that it is normally understood. He also has stressed that the chairs look Modern in their side view. However, turn them 90 degrees, and they become historical. This ambiguity is fascinating, and produces the 'messy vitality over obvious unity' that Venturi also sought. It is all a bit like cooking; take one part Modern Movement, and one part Historicism, put it into a pot, and something new and tasty emerges. Language can be created that way, though not always well. The American word 'meld' is a blend of 'melt' and 'weld'. Venturi 'melds', just as much as Arata Isozaki does, as we see in the latter's *Marilyn* chair, when he uses a Japanese process of taking two texts (Mackintosh Chair, Monroe's curves) and putting them together. It is a process present in, say, Paolo Portoghesi's architecture, when he too mixes elements from Borromini with others taken from Perret, and it is also implicit in Thun's concept of the Baroque Bauhaus. All these gestures are more or less using oxymoron to produce arresting self-contradictory design 'statements'.

Beyond such 'readings', Venturi's furniture has a sociological position as part of neoconservatism in a very wealthy country. He has 'Learned from Las Vegas', via a Caesar's Palace type of Classicism. Venturi's furniture is almost a theme-park or Disneyland view of two centuries of furniture history. America's attachment to the past is well known enough through popular films and television series such as *Revolution* or *George Washington*; maybe Venturi's furniture is Post-Modernism's equivalent of the historical romance. The chairs can be seen as instant, jokey antiques for a new rich consumer age, filling a place in history for a society anxious to prove its place within an historical context. The range may even be seen as furniture's answer to the well known American habit of tracing one's ancestry in Ireland, England, France, Germany or Italy. Venturi has also sought out roots, and this is a favourite American game.

The firm of Venturi, Rauch and Scott Brown has continued to produce designs since the Knoll venture. For Swid Powell, (formed in 1984 as the spin-off from Knoll), it has produced at least three ceramic designs. *Grandmother* is directly related to the Knoll fabric, whereas *Notebook* has a rich, veined black marble look that relates it to Memphis and indeed the marbled endpapers of such things as notebooks which are once again in fashion, the paper very often 'marbled' in Venice. Both these plates date from 1984. More controversial must be the *Village* set of 1986 for Swid Powell. This is based on a traditional Italian village, and is mimetic, in a Disneyland way, of types of architecture. Painted in gaudy colours, the coffee pot looks like a campanile, or tower, with a ball-topped cone roof for a lid; the teapot resembles a polychromatic Pantheon with pilasters in red and a flat yellow painted pediment; the sugar bowl is an ordinary house, the lid forming the yellow pitched roof; the cream jug is painted to look like a palazzo. Here, Venturi plumbs the depths of the souvenir shop, and all that was called Kitsch in design. Although they are all usable, they enter the realm of fairground art, with child-like colours. What would Wilhelm Wagenfeld say about this departure into the gladiatorial ring of bad taste? Venturi has said that 'they are representational, but not too literal', which one supposes is a blessing. As so often, Venturi pushes design towards looking like a tourist trinket. He does something similar with the *Campidoglio* part-gilded stainless steel tray for Alessi produced since 1985, though first designed in silver as a base for the solid silver *Tea and Coffee Piazza* of 1983. The Japanese architect Arata Isozaki had already quoted Michelangelo's famous Campidoglio pavement in Rome for his Piazza at the Tsukuba New Town of 1979-82. Isozaki reverses the emphasis of the pavement design, and in using it at all he ironically suggests the conflicts of culture and history that a Japanese might feel when working without the benefit of Western, or Renaissance, tradition.

When this same pavement is quoted in miniature by Venturi, we may question its validity. One supposes that he may be suggesting in a pun that the Renaissance is the 'base' of our culture. Apart from that, it is certainly a beautiful design source, and architects such as Paolo Portoghesi have been inspired by similar patterning of floors or roofs from the Baroque period. A flat pavement may inspire decoration, but Venturi has used it for a bowled, dish shape. Michelangelo's pavement and Venturi's tray are circular, but the former is flat and the latter is not; the 'pavement' design crosses the bowl and goes up the rim of the Alessi tray. Venturi has little regard here for the form of the tray – use, scale, and reference are all distorted – and the result, as with some of his Knoll furniture, is inevitably unhappy. The undeniable quality of the product is insufficient to save it from the accusation of camping up a tourist version of visual history. Venturi's designs could only appear in the age of prolific jet travel. They are excursions into history, trips to Italian cities and, as we shall see in his next effort, a visit to the Swiss Alps.

Venturi, Rauch and Scott Brown's latest offering is a *Cuckoo Clock*. This yellow and green clock was designed for Alessi in 1986 and produced in 1988. Venturi has written that 'Everyone knows what cuckoo clocks are and almost everyone loves them. It was a nice challenge to take what is at once a familiar form and a vivid symbol and retain its loveable qualities and make it new and fresh at the same time. We did this by diminishing its hand-craft qualities and abstracting its form, increasing its scale and intensifying its colours . . . this to create a bold kind of image appropriate for our time.'[62]

One suspects that this clock contains a few 'in' jokes, one such being that Le Corbusier, child of Swiss watchmakers, was never able to design a watch or clock. The other joke relies on the widespread knowledge of cinema's most slick aphorism, spun out in *The Third Man* by Graham Greene, which was directed by Carol Reed in 1949. There is a line by Orson Welles added to the film, which goes: 'In Switzerland, they had five hundred years of democracy and peace – and what did that produce? The cuckoo clock ', so one can also suppose that Venturi is asking us to think about the meaning of culture in the 1980s. Venturi is trying to provoke again; in *Complexity and Contradiction* he wrote: 'architects can no longer afford to be intimidated by the puritanically moral language of Orthodox Modern Architecture'. He does make us think about the meaning of culture, but with such an object as this clock he has gone so far from 'puritanically moral language' that one rather wishes it would return. Apart from the *Campidoglio* tray, some of Venturi's more accomplished designs have been for metalwork. An example is his variation upon the traditional baluster candlestick for Swid Powell, which imitates the 'cut-out' form and flat outline of some of his Knoll furniture.

He and his firm have produced some fascinating jewellery for Cleto Munari. When asked to 'explain the language' of this jewellery by Barbara Radice he said: 'My jewellery tries to combine different scales, it is bold in one way and delicate in

ROBERT VENTURI, *CAMPIDOGLIO* TRAY FOR ALESSI, 1985 AND CANDLESTICK, 1986 FOR SWID POWELL

another. I used architectural elements and I liked the idea of representing something else. It is against the abstract approach and it has not been done for some time'.[63]

One of the simplest is a ring in gold, the metal cupping two conjoined hemispheres of lapiz lazuli and turquoise. The two semi-precious stones form a sphere. It sets up a resonance with the Neo-Classical fascination with this particular 'solid', and makes one think of Goethe's *Altar of Good Fortune* (1777) at Weimar, which was a simple sphere on a cube. It also suggests an inspiration from Boullée's *Designs for a monument to Newton* (c 1790) and Ledoux's *Design for a Spherical House* of the same date. At the same time, Venturi has drawn a design for a jewel based on a straightened leaning tower of Pisa, complete with miniature arches. His best piece is a witty miniature Montgolfier balloon earring; the gold forms the basket, frame and silhouette of the passenger, and red agate the balloon itself. Venturi has summed up his concern with representation in the following way: 'Representation can work in the design of objects and it can be manifest in two ways: where a whole object looks like something it isn't – such as a clock that looks like a house – or where the appliqué on an object stands for something not necessarily inherent to the object. In these ways the object becomes aesthetically a sign in itself or a vehicle for a sign; the essential quality of this kind of object is less formal, structural or functional and more symbolic or ornamental. And the symbolic content is not necessarily re-lated to the formal, structural or functional quality of the object . . . In less historical ornament, a flower pattern, for instance, may allude to conventional wallpaper flowers rather than to real flowers; the extra layer of meaning makes the symbolism richer. Ornament in folk architecture is often representational high-art ornament simplified and rendered in two dimensions through painted patterns on flat surfaces, or through silhou-ettes. The jig-saw carpentry of American front porches or the cut-out boards of Alpine balustrades are examples. Economy and naïvety were probably the immediate reasons for this representational approach, but its aesthetic results were elo-quent expressions of the essence of style. In our time, economy and industrial standardisation on the one hand and lack of craftsmanship on the other justify this simplified, repetitive, and depictive approach to ornament. If we cannot construct historical architecture today or revive Revivalism, we can represent them through appliqué and sign. This goes for the design of objects too'.[64]

Venturi's lasting achievement in design as well as architec-ture is that he and his firm have managed such 'representation' and, usually with some irony, have brought colour, ornament, and history back into the arena of debate in the 1980s. Venturi is not Post-Modernism's best designer but he is, aside from Jencks, one of its father-figures. In the end, it is the thinking that lies behind his designs, rather than the objects themselves, that is important.

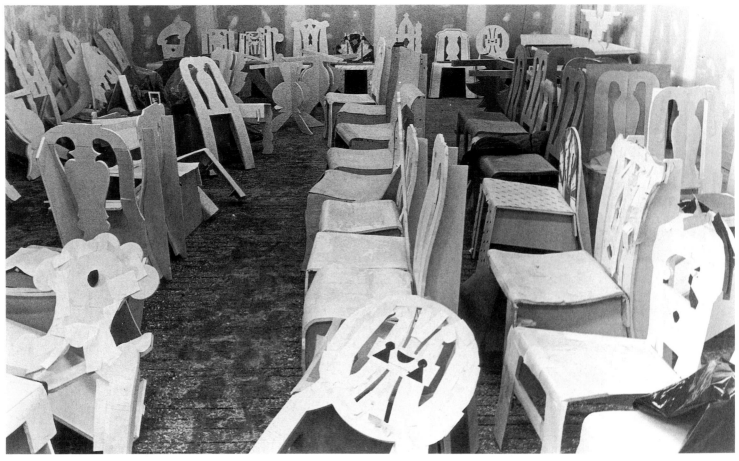

KNOLL INTERNATIONAL FURNITURE STUDY MODELS

ROBERT VENTURI, INTERIOR WITH *QUEEN ANNE* SUITE AND *TEA & COFFEE PIAZZA*, 1984

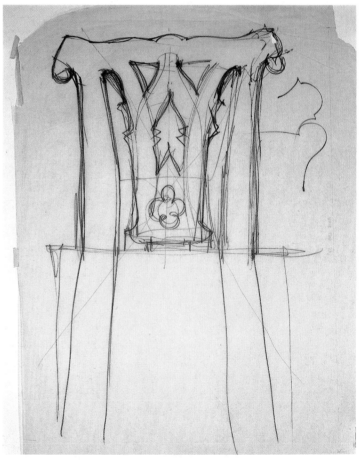

ROBERT VENTURI, STUDIES FOR *ART NOUVEAU*, *SHERATON* AND *CHIPPENDALE* CHAIRS FOR KNOLL INTERNATIONAL

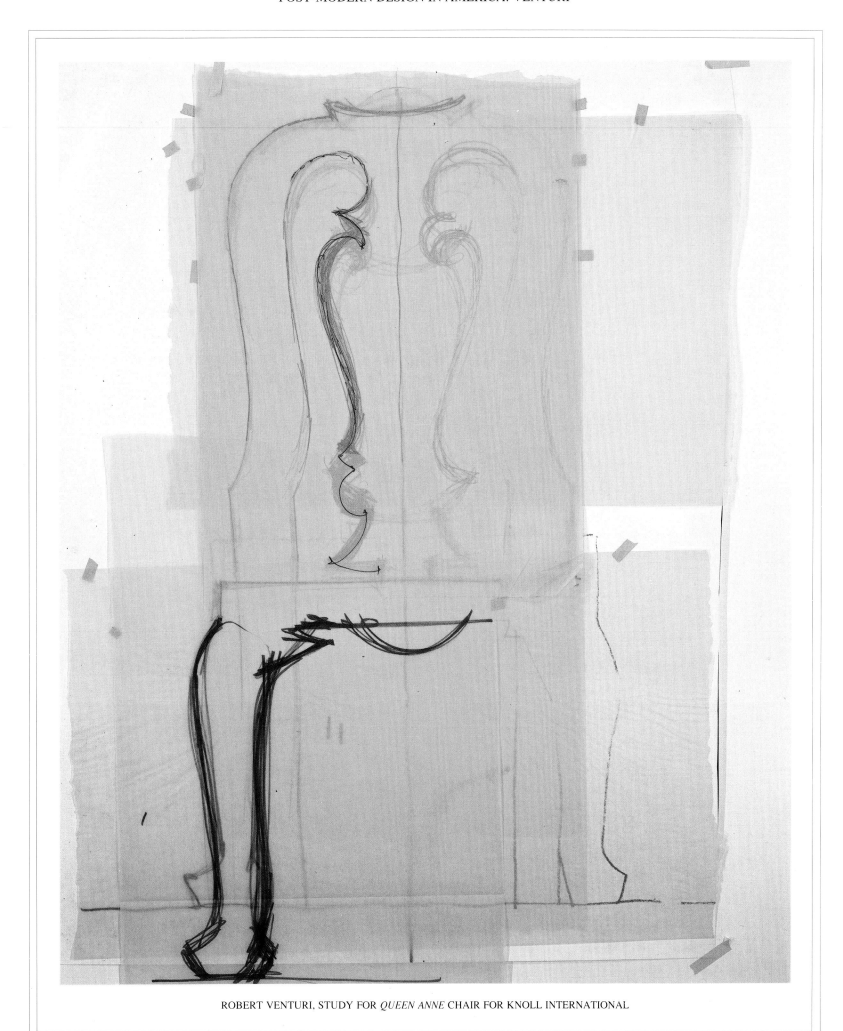

ROBERT VENTURI, STUDY FOR *QUEEN ANNE* CHAIR FOR KNOLL INTERNATIONAL

ROBERT VENTURI, COLLAGE STUDY FOR *LOUIS XV* LOWBOY FOR ARC INTERNATIONAL

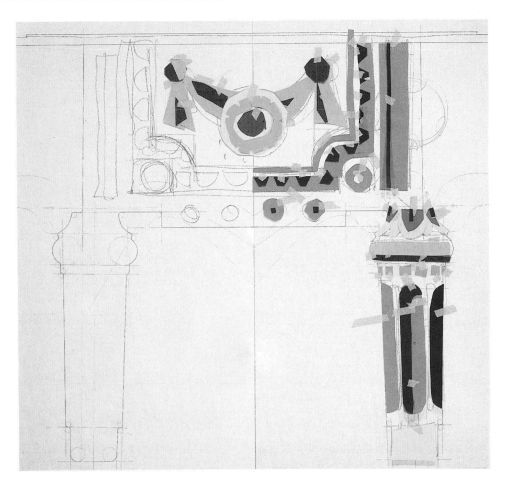

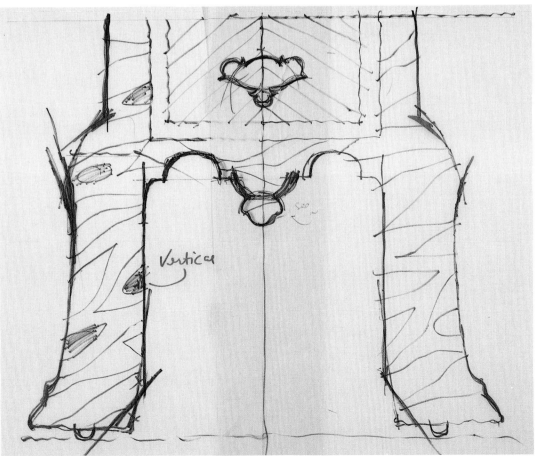

ROBERT VENTURI, STUDIES FOR *LOUIS XVI* AND *QUEEN ANNE* LOWBOYS FOR ARC INTERNATIONAL

ROBERT VENTURI, *SHERATON*, *CHIPPENDALE*, *BIEDERMEIER*, *GOTHIC REVIVAL* AND *ART NOUVEAU* CHAIRS, 1984 FOR KNOLL INTERNATIONAL

ROBERT VENTURI, *QUEEN ANNE* AND *LOUIS XVI* LOWBOYS FOR ARC INTERNATIONAL, AND *WILLIAM AND MARY* STYLE BUREAU, 1985

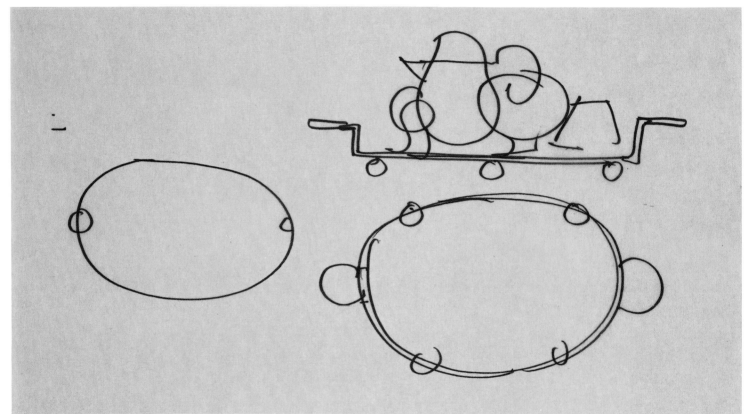

ROBERT VENTURI, STUDIES FOR ALESSI *TEA & COFFEE PIAZZA*, 1981

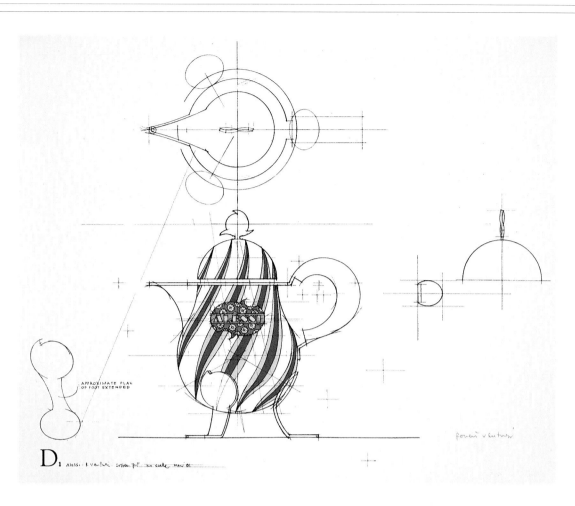

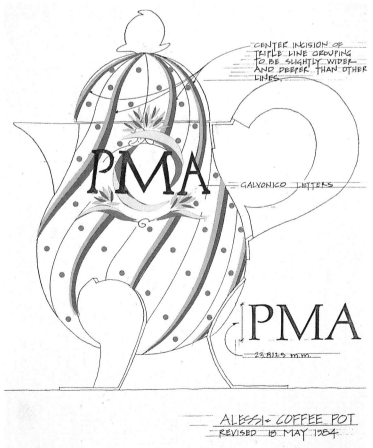

ROBERT VENTURI, STUDIES FOR ALESSI COFFEE POT, 1981-84

ROBERT VENTURI, MUGS (*TOP L*), GWATHMEY/SIEGEL, MUG (*CENTRE*) AND HAUSSMANN, MUGS (*TOP R*), AND VENTURI DINNERWARE, 1984 FOR SWID POWELL

ROBERT VENTURI, *NOTEBOOK* DINNERWARE, 1984 FOR SWID POWELL

CHARLES JENCKS, *SPRING ROOM* OF THE THEMATIC HOUSE, 1979-84

CHAPTER V

Charles Jencks · Michael Graves · Robert Stern · Charles Moore · Stanley Tigerman

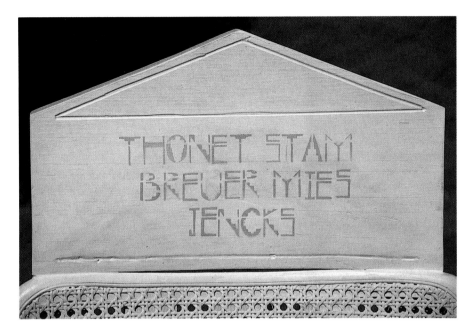

CHARLES JENCKS, *BREUER-JENCKS* CHAIR, 1984

Charles Jencks' 'ad hoc' and 'Late-Modern' furniture of the late 1960s has already been discussed, as well as his vital contribution to the literature and definition of Post-Modernism in architecture. If his work of 1968 can be read as progressive, then his architecture and design of the 1980s can be seen as a neoconservative about-turn. The *rappel à l'ordre* is revealed in its entirety in his own Thematic House in London, designed with British architect Terry Farrell from 1979 to 1984. This has rooms devoted to the seasons – spring, summer, Indian summer, autumn, and winter – as well as many others which are thematic, such as the Egyptian room and the Architectural Library. Jencks has designed symbolic furniture for his house, some of which has also been produced for sale, and unveiled by Aram Designs in London in 1985. Of late, a selection has also been produced by Sawaya & Moroni in Milan, and in 1985 Jencks' *Sun Chair* was made in Colorcore. The furniture is made of Medium Density Fibreboard (Medite), thereby using a modern material to manufacture historicist designs, and in that sense they relate to Knoll's use of plywood for Venturi's furniture.

Jencks' furniture works extremely well within its intended location in the Thematic House, as well as the pieces standing in their own right as individual objects of great merit. The symbolism is to be expected from a writer on architecture concerned with meaning and language – it is clearly apparent from Jencks' writing that his first degree, from Harvard, was in

English Literature. In the same year that his furniture was marketed by Aram, Jencks wrote that 'By 1985, after twenty years of practice, Post-Modernism has realised three basic achievements, and might be said to have reached maturity: it has formulated an urbanist practice, known as contextualism, which looks at the city as the basic public arena for architecture; it has reintroduced the full arsenal of expressive means such as ornament, polychromy and metaphor; it has synthesised a shared public language, Post-Modern Classicism, which, like the previous International Style is practised around the world with regional variation'.[65] Jencks' furniture draws in the main from 'Classical' inspiration ranging from Egypt, Greece, Neo-Classicism, Biedermeier, and Art Deco. His armchair, called the *Spring Chair*, designed initially for the Spring room in his Thematic House, has a shell-shaped back which conveys the idea of the first season, but perhaps, like Botticelli's *The Birth of Venus* in the Uffizi, Florence, where Venus is seen emerging from a shell, the image also has the connotation of the rebirth of learning. The rear of the chair has an inset Wedgwood shell-shaped plate, which Jencks calls 'a "found" industrial object which is used as a symbolic ornament'. His *Sun Chair* has a sunburst back, which echoes the Regency and Art Deco use of that motif, and is a compression of 1830s and 1930s furniture. Perhaps significantly, Jencks has a few original Biedermeier chairs in his house. This *Sun Chair*, conceived to go with his *Sun Table*, is most successful in the version without arm rests, and is one of Jencks' best designs to date.

The Symbolic range includes a witty *Egyptian Telephone Kiosk* and *Bookcases* with added turquoise scarabs from Egypt, which form the drawer knobs, the wood incised and painted blue, suggesting the waters of the Nile. His *Dice Table-Seats* are six square-topped seats, which, in echelon, can form a table. As one might expect from their title, each has an incised square, ranging in number from one to six, on their flat tops, while the bases resemble the triglyphs of the Parthenon and have the same proportions. Jencks not only takes inspiration from parts of architecture, but, in common with many other Post-Modernists, he suggests its form in 'micro-architecture'. The cliché of such a gesture has become the pitched roof, which Jencks uses for *Academy-Light* and the aptly named *Light-House*. It also appears in his marvellous *Slide Skyscrapers*, designed initially for his Architectural Library in the Thematic House. Since they house a collection of slides of traditional and modern subject-matter, one has a conventionalised man at its top, forming the letter 'T' and the other has an 'M' conventionally formed. The originals were partly 'ad hoc' in that the basic carcass was a standard steel unit, with added wood, and paint applied to simulate wood. They are now produced along with many other Jencks designs, by Sawaya & Moroni.

Jencks has explained his symbolic furniture in the following terms: 'Usually furniture is designed to be placed in many different contexts. As a result it is often banal . . . the most elegant furniture of this century, that of Mies van der Rohe and Charles Eames, is so general as to be equally at home in the airport lounge and the executive office . . . A symbolic furniture, still somewhat general but capable of specific meaning and function, might reassert its rightful place and give anonymous space a place and location'.[66] Jencks also asserts that his furniture 'is meant to have a multivalence lacking in the technosolipsistic furniture of our time'.[67]

As with much of his furniture, Jencks' silver service for Alessi is highly inflected towards Classicism, with its volutes, fluting, rams' heads and broken columns. The tray is stepped in a manner to suggest the base of a Greek temple. There are interesting precedents for the use of Classical columns in design, particularly in British silversmithing of the 1770s when, for example, certain tea caddy forms were fluted to resemble the drum of a column. As we have already seen, there are many columnar forms used in 1980s Post-Modern design and many will be examined in the work of Graves, Stern and others.

Jencks' set is highly learned in its use of the Classical Orders but betrays every lesson taught during the Modern Movement about 'form following function'. Despite Jencks' protestation that the set was designed to have black plastic and ebony insulation, the final version is of solid silver, and is likely to burn the fingers of the user. It remains an interesting fact that architects, before, during, or now after Modernism, have usually been better at designing furniture than other products.

His Alessi silver is an interesting curiosity and also a cautionary object. It demonstrates that learning should be wedded to sound ergonomics if a satisfactory design is to be produced. Function would not matter if this silver were purely ornamental, but the fact remains that it is a coffee and tea set. Such an object is too 'precious' in every sense.

Jencks has made a lasting contribution to Post-Modernism, especially in his writing, but this in itself can lead to problems when an actual design is produced. The set is too cerebral, and makes one applaud all the more the contribution of Michael Graves which is a more careful balance of a visceral approach with underlying theory.

It would be invidious to select the greatest niche in the future Pantheon of Post-Modernism for any one particular architect but, on the strength of Michael Graves' work, there is a strong chance the laurel will go to him. He has been principal of his own practice in Princeton, New Jersey, since 1964. His work in the late 1960s was, like many of 'The New York Five' or 'Whites', indebted to Le Corbusier's architecture of the 1920s. The rest of the group, Richard Meier, John Hejduk, Charles Gwathmey and Peter Eisenman, have essentially remained loyal to Late-Modernism. Graves began to abandon the Modernist aesthetic with his Snyderman House at Fort Wayne, Indiana (1972). This still retained a Le Corbusier-inspired grid, but used applied colour of light pink and blue. His conversion towards Post-Modern Classicism was complete by the time of the Public Service Building, Portland, Oregon (1982), the Plocek House, New Jersey (1978-1982) and the the Clos Pegase Winery, in the Napa Valley, California.

Although he was inspired by Cubism at the time of his conversion to colour, and particularly the paintings of Juan Gris, he gradually developed a return to the order of polychromy as applied in the nineteenth century. It is to be remembered that the Neo-Classicism of the late eighteenth century had relied on the monochrome 'noble simplicity and calm grandeur' of Greek architecture as it was understood by the generation of the great German art historian Johann Joachim Winckelmann. The discovery that Greek architecture was in fact polychromatic was revealed in J I Hittorf's *Architecture polychrome chez les Grecs*, for example, published in 1830. This coincided with the development of chromolithography, first used in books such as Hittorf's, and, most famously, in Owen Jones' *Grammar of Ornament* (1856). Equally important was the revelation that the Parthenon marbles had been coloured, a fact embraced with gusto in the painting entitled *Phidias and the Parthenon* by Lawrence Alma-Tadema (1868). Here, Alma-Tadema correctly depicted the frieze in bright colours.

Michael Graves uses colour symbolically in his architecture, and presses the nineteenth-century palette of earthbound reds, sky blues, and gold into service for his work. As Graves is relearning the process of colour, one could point him to, say, Michael Gottlieb Bindesbøll's facade for the Thorvaldsen museum in Copenhagen. The 1837 watercolour design for this has red Ionic columns with gold capitals, which visually

CHARLES JENCKS, MASTER BEDROOM OF THE THEMATIC HOUSE, 1979-84

MICHAEL GRAVES, *CORINTH* AND *DELOS* DINNERWARE, 1984 FOR SWID POWELL

protrude even further from the blue painted masonry because of the way red 'jumps forward' and blue, conversely, 'recedes into distance'. This device, known to every artist since the Renaissance, has had to be revived, since colour was essentially rejected by the International Style in favour of white or neutral tones, with the stress on texture rather than colour.

In Graves' case, it has been a highly rewarding process, especially as he is indebted to the colours and shape-making of Cubist painting in some of his designs. He uses sky blue, terracotta red, and green to suggest trees in his Sunar Furniture Showroom in New York (1979), although his *Easel Mural* for that showroom is more indebted to Purism than it is to nineteenth-century polychromy.

Between 1979 and 1981, Graves designed furniture as well as showrooms for Sunar. His conference table had fluted pilaster legs, with an elegant thin lozenge pattern on its surface. The chairs were reinterpretations of Art Deco, with a hint of Biedermeier, in the contrast between large areas of blond wood and dramatic ebonised sections. The wood was usually birds-eye maple, and his armchair and accompanying side chair, with wedge-shaped legs, delight the eye. The same may be said for his circular table for Sunar's London Showroom, with its square blond wood base and ebonised drum pedestal. The whole reminds one of Regency, or more particularly of Biedermeier 'loo' and 'library' tables of about 1820. A similar elegance was applied to his upholstered lounge chair for the same firm. Some of these splendid designs are still produced in Milan by Sawayi and Moroni.

His blond wood stool for Diane Von Furstenberg's boutique in New York has ebonised leg rails, and is topped by a cushion with tassels at its corners. The 'sabre' leg reminds one of 1830s' and 1930s' furniture, both popular sources of inspiration for Post-Modern furniture, but without the military connotations of the Regency and Empire period. Instead, it merely conveys the appropriate sense of luxury.

Graves is justifiably well known for his drawing, and his sketches for Post-Modern designs are among the best works on paper produced so far. He nearly always draws furniture or metalwork in plan and elevation, like miniature architecture, and some of his 'notes' of 1982 show his Post-Modern chairs for Sunar on a plinth, next to and therefore contrasted with a drawing of a tubular steel chair which broadly outlines the old Marcel Breuer, Mart Stam and PEL classics of the 1920s and 1930s. This ironic presentation accords with the gestures of Venturi and Knoll in the paradoxical presentation of their furniture next to Mies van der Rohe's MR or Brno chairs in publicity photographs. Graves also produced excellent designs for Memphis, notably his highly architectural *Plaza* dressing table (1981), and *Stanhope* bed (1982). Their very titles set up a resonance with Art Deco and the Jazz Age, and they differ from most Memphis work in that they are made of maple-root wood, which gives them an Art Deco look. The dressing table is a Hollywood fantasy with Art Deco style mirror-glass tesserae, the globe lamps are reminiscent of the 1930s, and the

six drawers and accompanying circular stool are painted in the blue that has become a characteristic of Graves' use of colour. Given the fact that both the dressing table and the bed have expensive price tags, they have sold relatively well; *Plaza* to eleven customers between 1981 and the end of 1986, and *Stanhope* to six buyers between 1982 and the end of 1986. They represent a return to high standards of production as well as design. Above all, as with other Post-Modern furniture, the use of blond wood evokes memories of 1830s' and 1930s' furniture, where Art Deco meets Empire or Regency.

Likewise, Graves' 1983 silver service for Alessi is full of witty art-historical references such as Neo-Classical fluting in metal, with just a hint of Hoffmann's interpretation of the same theme in his Wiener Werkstätte productions of the 1920s. The significance of Josef Hoffmann and the Wiener Werkstätte has been revealed in many excellent publications and exhibitions in the 1980s, and his work is quite justifiably admired in the United States. His significance lies in his ability to be multi-faceted. In the late 1970s, at the time of interest in High-Tech design and grid patterns, it was his early period and 'square' metalwork which was in vogue. In the 1900s Hoffmann had drawn inspiration from Mackintosh's 'square' forms, and was even dubbed 'quadratl' Hoffmann as a result. However, Hoffmann's use of Classical quotation and fluting in his metal and glass is now admired by contemporary architects as is his 'decadent' later phase of the 1920s, with its Rococo undertones. Hoffmann surely is the 'man for all seasons' and continues to exert posthumous sway over Post-Modernists such as Graves and Late-Modernists such as Richard Meier.

Graves' Alessi set is chunky, and the fluting makes it look as solid as marble. Graves again uses colour masterfully, in the blue glazed aluminium spheres which set off the corners of the silver, and provide the feet for the glass tray. This latter again looks very Art Deco, especially with its ivory-coloured handles. The handles of the coffee and tea pot, sugar basin, and cream jug are also mock ivory. Ivory, incidentally, was still used in the 1930s, but is today quite correctly illegal and recognised as immoral. One supposes that it is fair to imitate it, however. Graves' Alessi set was the most serious *rappel à l'ordre* in the range, and achieved notoriety through being admired by Nancy Reagan at the Whitney Museum's *High Styles* Exhibition in 1983. The problem is that it is 'high-style', and, as with the other submissions, made in a limited edition of 99 plus three 'artist's proofs'. The very term 'artist's proofs' used in the Alessi catalogue goes some way towards explaining the problem, for the set is limited in terms of numbers. Design could, and perhaps should be more democratic and less an 'affair of the élite' – Hans Hollein's description of architecture. Graves' set cost £11,390 in 1986, which was by any standard an élite price. It was therefore a welcome decision on the part of Alessi to mass produce a kettle designed by Graves in 1985, a design that has become one of Post-Modernism's most successful objects in commercial terms. 40,000 kettles were sold in one year, in spite of the fact that the design was for a non-electric device technologically in the rear of, say, Peter Behrens' electric kettle, marketed before 1910. It is perhaps a tribute to Post-Modernism that Graves' fun design can sell so well on style alone, and yet be static in terms of scientific achievement.

The kettle is made of stainless steel, and has a blue handle and a whistle in the shape of a red bird. Here, the metaphor of the singing kettle is taken to its humorous conclusion. Graves again uses his characteristic colours. The bird and the spheres which insulate the body of the metal are red, to warn the user of the hot parts of the object; commensurately the handles are blue, to convey coldness and safety to the touch. The only problem is that one thinks of birds as being sky bound, and would associate blue rather than red with them. Graves always seems to give much thought to his use of colour, but this causes problems when, as happened in 1988, a set is built around the kettle. Alessi have now issued a creamer and sugar bowl and spoon to match with the red of the earlier kettle, but this colour need not be used, as these two last objects do not retain heat.

Graves has also designed a stainless steel pepper mill, with orange coloured polyamide fins, produced by Alessi in 1988. These fins remind one of Oldenburg's *Swedish Wing Nut* of 1966-7 and, in turn, the ears of that much loved cartoon character, Mickey Mouse, who makes frequent guest appearances in Post-Modern design. In fact, the Graves design more closely resembles the wing nut, while Robert and Trix Haussmann have recently designed a pepper mill for Swid Powell, aptly called *Mickey*, with circular ears just like those of the famous Disney character. Unlike the Haussmann design, which is in plain metal, Graves' peppermill is again colour-coded, the orange immediately suggesting the hotness of pepper.

Swid Powell, established in 1984, have produced three excellent ceramics designed by Graves. Two are place settings and a series of plates with the apposite Greek names *Corinth* and *Delos*. The rim of the former is blue, with a conventionalised plant motif, and the bowl has characteristic stars. *Delos* is richer yet, with a star-covered white bowl, blue inner rim, rich red outer rim with conventionalised plants in black, and a plate with a gold painted circumference. Colour has not been used in this way since the days of Hittorf and Bindesbøll, and the stars remind one of Schinkel, as in the latter's gouache *Appearance of the Queen of Night*, a stage design for an 1815 production of *The Magic Flute* in the Staatliche Museum, Berlin. Colour, censored for too long during the Modern Movement, has returned with a vengeance. Graves' most interesting ceramic for Swid Powell is *The Big Dripper* (1986). This porcelain coffee pot has a cross-shaped foot and spherical body, thus setting up a dialogue with past work, such as the cross-footed ceramics of Bernard Löffler for Wiener Keramic of about 1905 at the time of Josef Hoffmann, and Marianne Brandt's famous Bauhaus metal teapot (1924), also with a cross-shaped base. The difference lies in the fact that Graves again uses colour in a symbolic and ornamental way. The base is red to signal that the object is hot, and the blue-green wavy line around the spherical body tells us that the vessel contains liquid, whereas

the gold ball at the top signals 'luxury'. Nothing could tell the Modern Movement to go away more than the presence of gold, with all its hierarchic connotations, and yet the form of Graves' coffee pot is heavily indebted to the Modern Movement. Here, indeed, is Venturi's 'complexity and contradiction' embodied in a fellow American's design.

Graves is, in any event, an excellent colourist. He can take as much from Cubism as he does from Victorian polychromy and his 'Grammar of Ornament' approach. For example, he has designed a table called *Variations on a theme of Juan Gris* which is almost an exact, if three-dimensional, interpretation of the Cubist painter's *Fruit Bowl & Carafe* (1914), now in the Kröller Müller, Otterlo, in The Netherlands. Cubism and Art Deco textiles have also inspired Graves' carpets for V'soske of 1979 to 1980, whereas his carpets for Vorwerk are rather more Post-Modern Classical.

Graves is also an excellent designer of lamps, most of which embrace the typology of lights used in the 1930s, from wall sconces to uplighters. He designed a *Tripod Lamp* for the Plocek House, New Jersey (1978-82), which has three tall upright supports stemming from a circular stepped base, and ends with a bowl-shaped uplighter. His *Ingrid Lamp*, originally for the same house, is equally vertical, with four wooden uprights stemming from a wooden cube base. The light section above the frame is onyx with four black spheres at the corners. This design is still available, though somewhat modified, marketed by Sawaya and Moroni in Milan. Graves has also designed a series of brass and frosted white glass lamps called *Baldinger*; the wall sconce is, self-effacingly, a reworking of 1930s' lamps. Some of these elegant lights have been used in the Humana Building, Louisville, Kentucky, in 1982. Graves' most 'archaeological' approach has been taken with his jewellery for Cleto Munari. Their dialogue is with the art of the museums, and when asked by Barbara Radice the question 'What ancient jewellery do you like most?', Graves replied 'Etruscan and Roman', at the same time explaining that his jewellery 'is not architectural. I'm making pieces of jewellery that are identified with different parts of the body. It is not terribly elaborate, no more elaborate than you would expect from archaic jewellery'.[68]

When compared with other submissions for the Munari range, Graves's designs can be seen to be completely Post-Modern Classical. He puts aside irony and humour, and instead dons the mantle of learning. The hard-stones are tooled with palmettes to suggest Classical ornament, and to link up with the long tradition of the signet ring. This archaism is somewhat mannered however since no one, apart perhaps from the odd lawyer or aristocrat, uses sealing wax; but nevertheless they remain enjoyable evocations of what jewellery used to look like. The best of them has a yellow gold shank, with a twisted effect simulating rope near the top of the ring, and an inset hematite with carved palmette flanked by a small spherical green agate on either side. Another has a cornelian with carved Classical urn and stars. Graves has, significantly, also designed

MICHAEL GRAVES, *BIG DRIPPER, SUGAR BOWL AND CREAMER*, 1986 FOR SWID POWELL

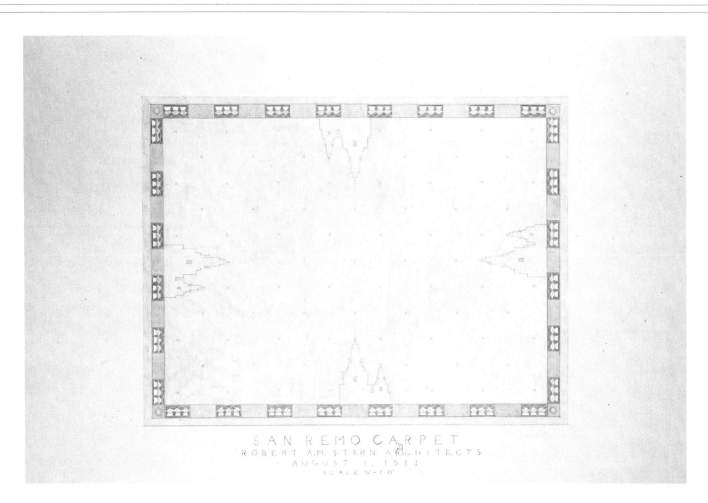

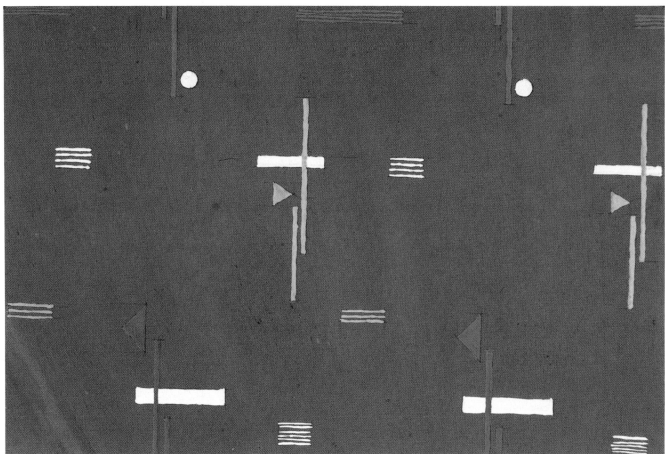

ROBERT STERN, *SAN REMO* RUG DESIGN, 1983 AND DEN CARPET DESIGN, 1986 FOR A RESIDENCE IN BROOKLYN

cuff links in gold and turquoise, gold and lapis-lazuli, and gold and black onyx. There has been a fashionable revival of such accessories, especially among the Preppies, Yuppies and other new breeds of young rich. The young fogey of the 1980s, who dresses in 'traditional' clothes, would delight in such items and, in any case, is likely to be the only type of person who can afford them. The rings cost over £700 each, and the cuff links are about £430 per pair.

Much the same has to be said for Graves' beautiful watch for Cleto Munari. This has a circular face, set into gold with a beaded edge, and the strap is attached with a bar surmounted by green agates at either end; the numerals are red, and the enamelled hands green. Graves, as always, uses colour very well, and the design is richer than the other watches for Munari by Sottsass, Hollein and Isozaki, though even at over £4000 it is not the most expensive. One of Graves' most accomplished designs to date has been the *Mantel Clock* for Alessi, conceived in 1986 and launched in 1988. This pendulum clock is of ebonised wood and maple-veneer, and the whole is 'micro-architectural'. As with the Munari watch, the numerals are red and the dial green. The face is square, set into a 'cube' of maple-veneer, with incised lines which resemble rustication, and this in turn rests on four squat ebonised Tuscan columns on a maple-veneer plinth. Graves has written that 'In designing the table clock, I was interested in exploring the well established tradition of seeing artefacts as miniature architecture . . . The pendulum exists in the void provided by the colonnade while the clock face exists in the space of architecture traditionally reserved for the "piano nobile". The two figures are then capped appropriately with the head or cornice of the composition. In this way we are able to attain readings of the clock as cabinet, the clock as architecture and finally the clock as clock'.[69]

Graves has come down heavily on the side of Post-Modern Classicism in his prolific design work and has rejected his earlier 'abstraction' for the sake of 'symbolic and mythic representation'. He has suggested that 'the loss of those figurative elements thought to be derived from classical analogies of man and nature leads to a sense of alienation or lack of association with the architecture. If we are to increase the participation in and identification with architecture by the culture at large, we must begin to re-establish the . . . somewhat classical mode of thinking which is capable of representing in physical form the symbolic and mythic aspirations of that culture'.[70]

Robert Venturi's ironic Post-Modern Classicism, and Michael Graves' rather more 'archaeological' approach are two sources of inspiration for other architect-designers in America. The most important of these are Robert Stern, Charles Moore and Stanley Tigerman whose individual styles form part of the larger Pluralism of the 1980s.

Stern established his own practice in New York in 1977, and his architecture has drawn inspiration from the Shingle style (the American term for the Richard Norman Shaw-influenced

domestic revival of the 1870s and 1880s), the work of Sir Edwin Lutyens, and Robert Venturi. Stern's designs have little of the latter's irony, and are somewhat nearer Graves' purer, historicist language.

Stern writes: 'As an architect, I am interested in designing objects for three principal reasons. First, because, like most architects, I believe that architectural design can extend beyond the bare walls to an idea of "total design" . . . Second, one of my fundamental approaches to building design – to transform traditional forms to suit contemporary use – can be applied to objects as well. A traditional salt shaker has to be scaled to a modern dinner table. Third, I am fascinated by miniaturisation, by taking an idea and condensing it to a scale at which it can be set on a table top, a process similar to making architectural models'.[71]

Stern, as with other Post-Modernists, is inspired by Art Deco and Classicism. His *San Remo* rug (1983) was designed for a living room inside the New York San Remo apartment building on Central Park West. The twin towers of the building are silhouetted on the carpet, while the border is indebted to terracotta decoration drawn from another New York skyscraper. The towers of the San Remo appear again in Stern's enamel and silver jewellery for Acme (1986).

He has also produced excellent designs for carpets, one of the best being *Dinner at Eight* (1983 to 1984) for the firm Furniture of the Twentieth Century. Of this Stern has written that 'The phrase "Dinner at Eight" evokes a certain genre of Hollywood film comedy that combined disingenuous innocence with metropolitan sophistication. This carpet . . . presents a highly formalised image within a proscenium-like frame of classical columns and theatrical drapes. The curtains are drawn, the doors about to open, and the music about to play as the comedy begins'.[72]

Stern's interest in textile effects manifests itself in his jewellery; *The Swag* and *Jabot* enamel and silver pieces for Acme (1986) derive, according to Stern, from 'traditional drapery motifs'. The *Majestic* necklace and earrings have a square buckle and clasp form, which relate them to Stern's ceramic design of the same name, for Swid Powell, in 1985. This plate has some of the richness of Graves' other work for the same firm and Stern suggests that 'the *Majestic* dinner plate, ruby red in colour and highlighted with gold leaf, emphasises, as do the silver pieces, richness of material. The plate's strap-and-buckle pattern evokes a family crest or medallion, yet remains anonymous by virtue of its abstraction'.[73] Like some of his *arriviste* houses, this plate is ideal for a new rich society – instant cachet, bought in this case fairly cheaply. One can read the non-specific crest ironically, but on the whole *Majestic* comes over as being rather Yuppie and élitist.

Some of Stern's best work for Swid Powell has been for their metal range. He has designed silver candlesticks, a water pitcher, and salt and pepper shakers. These were produced in 1984, and are 'stripped Classical' to the point where Modern (undecorated surface) and Classical (columnar) elements are held in perfect equilibrium. Stern has written that they are 'all based on the iconography of the column. The column of the ancient Minoan palaces, the Gothic colonnette, the classical columns – both in their pure geometries and in their stream-lined variations from the modern interpretations of the 1930s, are individually remembered in the various pieces . . .'[74] Stern's fusion of Classicism with Art Deco has become a common device in the arsenal of Post-Modern Design. His interest in Jazz Age and New York Art Deco gives his work a local accent, and in that sense, he is very much an American Post-Modernist working for an audience made up of people with New York tastes. He is also fully aware of the nature of capitalism, consumerism and demand, and has summed up his attitude to design by stating that 'The past offers the designer the best opportunity for comment on the present. The rediscovery of forms of the past, explored in interaction with present-day techniques and programmes, has opened up the dead end of "good design" as defined by the Museum of Modern Art in the 1950s and early 1960s. "Good design" was based on a false equation of economy and uniformity . . . Consumer capitalism is a fact, not an ideology, and as such is not so much to be overlooked or lamented as to be understood as part of our time and served by the designer . . . Fashion may not be the main thing, but it is part of what capitalism and industrialisation are all about – choice'.[75]

Stern's work can be read as neoconservative Post-Modernism, subservient to the most rampant form of capitalism, namely the taste trends of New York, but at least he is honest about consumerism in America. One senses, however accomplished his designs are, that they simply serve, in a somewhat venal manner, the desires of American consumerism. This latter word has a certain ambiguity, conveying eating as well as purchasing – highly suitable for many Post-Modern objects. Even the title of Stern's carpet, *Dinner at Eight,* has the resonance of a land of plenty, and it is significant that Swid Powell produce product designs for the dinner table. This is Land of Cockaigne design.

If Stern's work is very much part of the culture of New York, then other architects such as Charles Moore can be seen as serving different, perhaps more eclectic tastes. Moore is one of the elder statesmen of American Post-Modern architecture, and set up his own partnership practice from the early 1960s. He works from Connecticut and also California, where his firm is known as Moore, Ruble, Yudell. He is best known for his whimsical Post-Modern Classical Piazza d'Italia in New Orleans (1975-80). This historicist fantasy, designed with the local Italian community very much in mind, is a theme-park of Italian Classical architecture, mixed with elements taken from Schinkel, with the addition of bright colour and neon lighting. His *Corner Cupboard* for Colorcore is highly architectural, six foot in height, and massed upwards with steps and columns. It was produced in 1983, and its form is an abstracted mimesis of the massing and verticality of the steps to the Acropolis and the

Parthenon and temple complex.

Moore's recent work has embraced non-European culture, as well as craft, and his design is very much based on an awareness of layering and carving. For example, in 1986 he designed a wooden desk, with brass handles, in a form reminiscent of Empire furniture. It was made in India, in a traditional fashion, with no concession made to modern materials, unlike other Post-Modernists. Furthermore, the desk contains brightly painted wooden folk toys. It was shown at the *Golden Eye* exhibition at the Cooper-Hewitt Museum in New York, and in 1986, Moore produced his *Memory Palace* series for the touring Charles Moore retrospective exhibition. Nearly all these designs resemble his Colorcore cupboard in that they are stepped up, large-scale structures, with titles such as *Walls that Layer* or *Space that leaks up and out.* As with his Indian desk, many have painted wooden figures, toys and animals. *Stairs that climb and Spread* has naively painted and carved figures, some quite out of scale with each other, standing on steps. They spark off a memory of people, say, on the stairway of the Great Mosque at Delhi, or pilgrims descending to bathe in the sacred Ganges at Benares. This folk-art based, non-Eurocentric approach to eclecticism is a welcome change from the slicker products of Post-Modern Classicism. Moore had, in 1985, designed a prototype *Layered Coffee Table* for Stendig which has some of the qualities of the *Memory Palace* series. In a circular recess in the square table, Moore has filled the space with a child-like world of toy houses, brightly-painted figures and an elephant, while a model of a train like Stephenson's 'Rocket' is on a track along the outer circumference of the recess. Its lack of sophistication would please the child in all men, although at another level, it is, like nearly all his work, about layered space and the nature of plasticity through the full exploration of three dimensions.

Moore's *Recamier* sofa (1986) is equally plastic in its use of solid and void, indentation and contour, though as the title suggests it is a Post-Modern Classical design. It is reminiscent of the typology of such furniture depicted in the two paintings of Madame Recamier, one by Jacques-Louis David of 1800 and the other by François-Pascal Gérard of 1802 which show her reclining on Neo-Classical furniture, though it is not specifically based on these paintings. He has written that 'the incomparably rich heritage of 2,500 years of Latin and Post-Latin languages, redolent of all the amazing things they have conveyed to us, reasserts itself'.[76] Moore's contribution to eclecticism is that he casts his net widely, and gathers in much of the goodness that this rich heritage has to offer.

Moore's use of figures and animals, not present in the work of Graves or Venturi, links him to Stanley Tigerman. Tigerman was born in Chicago and set up his own practice there in 1964. His anthropomorphic and zoomorphic humour became well known through such houses as Hot Dog House in Illinois (1973), and his aptly named Animal Crackers house in the same State in 1978. His practice, known as Tigerman, Fugman, McCurry has also designed prolifically and, as with Charles

CHARLES MOORE, 'MINIATURES THAT MAGNIFY', *MEMORY PALACE*, 1986

STANLEY TIGERMAN, *QUICKSILVER* CANDLE HOLDER, 1984 FOR SWID POWELL

Moore, he and Margaret McCurry rely on a child-like approach to much of their work. There is little of Graves' later *gravitas*, or Stern's Art Deco and Classicism.

Tigerman's designs often reinforce the human presence that was missing from architecture for so long. He writes of his wish 'to relate buildings and their structures not only to human configuration but to the human spirit as well. Thus, I am less interested in directly tying my work to classical allusion on the totemic side of the history of architecture . . . than I am to the aedicular theory which celebrates the human being as a frail finite creature . . .'[77]

Tigerman is thus highly ironic about Classicism, and treats it with a sense of humour, as he does most of his work. His drawings for his *Barcalounger* chair of 1982 show designs for a colourful armchair with fluted back and headrest, formed alternatively of Doric, Ionic and Corinthian capitals. Like other Post-Modernists, he has clearly been inspired by Surrealism and has a jokey interpretation of it. A publicity photograph of his office in Chicago shows an oversize *trompe-l'oeil* pencil on the ceiling, and Magritte-like apples and hats placed on the desks. His silver set for Alessi is also quasi-Surreal. This was produced in 1983, and has a coffee pot with quite literal 'lips' and a handle formed to resemble plaited hair; the sugar basin has ears for handles and, to further the use of dismembered parts, the tray has hands clasping its outer edges. Tigerman's set pursues the concept of the tray as a 'carried object' and his working drawings for the set explore the idea of the hands fully. The result should be compared and contrasted with Hans Hollein's set, to be discussed later, where the pun on the concept of the tray as 'carrier' is taken to extremes, with a base shaped like an aircraft carrier deck. Tigerman has produced a drawing showing the parts of this set each within a grid frame, set against a backdrop of Magritte-like sky and clouds; a characteristic winged Tigerman figure suspends the vessels and tray from the clouds, and below, more figures hang from them, almost like figures at the base of a parachute. Such figures and clouds reappear again, as we shall see, in his ceramic designs for Swid Powell.

In 1983, Tigerman designed his *Tête à tête* double chaise longue for Colorcore. He states that 'The design was intended for an intimately related couple who could read the same page of the Sunday New York Times simultaneously on opposite sides of the page'. Its profile sets up a resonance with the indentations and contours of Classical mouldings, though the chair as a whole has an uncanny human presence, even when empty. Tigerman's playful Classicism can be seen in his drawings for the projected rocking chair for Knoll of 1979-81, which was prototyped but never completed. The larger chaise had a pedimented head with a backrest of flat pilaster form and pierced fluting. As a companion to this larger *Papa Bear* rocker, the *Mama Bear* was more ironic, and somewhat reminiscent of Alchymia's anti-design. In the second rocker, the back would have been of Magritte-like cloud form, with clouds flopped, like a soft object from a Dali painting, over the arms.

The full range of Tigerman's humour can be seen in his work for Swid Powell, especially in his many ceramics, even if the joke is just a one liner that wears thin fairly quickly. His plates entitled *Sunshine* and *Verona* also have clouds and blue sky inspired by Magritte; the former has, as its title suggests, a sunburst with, in addition, a characteristic winged Tigerman figure in the top cloud. *Pompeii*, as the title suggests, has 'Classical' colours, red and black, reminding one of Attic ceramics, and a design of amusing frog-like characters who support the red bowl of the plate like so many Atlas figures around the rim. *Tigerpause*, in the same colours, is a rebus on the architect's name, with black tiger paw prints on the red plate; the same rebus which he uses on his firm's stationery. He has also produced a salt and pepper shaker, paired in echelon as two halves of a bisected, Oldenburg-like screw; this relates to the bisected heart he designed for Alessi – a salt and pepper set that fits together again to rejoin as a heart, and also to look like an embracing couple. These quasi-Surreal, anthropomorphic and dismembering gestures are amusing, if somewhat transient in the pleasure they give.

This 'dismembering' technique appears in his equally strange jewellery for Cleto Munari. He has designed a pair of rings, in the form of two halves of an Ionic capital which, when placed on adjacent fingers, can be made to join again. This strange alienation effect has been explained by Tigerman: 'The idea . . . was to establish "distance" from, while seeming to employ, the Classical Language. By imposing an ironic stance on the jewellery designs, classical orders, at a much diminished, "decorative" scale, are perceived in entirely new ways from the original ones. Columns are presented as no longer being obliged to support anything, entablatures bear on nothing more than the wearer's breastbone, and keystones no longer take the weight of walls bearing down on them . . . the seemingly "useless" quality attached to jewellery is questioned by paired rings, for example, that disrupt an ionic (or is it "ironic") capital . . . metaphor is at the root of the design of these objects'.[78]

Tigerman's gold bracelet for Munari (1986-7) has rather threatening miniature Tuscan columns, which lie flat, or stick out, somewhat reminiscent of a Punk's spiked collar. In another bracelet, a fluted pilaster is curved to fit the shape of the arm. He has explained these ironic images to Barbara Radice by suggesting that 'The feature most representative of this epoch, especially in America, is displacement, exile. And Post-Modernism reinforces exile in the sense that it is disillusioned with its own epoch. As in the Renaissance, we are looking back to another time'.[79]

The words in Tigerman's vocabulary, 'disrupt' or 'displacement', are somewhat negative, and set up a suggestion of a similar tendency within some aspects of 'deconstruction' which will be examined shortly. Tigerman writes that 'The nature of "Post-Modernism", that fascinates me most, is the disjunction extant in a time whose most salient feature can be said to reside in dissimulation. The yearning for an earlier state of innocence, represented by the historicist side of Post-

Modernism, as reflected in the design of objects that look over their shoulder for verification, for example, indicates a desire for verification, even if it infers a dissillusionment with the nature of the present. The use of history to authenticate permeates this kind of design.

'The equal, but opposite, interpretation of Post-Modernism, ie the expression of that dislocation endemic to our epoch by the exploitation of disjunctive strategies ("deconstruction", for example), represses a hopelessness that intrinsically goes against the optimistic tendencies I find indigenous to both architecture and design'.[80] Tigerman's attitude is therefore ambivalent, lying somewhere between the *rappel à l'ordre* of neoconservative Post-Modernism and what he perceives as the negative aspects of deconstruction. He states that 'The use of history alone is, for me, simply too retrograde an operation to be believable any longer'. Neither with or without belief, Tigerman sits on the fence between, say, Graves on the one hand, and Eisenman on the other, no doubt with a wry smile.

CHARLES JENCKS, *SPRING CHAIR*, 1984 (*DETAIL*)

CHARLES JENCKS, *ARCHITECTURAL LIBRARY* OF THE THEMATIC HOUSE, 1979-84

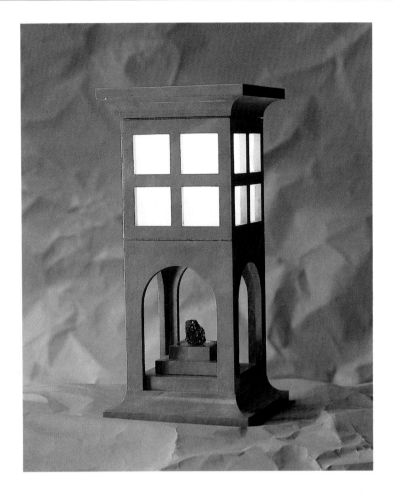

CHARLES JENCKS, *DANAE LIGHT*, *LIGHT-HOUSE*, *HOUSE-LIGHT* AND *FIRE-LIGHT*, 1984

SYMBOLIC OBJECTS
Charles Jencks

CHARLES JENCKS, *SUN-DIAL TABLE* AND *COLOSSEUM CHAIR AND STOOL*, 1984

Most functional objects are designed to disappear, mentally if not physically, and this is as it should be according to the most enlightened doctrines of Adolf Loos and Le Corbusier. 'Equipment', as the latter christened utilitarian objects, should not make unnecessary demands on our time and consciousness: it should be used and thrown out when no longer functional, or replaced by more efficient inventions. Furthermore, a room of such objects should be quiet and restful – a background for living or working, and not a zoo of animals all clamouring for attention. Loos advocated the silent butler function for such objects. They would be present but unnoticed, serving a required role with a well-trained discretion. Braun, Dieter Rams and a few other Modernist firms have made a virtue of such invisible servants and our business environment is, as a result, full of such wonderful emptiness. But an environment totally furnished in this way leads to a paradox: our attention is freed to focus on nothing. A perfectly silent, functional room devalues the meaning of function itself. Only where there is something to engage the eye and mind – a painting, hearth, chair or sculpture – does this background efficiency gain strength. Any room needs a few symbolic objects which have been carefully designed and crafted to give point to the ephemeral background. Let us posit a ratio of nine to one, a vast majority of silent butlers and a few assertive guests.

*   *   *

In the design of symbolic objects we have used very simple forms and proportions, the main Platonic solids and such ratios as 1:1:2:3:5. Furthermore we have kept to simple colours which relate to the background, and minimal articulations such as the incised line, and the layered overlapping of flat planes. This simplicity is partly sought to heighten the effect of the central symbol – the eye-catcher – and partly meant to harmonise with other forms. In effect minimalist abstraction is used, not as an end in itself, but as a rhetorical means of contrast. The eye-catcher, in the case of a series of lights, is a polished stone, mass-produced item or precious object. It becomes the visual and semantic focus of the composition, taking our mind away from the function. Its role is to displace meaning, disrupt continuity, become an exception, or 'other'. It is outside design, shares a taste and skill different from that of the designer. Furthermore, it is precious, beautifully made and cheap: the point of prefabrication, either by nature or man, is to mass produce beautiful objects that could not be made as well by hand. In Egypt they sell small onyx pyramids in several different contexts – most appropriately as a gnomon for a sun dial, as the geometric point which casts the shadow. The sundial, whose lines were determined by Mark Lennox Boyd, has an onyx pyramid above and an onyx obelisk below, two traditional signs of the sun. Thin columns form a half-temple to enclose the obelisk and mark out the passage of time, which is also symbolised by stylised zodiacs. The sun dial also functions as a focus to the view south and as a table, since seats ring it on one side, it acts as a visual stimulant when the mind wanders.

If furniture can disappear, it can also become a monument. Several High-Tech designers such as Norman Foster play on the contradiction 'disappearing monument', as their ultra-light tensile structures both call attention to themselves and like to tip-toe out of the room, a silent butler on stilts and moon-pods. In several large, heavy chairs we have taken the opposite approach and made them like masonry buildings, or tombs. The *Colosseum* chair and stool are meant to recall several different archetypes of architecture and be ambiguous because of this multivalence. The round-backed chair is a traditional form stemming, I suppose, from two sources: the idea of the circle, and resting one's arms and back against an embracing shape. At once comfortable and geometric it leads to the idea of a perfect circle and then to a full globe: the sphere and arch forms. Hence the Colosseum which had a canopy suspended across it from time to time. Invert this tensile structure and you produce a dome. Design a domed stool and place it, with centred oculus, and you have the Pantheon. Repeat arches and there is an aqueduct. Put the stool inside the chair and the result is an enigmatic object with several overtones. Sit in it, close the gates and you're imprisoned in a sixteenth-century stock. Add hinges and a columnar order and it becomes, again, a colosseum with major and minor arcades. It is also quite comfortable for reclining.

The idea of treating furniture as a small building has a long history, since architecture naturally lends its language to constructional forms and various scales. One can even imagine jewellery designed as buildings, and John Hejduk has actually produced tiny houses that fit in his pocket. Charles Rennie Mackintosh inverted this formula from time to time and produced, for instance, a doorway like a blown-up brooch. The reversibility of architecture and furniture can result, in any case, in the small object becoming a monument and as such it might have the presence of a strong, permanent building. Alberti and other theorists recommended primary shapes and symmetrical compositions for the monument, and we have followed his formula in many cases. Thus the cabinet, *Tempus Stasis*, symbolises at once a podium, grave, stela and skyscraper. It is symmetrical on both axes and it forms the basis for the eye-catcher, which in this case is a nineteenth-century clock. The symbolisation is again divergent. As well as a building, it relates to the metaphor of a body with a head. The inscription 'As if you could kill time without injuring eternity', by Thoreau, is handled in an architectural manner since the letters are massive and divided up into chunks, not correctly into words. The Romans used this convention to give their inscriptions an architectural metaphor. The phrase *Tempus Stasis* obviously plays on the contradiction that 'time flies' (*Tempus Fugit*), but the clock stays still in one place. Inscriptions often can assert the truth best when they state a clear falsehood that reveals a latent meaning. Magritte's paradoxical

painting of a pipe called *This is not a pipe* reveals that you can't smoke a painting. Inscriptions – a fundamental adjunct to symbolic objects, because they clarify an ambiguous visual code – are most effective if they have more than the ostensible meaning.

A set of lights we have designed makes use of the foursquare window motif which proportions the overall volume and alludes to a little house. The light shines up through the paper and down on various objects that join the view, and it usually sits on a desk or perhaps at the end of a vista. But equal with these functions is the metaphysics of light, its traditional role of symbolising 'enlightenment', 'truth', and 'seeing the light' – 'getting the idea' (itself signified by a light bulb). 'Let there be light', or Goethe's last words, 'more light', are characteristic demands of a metaphorical nature and we can find a Christian metaphysics of light elaborated by St Augustine, Abbot Suger and many artists and philosophers who have stressed the inherent meanings of stained glass and glistening objects. Merely to light a space misses half the point. Several lights were designed symbolising these metaphysicians of enlightenment but the only personification shown here is of Danae, the mythical character who was locked up in a bronze house to keep her from having a son. Unfortunately for her father the top of the house was left open to the sky and Zeus was able to impregnate her with a shower of gold. This is symbolised in the *Danae* light by the open top and the little piece of pyrite which is lit from above and sparkles. This is appropriately called 'fool's gold' because it is very cheap.

The *Light-House* and *House-Light* also make use of readymade objects which are quite beautiful and inexpensive – in these cases white and green alabaster eggs. The cosmic egg is a symbol which recurs in several cultures (and even the architecture of Lethaby) and here we have used it as a divergent sign as a contrast to 'light' and 'house'. The sky-blue of the *Light-House* and the green base of the *House-Light* are signs convergent with the overall shapes and meaning. The *Academy Light*, for Academy Editions, uses a stylised A and a tiny red book, again as convergent signs to reinforce the overall idea of a 'publishing house' while the *Fire-Light* and *Sun-Light* use semi-precious stones to set up readings which slightly diverge from the overhead images of sun and fire. Basic to all these lights is a triple code – light/building/eye-catcher – which gives the object more than functional meaning. The idea, however, is to use the inherent meanings of lighting as one of the departure points and find out what other images, and shapes, can add to or conflict with this utilitarian function. People may use objects in unexpected ways – as uplighters, or desk lights that also hold smaller things such as pencils and paperclips – and the Milanese company (Sawaya and Moroni) that produces small numbers of selected ones, makes them in different woods and colours (amarillo, lemon wood, a white bird's-eye maple). So the symbolism does not predetermine use or absolutely dictate colour. Because functional objects will be used in different contexts, they must have a certain abstract sobriety about them; they must be general and digni- fied enough to fit into several different kinds of room. But because symbolic objects are more than utilitarian and should be kept (or at least not destroyed by a change in fashion or technology) they can afford to be specific and meaningful in some parts. They exist then somewhere in this growing realm between the mass-produced item and the art object, the throw- away and antique, and quite a few designers and consumers are now becoming more interested in the middle territory. Among the former we might mention Tom Beeby, Hans Hollein, Robert Venturi, Mario Botta and occasionally Italian designers including Memphis (although their work is more often aes-

thetically than symbolically motivated). In any case, there is an increasing demand for objects which have character and will last, which can occupy a special place in a room among ephemeral and background furniture. Hence the recent growth of many firms specialising in such objects, or even the addition by large firms of limited ranges. The Modernist idea that mass- production would entirely destroy hand-crafted furniture has proved as one-sided as their over-emphasis on complete ano- nymity. As far as furniture is concerned most people want a judicious mixture of silent butlers, transitory acquaintances and permanent members of the family.

CHARLES JENCKS, *TEMPUS STASIS* CLOCK PODIUM AND CABINET, AND *COLOSSEUM CHAIR AND STOOL*, 1984

CHARLES JENCKS, STUDIES FOR *SUN TABLE*, *SPRING CHAIR* AND *SPRING SOFA*, 1983-84

CHARLES JENCKS, *SUN CHAIR*, *COLOSSEUM CHAIR* AND *STOOL*, AND *DICE TABLE*, 1984

CHARLES JENCKS, *EGYPTIAN ROOM* OF THE THEMATIC HOUSE, 1979-84

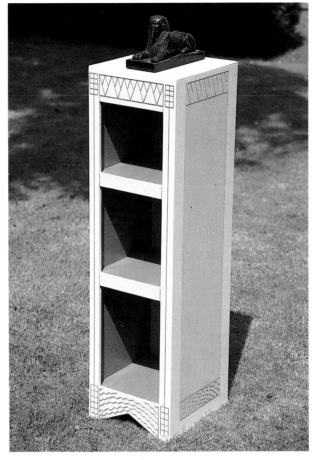

CHARLES JENCKS, *EGYPTIAN KIOSK* AND BOOKCASE, AND THREE CHAIRS, 1984

MICHAEL GRAVES, *COFFEE TABLE* AND *CONFERENCE TABLE*, 1979-81 FOR SUNAR

MICHAEL GRAVES, ARMCHAIR, 1979-81 FOR SUNAR HAUSERMAN

MICHAEL GRAVES, STOOL, *VARIATIONS ON A THEME OF JUAN GRIS* TABLE AND LOUNGE CHAIR

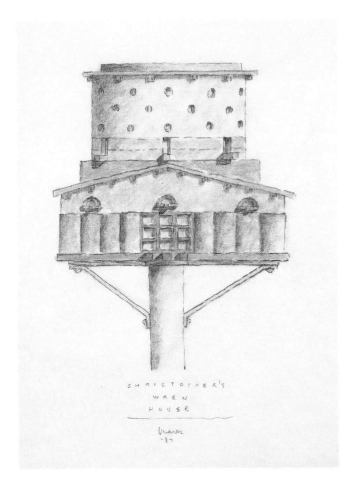

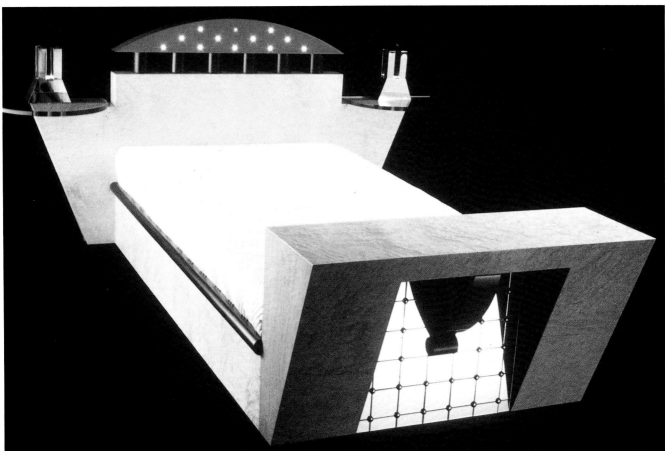

MICHAEL GRAVES, *CHRISTOPHER WREN'S HOUSE* ELEVATION, 1987, *PLAZA* DRESSING TABLE AND *STANHOPE* BED, 1982

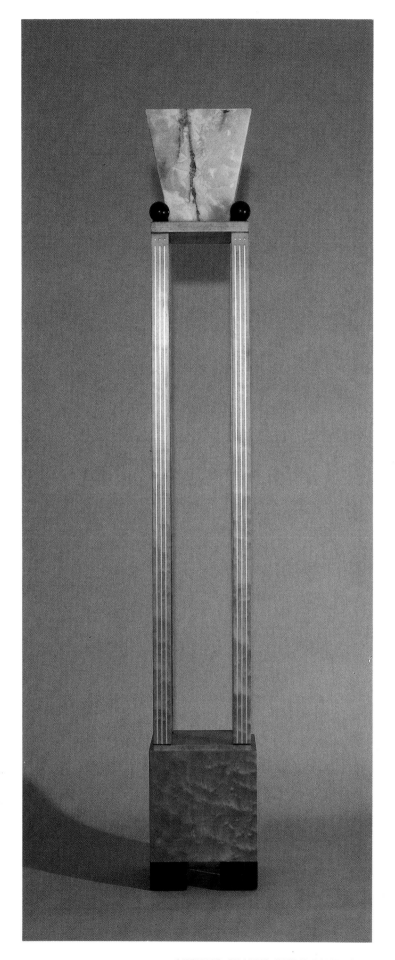

MICHAEL GRAVES, *INGRID LAMP* FOR PLOCEK HOUSE AND *BALDINGER LIGHTS*, 1982

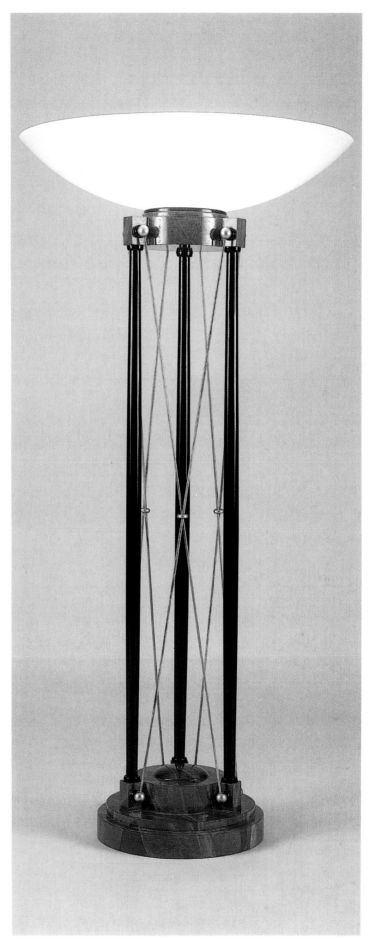

MICHAEL GRAVES, *BALDINGER LIGHTS* AND *TRIPOD LAMP* FOR PLOCEK HOUSE, 1982

MICHAEL GRAVES, *MANTEL CLOCK*, 1986-88 FOR ALESSI, MODEL

MICHAEL GRAVES, KETTLE, SUGAR BOWL AND CREAMER, PEPPERMILL AND PRESS-FILTER COFFEEMAKER, 1985-88 FOR ALESSI

MICHAEL GRAVES, DESIGNS, LATE 1980s FOR VORWERK CARPETS

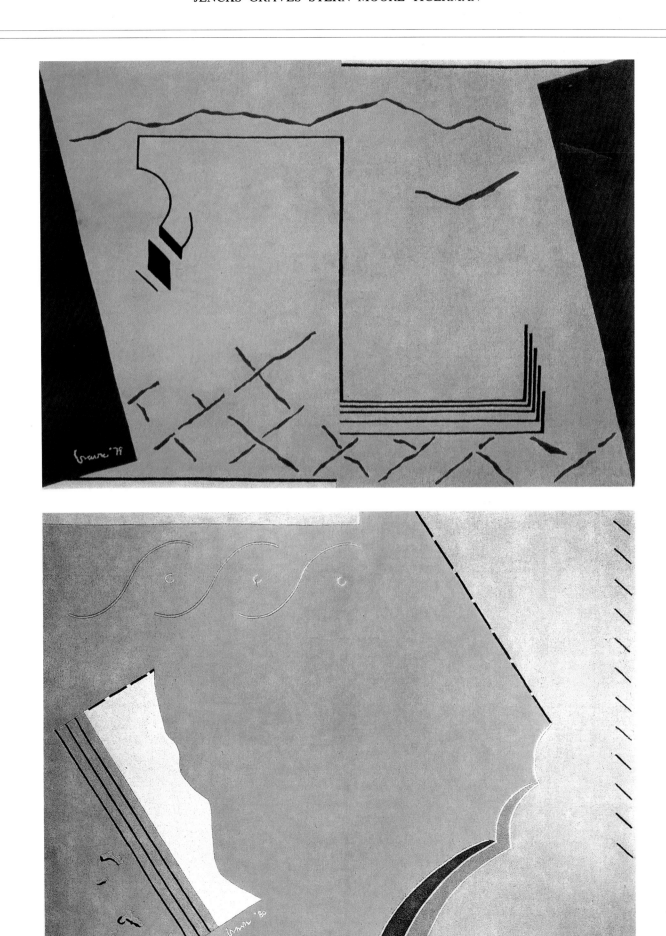

MICHAEL GRAVES, V'SOSKE RUGS, 1979-80

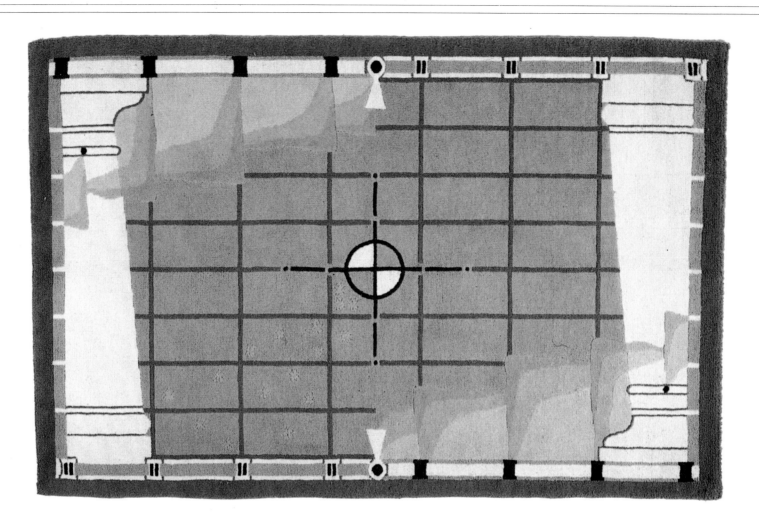

ROBERT STERN, *DINNER AT EIGHT* CARPET, 1983-84

These studies are for carpets designed for a suite of formal rooms in an Italianate villa under construction in New Jersey. In keeping with the character of the house, the designs were based on the geometries and palette of Pompeian frescoes. Shades of blue, red and grey relate each rug to the colour scheme of its corresponding room while gold, used in all three rugs, serves as the common colour to unite the enfilade and reflect the sunlight which enters through large windows opening onto the south garden. The focus of the living room rug, a large medallion, marks the point at which the main garden axis crosses the axis of the three rooms to unite the whole, creating a centre to rooms to the left and right . . .

The phrase 'Dinner at Eight' evokes a certain genre of Hollywood film comedy that combined disingenuous innocence with metropolitan sophistication. This carpet seeks to recapture the mood of those films – their heightened sense of romance, their use of theatrical convention and of exquisitely ambiguous euphemism,

It presents a highly formalised image within a proscenium-like frame of classical columns and theatrical drapes. The curtains are drawn, the doors about to open, and the music about to play as the comedy begins.

Robert Stern

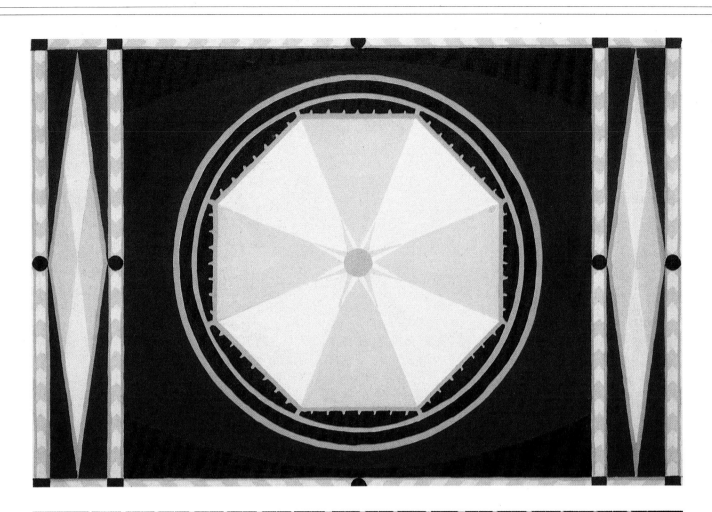

ROBERT STERN, DINING ROOM AND LIVING ROOM CARPET STUDIES FOR A RESIDENCE IN NEW JERSEY, 1983

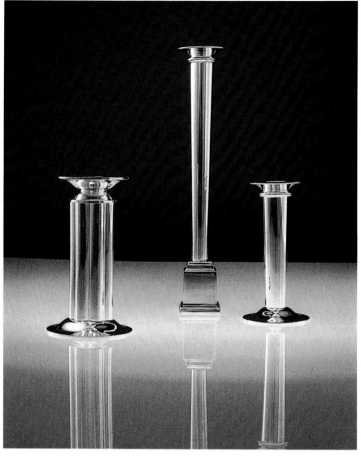

ROBERT STERN, SALT AND PEPPER SHAKERS, CANDLESTICKS, BOWL AND PITCHER, 1984 FOR SWID POWELL

ROBERT STERN, *MODERNE* DINNERWARE, 1986, *SWAG*, 1984, AND *MAJESTIC*, 1985, PLATES FOR SWID POWELL

ROBERT STERN, STUDIES FOR GOLD AND SILVER CUFFLINKS AND A SILVER FRUIT BOWL, 1987 FOR CLETO MUNARI

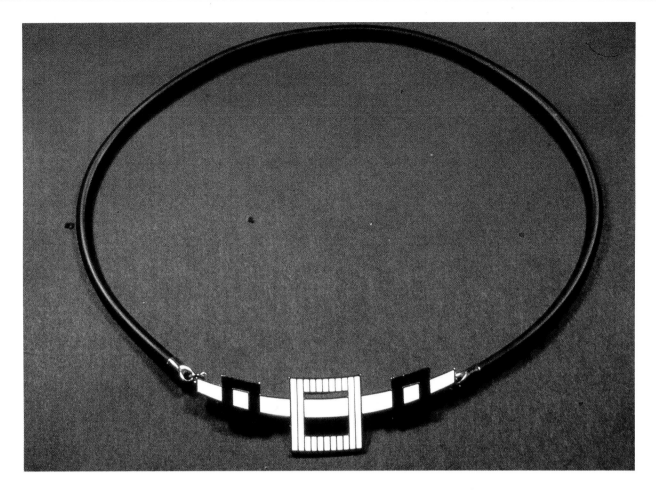

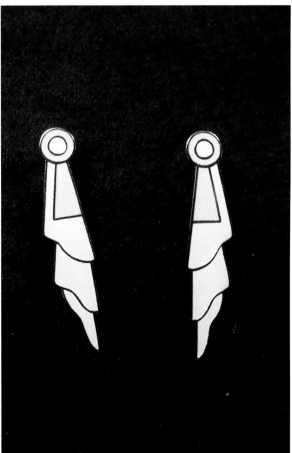

ROBERT STERN, *MAJESTIC* NECKLACE, *SAN REMO* BROOCH AND JABOT EARRINGS, 1986 FOR ACME

CHARLES MOORE, *LAYERED COFFEE TABLE*, 1985 FOR STENDIG

CHARLES MOORE, 'WALLS THAT LAYER', *MEMORY PALACE*, 1986

CHARLES MOORE, 'STAIRS THAT CLIMB AND SPREAD' AND 'WALLS THAT LAYER', *MEMORY PALACE*, 1986

CHARLES MOORE, 'LIGHT THAT PLAYS', *MEMORY PALACE*, 1986

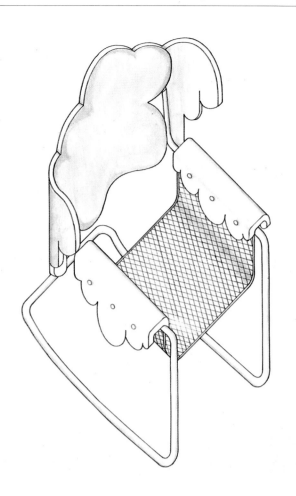
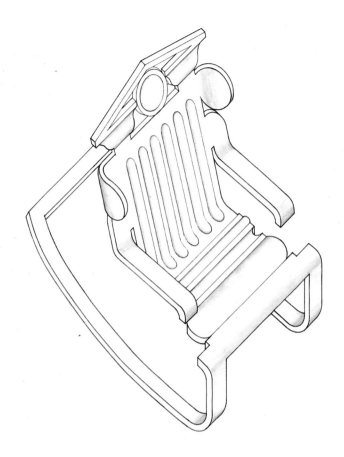

STANLEY TIGERMAN, STUDIES FOR *MAMA BEAR AND PAPA BEAR ROCKERS*, 1979-81 FOR KNOLL INTERNATIONAL

Objects of Desire

There is something seductive in designing in miniature as opposed to designing 'full size'. Perhaps it is comparable to teaching small children as opposed to educating adults. Maybe it has something to do with the compelling quality apparent to many in Frank Lloyd Wright's Coonley Playhouse project.

There is something of the child in us all such that diminutive scale not only attracts our attention by virtue of its reductive intensification, but also evokes the memory of a time when this idea of 'the small' was just the right size for us because we too were small. I suspect that all of these feelings of reverie are an unnerving reminder of the 'loss of innocence' intrinsic to 'fullsized' objects and the implicit appearance of 'educated' design.

Architecture for me has always been invested in making something out of nothing, ie 'daydreaming'. The innocence in creating objects of desire – buildings – has always seemed to have an attractive quality in that innocence itself (a state by definition removed from cynicism) suggests the making of an 'original'. And when one is connected with such things – originals, that is – Eden, and the original state of innocence cannot be far behind.

So when I am asked for an involvement in the design of objects of desire, I am once again innocent. The objects there shown are a product of that state. Much more of the child in me (I am happy to say) is present in this work than in much else of what I design. For all that I try to invest 'full size' objects with a condition of innocence I can never apparently return to an earlier time or a place where my own size was once concommitant with the scale of the small objects of desire.

I continue to try to achieve a state of innocence in my full size works knowing that even as I try to consciously achieve such a state, the nature of consciousness neutralises my ability to achieve the very innocence that I so desire. I am bound to repetition and doomed to perpetual failure in a full size arena defined by adulthood and denied to those who have achieved a scale themselves that is detached from the innocence of things small.

Stanley Tigerman

STANLEY TIGERMAN, *PAPA BEAR ROCKER*, 1979-81 FOR KNOLL INTERNATIONAL

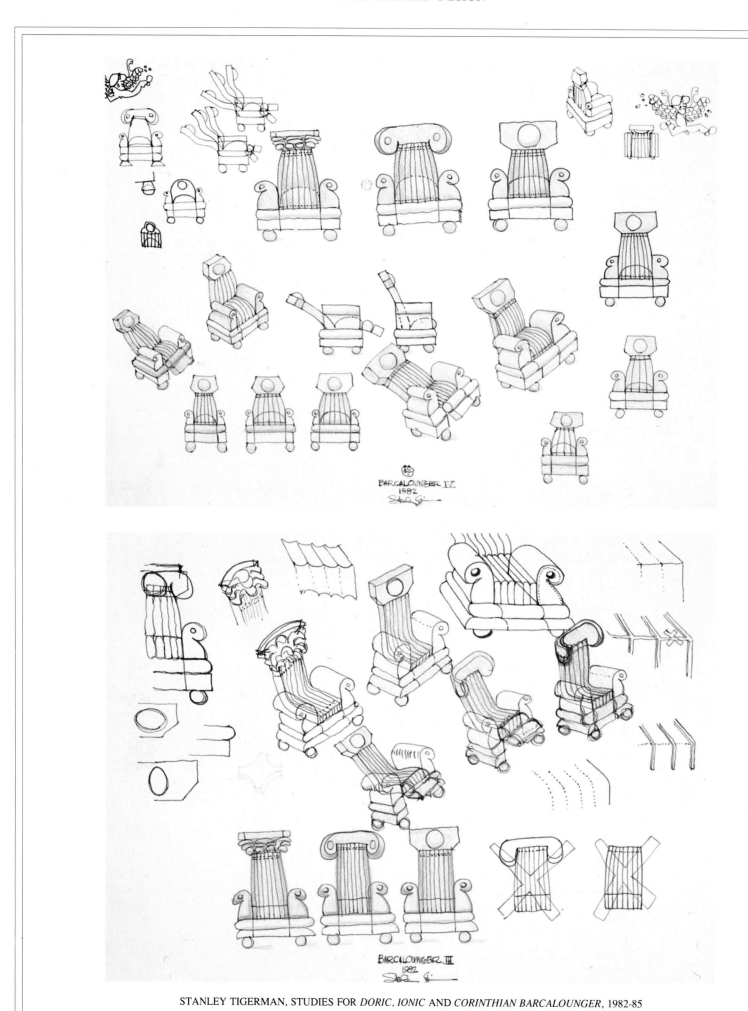

STANLEY TIGERMAN, STUDIES FOR *DORIC*, *IONIC* AND *CORINTHIAN BARCALOUNGER*, 1982-85

STANLEY TIGERMAN, *CHAIR WITH BUILT-IN OTTOMAN*, 1985-87 FOR HERMAN MILLER

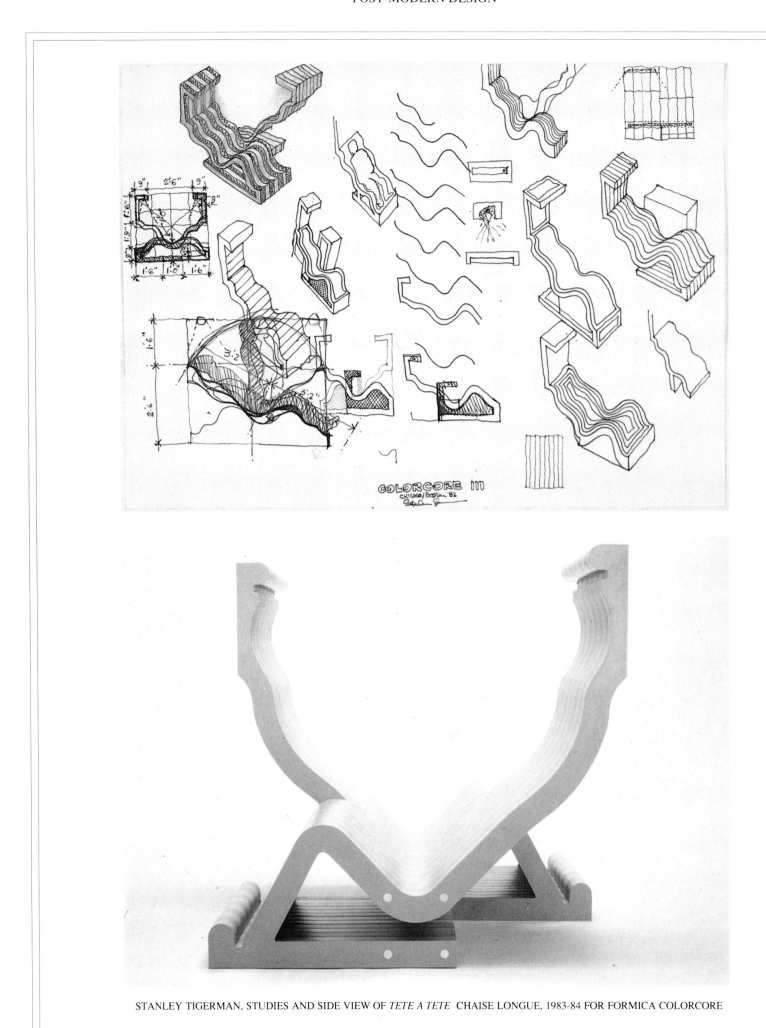

STANLEY TIGERMAN, STUDIES AND SIDE VIEW OF *TETE A TETE* CHAISE LONGUE, 1983-84 FOR FORMICA COLORCORE

STANLEY TIGERMAN, *TETE A TETE* CHAISE LONGUE, 1983-84

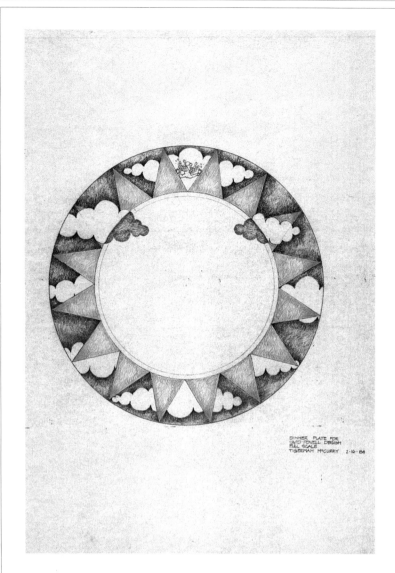

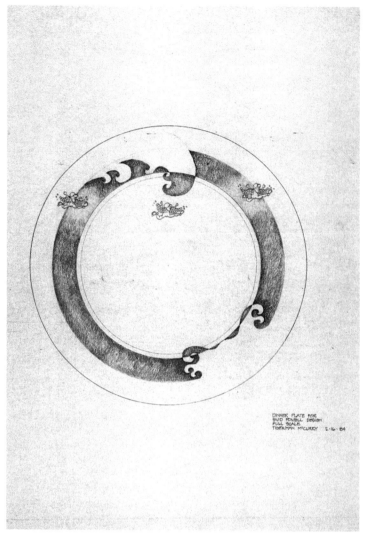

STANLEY TIGERMAN, STUDIES FOR *HEAVEN* AND *SUNSHINE*, AND *POMPEII* AND *TIGERPAUSE* PLATES, 1984-86 FOR SWID POWELL

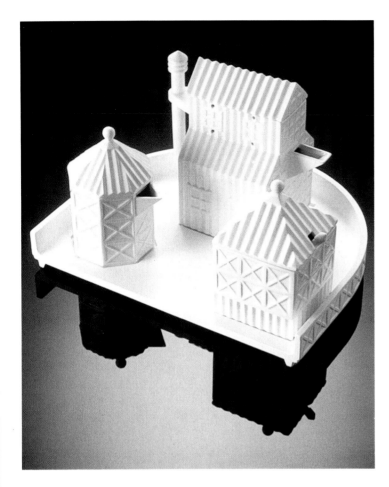

STANLEY TIGERMAN, TEA SERVICE, SALT AND PEPPER SHAKERS AND PICTURE FRAME, 1984 FOR SWID POWELL

STANLEY TIGERMAN, TEA SERVICE, 1980-82 FOR ALESSI

STANLEY TIGERMAN, PROTOTYPE TEA POT, 1980-82 FOR ALESSI

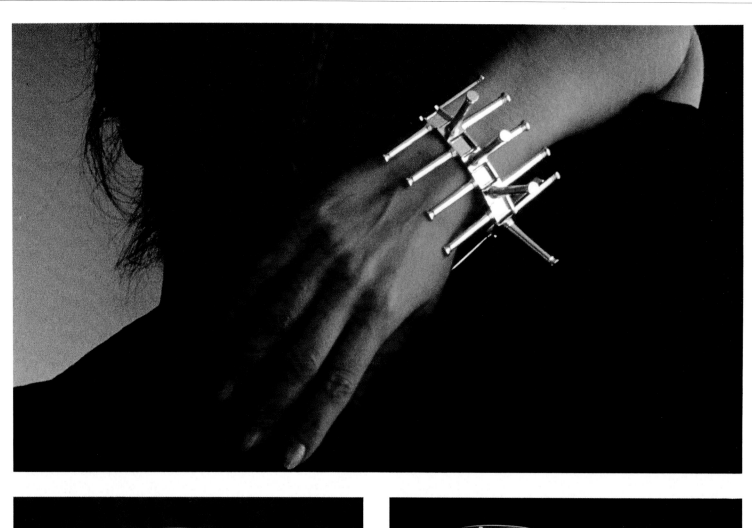

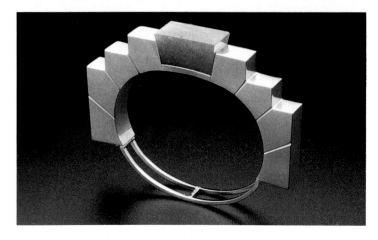

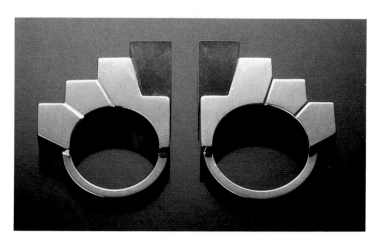

STANLEY TIGERMAN, JEWELLERY, 1986-87 FOR CLETO MUNARI

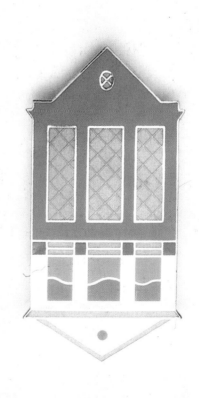

STANLEY TIGERMAN, FABRIC DESIGNS, 1984-85 FOR HAMANO, AND PINS FOR ACME, 1986

FRANK GEHRY, *RYBA* LAMP, 1983 FOR FORMICA COLORCORE

CHAPTER VI

Deconstruction, Deconstructivism & Late-Modernism

CHARLES GWATHMEY AND ROBERT SIEGEL, *TUXEDO* DINNERWARE, 1984 FOR SWID POWELL

Deconstruction, a post-structuralist development, is indebted to the writing of Jacques Derrida, a French philosopher who has done much teaching in the United States. The full effect of Derrida's ideas was felt in 1988 with a conference on Deconstruction held at the Tate Gallery in London, and an exhibition on Deconstructivist Architecture at the Museum of Modern Art, New York, between June and August, under the auspices of Philip Johnson, assisted by Mark Wigley. This exhibition featured the work of, among others, Bernard Tschumi, Peter Eisenman, Frank Gehry and Zaha Hadid. These last three also design objects. Any interpretation of deconstruction in the visual arts is fraught with difficulty because of the way in which the Derridean influence has been appropriated, and elided with that of Soviet Constructivism – as revealed in the dispute over terminology embodied in the two tags 'Deconstructivism' and 'Deconstruction'. All of the 'Deconstructivist' architects essentially draw on the designs of Soviet architecture, but, in the Late-Modern manner, regard their work as an unfinished programme. As Mark Wigley says in his catalogue introduction to the MOMA exhibition, 'It is the ability to disturb our thinking about form that makes these projects deconstructive. It is not that they derive from the mode of contemporary philosophy known as "deconstruction". They are not an application of deconstructive theory. Rather, they emerge from within the architectural tradition and happen to exhibit some deconstructive qualities.'[81]

While the original Soviet Constructivists fragmented volumes into their constituent components as a preliminary to reconstructing these into rational assemblages, the 'Deconstructivist' strategy is to reject the second stage and actually build the exploded and fragmented forms of the experimental stage. This is rationalised through the superimposition of the Derridean brand of deconstruction. Derrida's method of 'deconstructing' texts reveals how they necessarily self-destruct through internal contradictions and thus demonstrates the impossibility of a transcendent metaphysics, while remaining silent on questions of value. This has been taken (or mistaken) as being in itself a metaphysical position, and Derrida's talk of 'absence' and the 'void' has been matched with the social theory of Jean-François Lyotard's *The Post-Modern Condition* to breed a rather terrifying mongrel – a kind of 'deconstructed' condition, from which meaning, transcendence and coherence are forever banished. In their place is absence, rupture and the arbitrary. Deconstruction is rather like psychoanalysis, to which Gehry and Eisenman are indebted, in that it ceases to believe or assume that the subject (or text) is in total control of its ideas and arguments, and looks for ways in which it undermines and destabilises itself. Where Post-Modern man saw a happily though bewilderingly plurivalent world and light-headedly relished the plenitude of choice it offered, the Frankenstein's monster of deconstruction must withdraw from this clamour, unable to express anything but the ultimate emptiness and arbitrariness of the act of choosing, yet clinging to the stripped skeleton of form in mute despair.

In this there is a strong kinship with the interventions of Marcel Duchamp and his ultimate withdrawal. Duchamp's gestures remain significant and his ironic exploration or de-construction of value, originality, signature, authenticity and hierarchy can be seen as a precedent for the approach taken by the American architects Frank Gehry and Peter Eisenman. Absent from their work is the figure and Classical reference or learning. Instead, abstract modes of presentation continue, especially with Eisenman. The shared Jewish origin of Der-rida, Gehry and Eisenman could be seen as placing them within the abstract tradition which eschews the human form as a direct result of the biblical prohibition 'thou shalt not make a graven image.' Without resorting to racially stereotypical commen-tary, this abstraction has been seen as essential to, say,the work of Rothko, while, conversely, it is not a factor in the equally Jewish qualities of, say, Ron Kitaj. Jewishness may also contribute to the cabbalistic language, individualistic gestures, and outsiderism of Gehry and Eisenman, whose work can be seen as much in opposition to Post-Modernism as it is to any other historical system.

Frank Gehry, the Toronto-born architect, who practises in Los Angeles, has collaborated extensively with artists such as the painter Ron Davis (for whom he designed a house in the Malibu Hills in 1974), the late-Minimalist sculptor Richard Serra and, in 1984, with the Pop Artist Claes Oldenburg at the Ronald McDonald Camp for Good Times, Malibu. As Barbara Diamonstein observed in 1981, 'it was his corrugated card-board furniture designed in 1972 that first brought him wider public attention. Exhibited in the Musée des Arts Décoratifs in Paris and sold in Bloomingdales, it is also in the MOMA design collection'.[82] This *Easy Edges* corrugated cardboard 'Chaise Lounge (*sic*)' has a highly sculptural quality and Gehry has written, 'I share with contemporary American sculptors, an interest in materials. I'm easily seduced into extensive research into new materials. As in the case of the chain link, or as in the case of the chain link fence and cardboard, I get interested in material that the culture denies . . .'[83]

It should be noted that some of Claes Oldenburg's most innovative work uses corrugated card, which Gehry also presses into service for his *Little Beaver* chair of 1980, made by Vitra. In sharp contrast to *Easy Edges*, the second chair is rough, serrated and jagged, with uneasy edges and almost literal deconstruction of the silhouette. Even more deconstructed, again in a literal sense, is Gehry's series of Colorcore lamp 'sculptures' entitled *Ryba* of 1983; one senses that the smashed and reassembled material has more than an echo of Mikhail Bakunhin's famous anarchic phrase, 'the passion for destruc-tion is also a constructive passion.' Gehry has admitted his debt to Surrealism in stating that 'in everything I do, Surrealism interests me, but not in the sense that everything is surreal.'[84]

In these Colorcore fish lamps there are elements of an Arpian approach, during the latter's Dada period. As Hans Richter recalled , 'Dissatisfied with a drawing he had been working on for some time, Arp finally tore it up, and let the pieces flutter to the floor of his studio . . . some time later he happened to notice these same scraps of paper as they lay on the floor, and was struck by the pattern they formed. It had all the expressive power that he had tried in vain to achieve.'[85] There is also a vital difference in that Arp's process is a natural metaphor of chance, like leaves falling on the ground or pebbles found in a brook, whereas Gehry's is artificial and man-made chance – the hazards of explosion and anarchic destruction. Gehry's approach also has a resonance of the continuation of such Surrealist gestures in, say, the 'fold-in' or cut-up technique of the writings of William Burroughs and the random selection of the music of John Cage, which extend the tradition of Arp's 'laws of chance'. The image of the fish contains some very cabbalistic and, in Gehry's case, private language. As Charles Jencks has observed, 'As a young boy he (Gehry) suffered several humiliations for being a "fish eater", for "smelling of fish", in short, for being a Jew in a tough Catholic neighbourhood of Toronto.'[86] As Gehry himself says, 'if everybody's going to say that Classicism is perfection then I'm going to say fish is perfection, so why not copy fish? And then I'll be damned if I don't find reasons to reinforce why the fish is important and more interesting than Classicism. That's intuitive . . .'[87] Beyond Gehry's obvious pun, 'fish scales are the right scale for buildings', one should note that the term 'fish scale' is used to describe the hexagonal slates traditionally used and overlapped to roof a Victorian bay window, and that for Jews, only certain fish are in fact Kosher, while others are not; among other factors scales are important in allowing fish to be acceptable in the strict diet.

Here we have two different ideas implied: Jencks' sugges-tion that the fish is personally and psychologically significant; and Gehry's, that the fish is arbitrary, 'why not copy fish?', and then subsequently rationalised. If, indeed, the fish is arbitrary, then his argument fits in with despair of a 'shared symbolic order'. If the fish is, however, personal and psychological, the issue is not about despair, but about refusal. The image is then not an expression of void, emptiness or the arbitrary, but rather of the self and self-assertion. If Gehry's ordering system is his own sense of order, his stance is not Deconstructivist, but is instead existentialist. Gehry's architecture may be Decon-structive but he does not use deconstruction. He is anti-Post-Modernist, Surrealist and an individualist.

In essence, the fish sets up an oppositional paradigm to Post-Modern Classicism. As Gehry has written, 'my ordering sys-tem is personal, unconscious, and intuitive. I become frustrated with people who appropriate ordering systems from the Ren-aissance, or when people throw Palladian order at me as the most relevant thing. An ordering system should be one's own sense of order.'[88] Above all, in the few objects that he has designed Gehry sees himself as an artist; as he says, 'it is like a painter facing a white canvas. In doing so, I confront myself, my priorities, my imagination, my *tabula rasa*: "Where do I

FORMICA COLORCORE 'SURFACE & ORNAMENT EXHIBITION', 1983, NEW YORK CITY

PETER EISENMAN, DOOR HANDLE, 1986 FOR FSB DESIGN WORKSHOP

come from? Where do my ideas come from? How do I make a building?" There are very few crutches to lean on. When I'm at that point, I find I'm fascinated by how much I turn to painting and sculpture, and how I draw on the work of people working and living at this point in time and not just the past'.[89]

It is as if he only acknowledges the present, and rejects anything that resembles the order of the past. This highly individualistic and somewhat anarchic stance, Gehry's Gauguinesque cry, 'where do I come from? Where do my ideas come from?', which has a psychoanalytical inflection, and his rejection of historical reference place him in opposition to Post-Modernism. The latter's Classicism or potential for shared symbolism is rejected by Gehry in favour of wilfully self-referential and personally artistic design.

If Gehry's objects are sculptural, and sometimes independent of his architecture, the same cannot be said for those designed by Peter Eisenman. Born in Newark, New Jersey, and practising from New York, Eisenman established a reputation for 'White' abstract and Modern buildings in his 'numbered' Houses, from House I in Princeton (1967-8) through to the project for House X (1977). At first one might read his work as analogous to the art of Sol LeWitt or Carl André – that is, as an American Minimalist. Sol LeWitt, for example, used cube frames and architectural, geometric form in a similar manner. Eisenman clearly saw the equilateral cube as a perfect structure – but since then the leitmotif in Eisenman's architecture became the 'L' shape (els) which he then used in names for his later houses, for example House LLa and House EL Even Odd. The 'L' is also used in Derrida's writing, significantly in 'Lemmata' in his *La Vérité en peinture*, where it is dispersed as a beginning and ending to his paragraphs. The 'L' is used in Derrida's text to represent the frame device or 'parergon', the device by which we demarcate areas of discourse and language spaces. The frame is necessarily broken, its corners only being present to represent the interface and intermingling of internal with external, the inability of a frame to isolate entirely its chosen area. Likewise in the house, this could represent the rejection of the cubic house's rhetoric of self-containment. A house is part of a wider cultural structure and the 'L' represents this partial quality and the inability of the house to be a complete 'little world'. In Eisenman's case this relates to his interest in the *unheimlich*, the uncanny and uncomfortable elements that exist within the house. Eisenman and Derrida derive some aspects of their respective work from Freud and psychoanalytical theory. Derrida has in fact collaborated with Eisenman and Bernard Tschumi in the latter's recent *Parc de la Villette* in Paris, which Tschumi has described as the practice of 'a strategy of disjunctions.' Tschumi, who began the project in 1983, also sees the work as 'the largest discontinuous building in the world'.

In terms of design, there is a greater coherence in Eisenman's work than in that of Gehry and, when writing about his jewellery for Cleto Munari, he says that 'they are part of a scale continuum of objects from the ring to a building.'[90] In short,

this would seem to describe a form of micro-architecture, a method of design he has in common with some of the Post-Modernists. Eisenman's design is a smaller version of his building, particularly his houses. He dislikes Post-Modern logocentrism, anthropomorphic reference and does not share in the *rappel à l'ordre*.

Eisenman has designed extensively, from a projected plate for Swid Powell, to a menorah for the Israel Museum, a door handle for FSB in Germany, and jewellery for Cleto Munari. His menorah for the Jewish Chanukah festival is, as one might expect, the most cabbalistic and spiritual of all his objects, and his text for the accompanying catalogue of 1986 goes a long way towards explaining his intentions. Eisenman writes, 'Even the elements that make up this menorah are unstable. Each element being an "L" shape, which is either growing to a full square or reducing itself to a point. The materials of the menorah further represent the instability of presence. They are made up of different types of steel, the absence of presence is untreated steel which can be allowed to rust and erode, while the smaller and larger scales have a brushed and polished finish respectively. The structure is in copper.'[91] The instability, the Derridean shimmering absences are all pressed into service to convey an abstract theology, and perhaps the emptiness of being a post-Holocaust Jew. Eisenman himself has written, with almost biblical incantation, 'the beginning and the end, and the beginning again: the light for one day that became the light for eight days lit by the one that burns each day. The symbol of what has been and what will become, represented in the present by a light with no being.'[92] In his menorah, Eisenman uses solids and voids to convey absence, and the instability of presence, with great power. For the FSB door handle as well as the Swid Powell plate, Eisenman uses layering, rather than over-emphasis upon the solid and void. Eisenman spelled out his 'motto' in the attendant publication *Doorhandles, Workshop in Brakel* of 1987 as 'my objects aim to do away with the illusion that architecture should ape human form, scale and proportion. I try to exclude decoration and representation and instead blend my objects into a single scale embracing everything from the door handle to the building itself.'[93] Eisenman's emphasis on the non-mimetic has resulted in a highly geometric and abstract door handle, which is to be perceived cerebrally, rather than handled conceptually. In common with so much 1960s' sculpture, the result, perhaps unfortunately, is that one wishes to look at it in preference to touching it. The problem here is that a door handle *has* to be touched, and Eisenman's is uninviting, almost an 'un-doorhandle'. Eisenman does explain that 'most door handles nowadays are based on an ergonomic and anthropomorphic philosophy that I do not share. I wanted to create an abstract work of art, realising all the while that art and function are actually opposites.'[94]

During a design discussion held at the FSB factory in September 1986 between critics and the other participating architects, including Botta, Hollein, Mendini and Rams, Eisenman delivered a characteristic attack on Post-Modern design and the whole emphasis upon 'designer' as a prefix: 'I'm heartily sick of being invited round to friends who've been completely taken over by design. No sooner are you through the front door than you're confronted with a Mendini on the wall, a Hollein on a column, a Rams on the windowsill, and not a square inch in sight untouched by design . . . It's my view that, in the late 80s, we are being subjected to the cynicism and decadence of the consumption of good form (aesthetic function).'[95] In the same outburst, Eisenman insisted that one should talk about the 'commonplace' which he equated with the 'archetypal', though not in the Purist's sense of archetypes – plain objects refined in their simplicity by centuries of use. As Siegfried Gronert observed in his commentary, 'Eisenman uses a "syntax" of geometrical forms to produce formal structures that adhere to highly rational principles without being identifiable with the human body or any straightforward concrete notion.'[96]

Eisenman summed up his approach by stating that 'I believe you can design a door handle without symbolising the object's relationship to man. In my current projects in West Berlin and elsewhere, I am attempting to build homes that do not symbolise "home", trying to design comfort without symbolising it. I don't regard home and comfort as art. Art is a field unconnected with human well-being. This door opener derives its status neither from the door nor from the act of opening but from a self-referential object world. We see here very small-scale components and an extremely indeterminate form; the L shape is unstable, no longer being a full square. Although you can open the door with it, it's a form that does not indicate that function in any way. It is a geometric landscape of the mind.'[97] This 'geometric landscape of the mind' seems to extend to Eisenman's jewellery for Cleto Munari; in common with the other architects' work, gold is the major material.

Eisenman's designs include a ring with cubes of turquoise, lapis-lazuli, and black onyx, a circular pendant with small squares of turquoise and black onyx, and an earring and bracelet in plain gold. His finely worked drawings and blueprints reveal a mathematical layering of surfaces, and all the objects rely on a subtle, proportional plasticity. In another sketch the layers are labelled 'present, future, past' with an under-notation 'not in centre'. When questioned by Barbara Radice about 'what kind of woman did you have in mind when you designed your jewellery?', Eisenman replied: 'I was not thinking of any woman. These pieces propose a different relationship to the human wearer. They are not mimetic of human form or proportions. Their scale is not taken from the scale of a person. As such they deny any connection to or embellishment of human form. They are not in the least decorative. Neither are they representational.'[98] When asked to 'explain the language of your jewellery' by Radice, Eisenman continued, 'Since Freud, since the unconscious became known, man has been psychologically different. He's no longer "in the centre" as in the Renaissance because he's studying himself. I

would like my jewels to be the archetypal symbol of this decentred man and his unconscious.'[99] Eisenman is very liberal here in his mishmash of references to Freud but what is clear is that he is rebelling against Renaissance and subsequent humanism in favour of decentred man.

On a first 'reading', Eisenman's jewellery is simply beautiful in a mathematical, minimal way. The fact that his designs symbolise voids, an emptiness of centre and say something about the human condition, becomes apparent only on closer examination; hollow gold, given by hollow men to decentred women. Lonely, existentialist and uncanny, they are in effect a form of 'unjewellery', in a way analogous to Eisenman's *unheimlich* (uncanny and also unhomely) buildings. The many negatives form a strong oppositional paradigm to Post-Modern work, checking, if not check-mating, the latter's hedonism and return to humanist and anthropomorphic reference. As with Gehry, Eisenman side-steps tradition for the sake of self-exploration. Their objects are polemically intended as a counter to Post-Modernism; it is as if its ingratiating qualities have proved too cloying in the Post-Modern repression of the menacing ambiguities of experience.

If Gehry and Eisenman can be read as anti-Post-Modern, on a more positive level the architecture of both, and that of Zaha Hadid, can be seen as continuing a dialogue with Soviet Constructivism. This has led to their work being labelled simply as Late-Modern, whereas in fact it needs to be stressed that they are in the main quite firmly *against* neoconservative Post-Modernism.

Eisenman was, significantly, along with early Graves, John Hejduk, Richard Meier and Charles Gwathmey, one of the 'New York Five' or 'Whites' in the 1960s. Richard Meier and Charles Gwathmey in their designs continue this adherence to Late-Modernism.

Richard Meier worked for two great 'Modern' practices, namely Skidmore, Owings and Merrill from 1959 to 1960, and Marcel Breuer and Associates from 1960 to 1963, before setting up his own firm in New York in 1963. His designs are indebted to a 'pioneers of modern design' viewpoint, and he draws inspiration from the work of Josef Hoffmann during the latter's 'quadratl' phase, and, as with the Deconstructivists, the work of Kasimir Malevich; though unlike the Deconstructivists he is not concerned with the preliminary volumes of the early Soviet architects and designers. Thus Meier designed a range of black lacquered wood furniture for Knoll between 1982 and 1985 that owes much to early Hoffmann. The chair is quite a homage to Hoffmann's typology of the chair for Thonet and J & J Kohn of about 1905. The chaise on the other hand is a curious amalgam of the reclining position used in Le Corbusier's chaise longue commonly known as *LC/4* of 1928 with a 'quadratl' base more redolent of Hoffmann.

Richard Meier's design for Alessi for the *Tea and Coffee Piazza* of 1983 is a direct homage to Kasimir Malevich. Meier's silver set echoes the latter's famous, but highly experimental, porcelain teapot of 1923, fairly directly, though we see

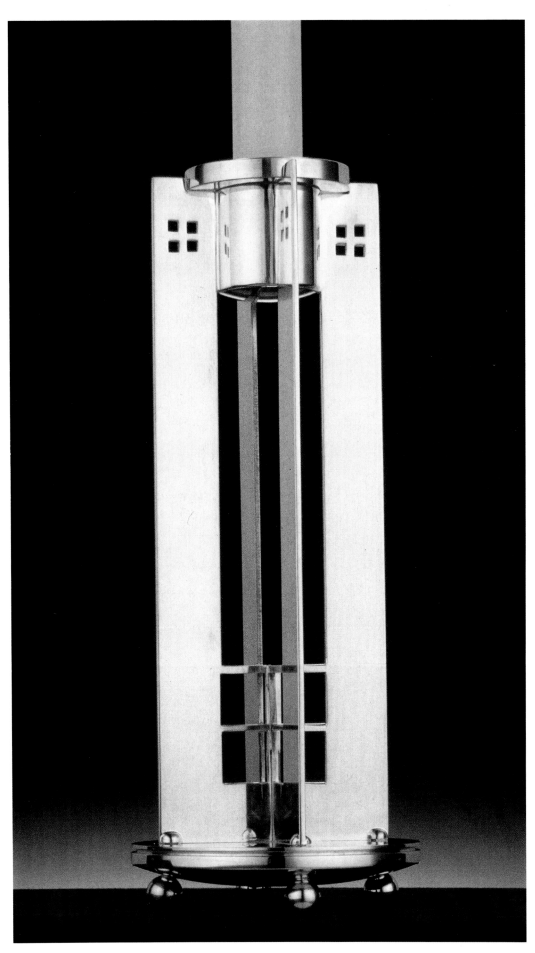

RICHARD MEIER, DETAIL OF SILVER CANDLESTICK, 1984 FOR SWID POWELL

the shape 'translated' from ceramic to metal. The result is a Late-Modern 'Modern Revival'.

Meier has designed extensively for Swid Powell from 1984, and provided further references to Hoffmann, Kolo Moser and Wiener Werkstätte designs of about 1904 to 1910. It should be added that the Wiener Werkstätte is highly fashionable, particularly in New York, with many dealers specialising in its products. In fact it is easier to see in New York than it is in its native Vienna.

Meier's candlesticks, bowls, serving trays, dishes, letter rack, opener and pencil cup all work well *en suite*, with no surface decoration and pierced squares in the manner of Hoffmann or Mackintosh. Meier has also designed two boxes which rely entirely on the repetition of squares for effect. His drinking glasses are equally self-effacing and simple, as are most of his ceramics. *Signature* has a simple, thin black cross on white circular dishes. These are very basic designs and run counter to the Classical or Art Deco decoration present in the respective work of Graves and Stern for the same firm.

Much the same can be said for Charles Gwathmey's few designs for Swid Powell, produced with his partner Robert Siegel. Their practice was established in New York in 1968, and their ceramic *Tuxedo* is also Hoffmannesque in its simple black squares on a white ground.

The Swid Powell products, when seen as a whole, reveal nearly all the 'isms' of 1980s' Pluralism. Ironic Post-Modernism is demonstrated by Venturi; *rappel à l'ordre* historicism by Graves, and to an extent by Stern; humorous anthropomorphic and figurative Post-Modernism is present in the work of Tigerman; Meier and Gwathmey are Late-Modernists. The Florida practice Arquitectonica, mentioned earlier for their Memphis design, have produced an equally bright ceramic for Swid Powell, appropriately named *Miami Beach*. As we shall see, the firm have encouraged European Post-Modernists such as Hans Hollein, Robert and Trix Haussmann, the Japanese Post-Modernist Arata Isozaki, and European Neo-Modernists such as Sottsass and Sowden. Swid Powell have proved to be the Memphis of American design in the 1980s, with a catholic range of products to suit all the taste cultures of a complex, consumer society.

RICHARD MEIER, *PROFESSOR* GLASSES, 1984 FOR SWID POWELL

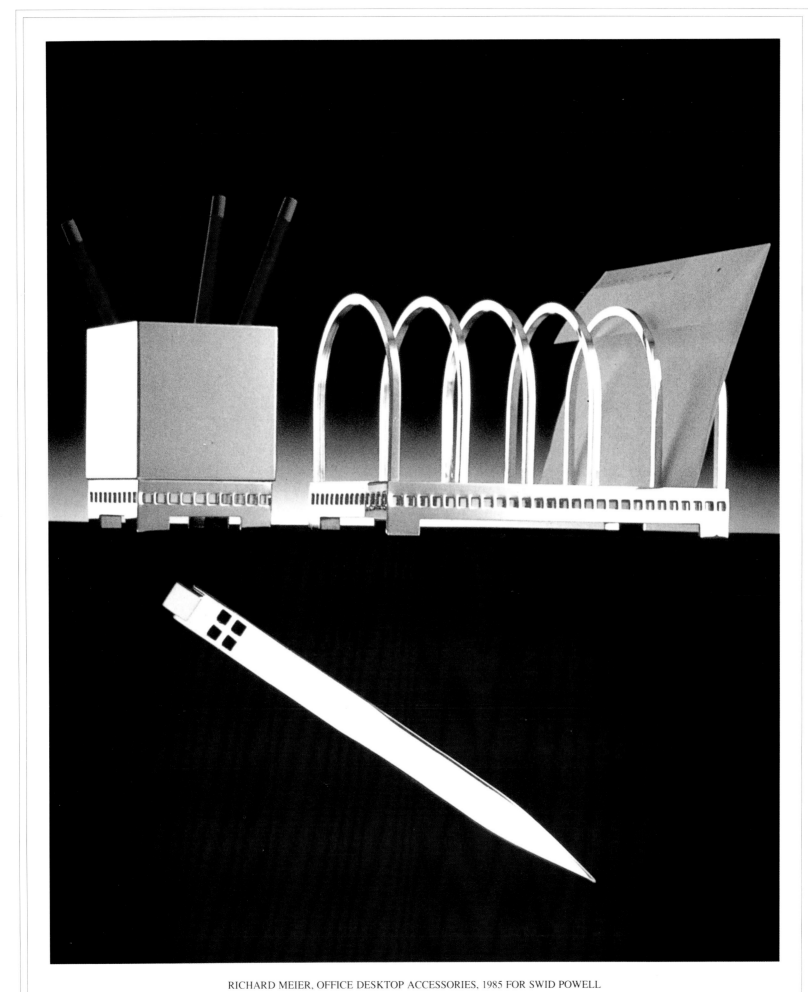

RICHARD MEIER, OFFICE DESKTOP ACCESSORIES, 1985 FOR SWID POWELL

PETER EISENMAN (*TOP*) AND ETTORE SOTTSASS (*ABOVE*), MENORAHS, 1986 FOR THE ISRAEL MUSEUM

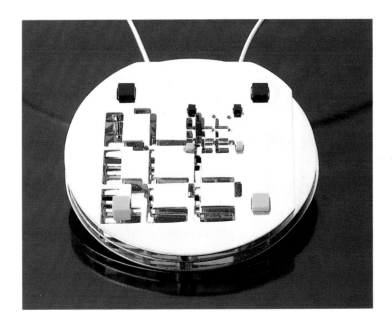

PETER EISENMAN, JEWELLERY, 1985 FOR CLETO MUNARI

TOP: PETER WILSON, *PUNCH SOFA*, 1987, FOR TENDO; *ABOVE*: HELMUT MATYSIK, TABLE AND CABINET, 1988

HELMUT MATYSIK, CABINET, 1988

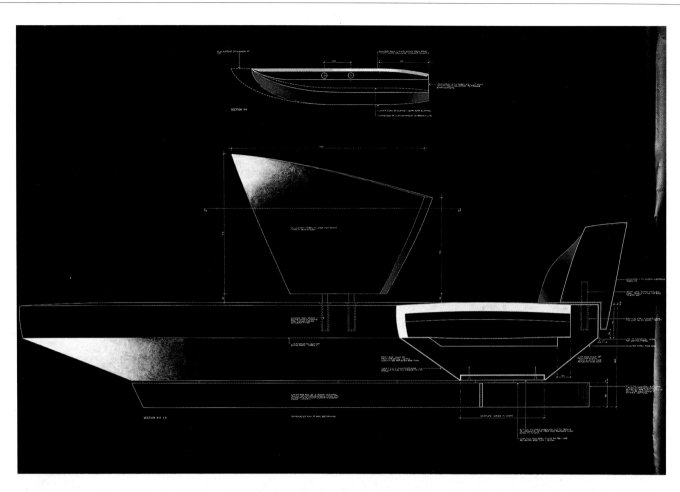

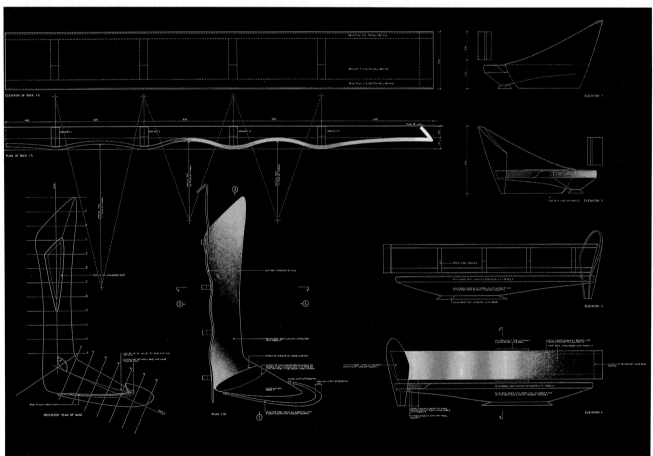

ZAHA HADID, WORKING DRAWINGS FOR *WHOOSH* SOFA AND *WAVY BACK* SOFA, 1987-88

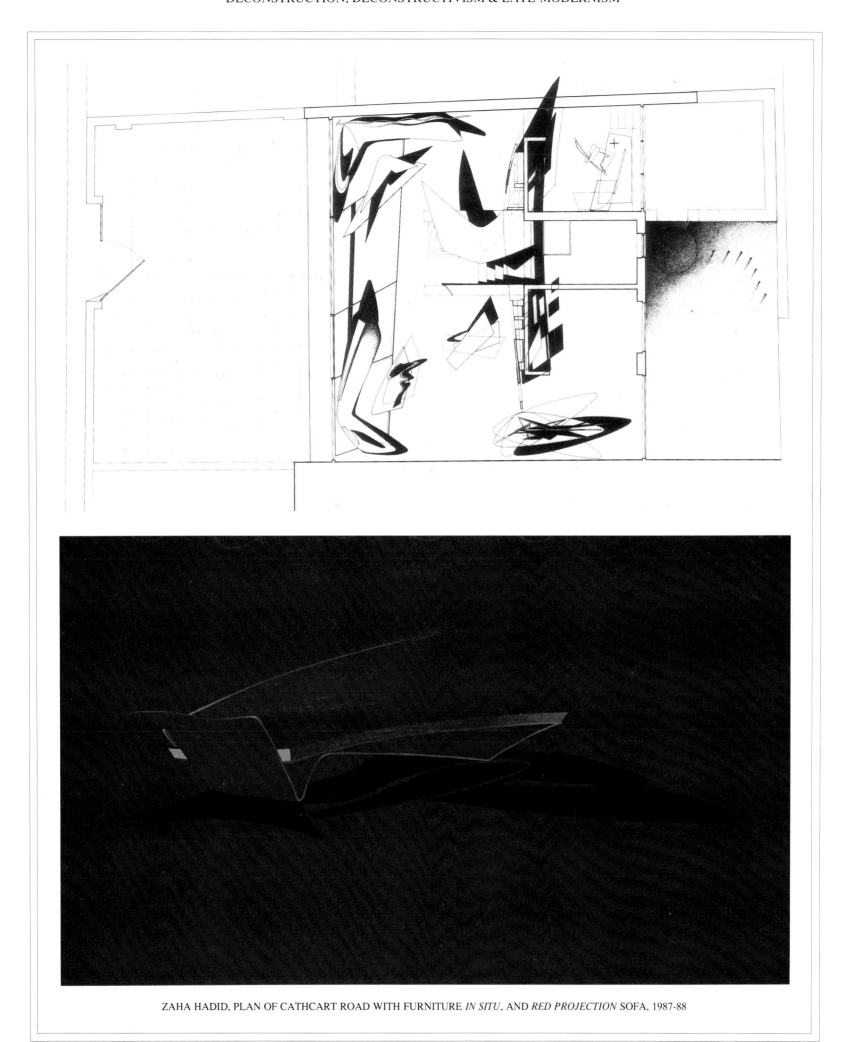

ZAHA HADID, PLAN OF CATHCART ROAD WITH FURNITURE *IN SITU*, AND *RED PROJECTION* SOFA, 1987-88

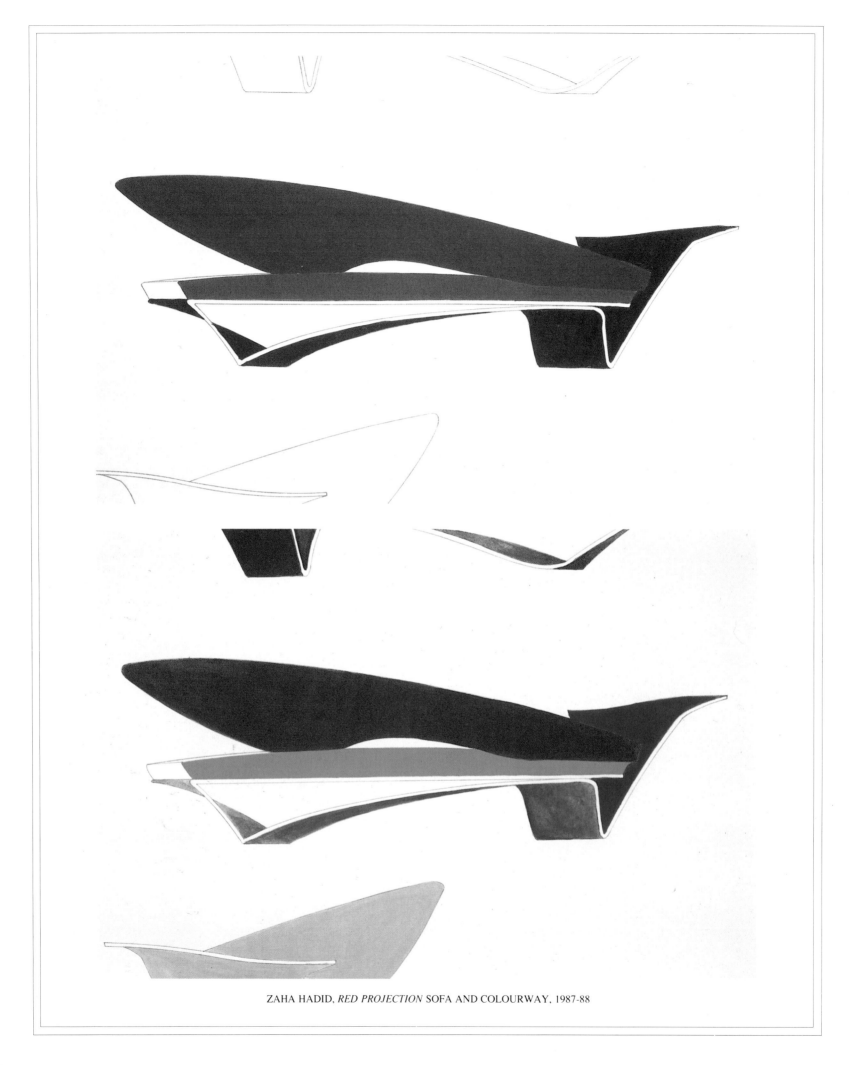

ZAHA HADID, *RED PROJECTION* SOFA AND COLOURWAY, 1987-88

ZAHA HADID, *WAVY BACK* SOFA, 1987-88 FOR EDRA

ALDO ROSSI, *TEA & COFFEE PIAZZA*, 1979-83 FOR ALESSI

CHAPTER VII

Paolo Portoghesi & Aldo Rossi

PAOLO PORTOGHESI, *ALDEBARHAN* TABLE, 1986 FOR TRAVERTINO ROMANO

Paolo Portoghesi, born in Rome in 1931, established his practice in 1958. He is the most learned and academic of all Post-Modernists, having taught History of Criticism at Rome's faculty of architecture from 1962 to 1966, and having been Professor of Architectural History at Milan Polytechnic from 1967 to 1977. He has published material on a wide range of architectural history, from *Guarino Guarini (1624-83)* (1956), *Francesco Borromini (1599-1667)* and many articles and publications on the Baroque in Rome. In the late 1960s his writings covered nineteenth- and twentieth-century themes, and included *Victor Horta* (1969), *The Art Nouveau Album* (1975), *The Twenties Album* (1976), *The Fifties Album* (1977) and *The Thirties Album* (1978). At the same time he developed the theme of Post-Modernism in *The Inhibitions of Modern Architecture* (1976), *After Modern Architecture* (1980) and *Post-Modern* (1982). His major contribution came when he organised the 1980 Venice Biennale on Post-Modernism, with the resulting *Presence of the Past*, the 'Strada Novissima' and the general subtitle 'The end of Prohibition'.

Portoghesi's architecture is as learned as his writing, though it is far from being purely 'archaeological'. In fact, he enjoys throwing elements from history together, as he did in one of his first buildings, the Baldi House (1959-60) at Labaro. Here, forms from Michelangelo, Borromini, Rietveld and Le Corbusier collide and result in a hybrid building. Portoghesi has written of 'this craze of mine to contaminate, to put vastly

removed, and sometimes highly contradictory things together, convincing them to love each other ... The town hall of Civitacastellana, designed for a third-year exam in 1954, forced Borromini and Perret to join together ... The Baldi House ... postulated the marriage between the Schroeder House of Rietveld and the S Ivo lighthouse; witnesses at the wedding, the little temple of Venus at Baalbeck and a Mies plan of 1929. From that date the game became a rite'.[100]

Portoghesi's technique, part Modern and part historicist, was applied to his furniture for the Baldi House between 1959 and 1961. This was similar to the eclectic mixture in the architecture, with a plywood desk with Aalto-like curves and Rietveld-inspired overlapping planes. Other pieces, also using plywood, were more idiosyncratic, combining Baroque forms with fashionable Neo-Liberty and a hint of Gaudí. The result was strangely contradictory – a kind of 'Baroque Bauhaus' twenty years before that term was coined by Matteo Thun (who also uses such contradictions as the marriage of a Morris textile on a thirties style sofa). In fact, if one has to find a first in Post-Modern design, the laurel goes to Portoghesi. This 'melding' has already been examined in the part Modern, part ironic historicist furniture that Venturi produced in 1984. It is a technique used, in a slightly different way, in Arata Isozaki's *Marilyn* chair, where the Japanese architect married the form of a Mackintosh high-back chair, with curves taken from nude photographs of Monroe. Isozaki's methodology will be examined later; Portoghesi's desire to 'contaminate' and 'contradict' has more than a hint of Venturi's similar desire expressed in *Complexity and Contradiction in Architecture*.

Portoghesi also talks of 'lap dissolves' and illustrates his work next to others of different periods; for example the marble of Fiesole Abbey, Behrens' decorative marble, and Hoffmann's Viennese decoration with Portoghesi's ENPAS hall of 1959 in Florence. Portoghesi's prolific designs still use the oxymoron, but on occasions he has steered a course towards a purer historicism and *rappel à l'ordre* of a type one might expect from a scholarly historian of architecture. He has maintained a strong interest in Art Nouveau stained glass, and paid homage to it in the glass in his own house in Rome (1979), and many other buildings. He designed Neo-Liberty, or more particularly neo-Tiffany lamps in brass and leaded-glass for Fratelli Tavani (1981-82). The bases remind one of Henri Van de Velde's Jugendstil lamps, and the glass of Tiffany's exotic creations in New York.

At the same time Portoghesi has designed extensively for Poltronova, and his work has maintained a Neo-Liberty inflection. In 1980 Poltronova produced his plywood table, with oval glass top; its base sets up a reference to Thonet and the bentwood furniture of Vienna, so admired by Portoghesi. They also manufactured a wooden display case with an assertive circular surround which reminds one of 1900s' furniture in France, Belgium and Germany, and Guimard's rare, circular-surround Métro entrances of the same date.

Of late Poltronova has issued Portoghesi's *Liuto* range. This includes armchairs, and two-, three- and four-seater sofas, all with curved cherry wood, or white lacquered wood frames. *En suite* are several different glass-topped tables, their bases with four curved supports of the same design as the chair and sofa frame. The furniture is available in upholstery with a Morrisian 'willow' pattern, or a pink Art Nouveau pattern with conventionalised tulips in the manner of Voysey, or the eponymous Liberty fabric studio. It is also available in a dramatic black and white upholstery, reminiscent of Hoffmann, Kolo Moser and the Wiener Werkstätte, with a horizontal running band of black and white lozenges just beneath its cushion. This latter black and white lozenge pattern was first used by Portoghesi in his already mentioned ENPAS hall of 1959 as an interior leitmotif. It appeared again as enamel decoration running round the *Tea and Coffee Piazza* set designed for Alessi and produced in 1983. In this set, somewhat micro-architectural vessels cluster together on the tray, rather like a small church with apsidal chapels around the centre formed by the tea pot. Of all the submissions, Portoghesi has commanded the grouping of the vessels in the most intelligent manner, and conceived of it as a gathered whole. The black and white lozenge also appears, finally, in a laminate designed by Portoghesi for Abet in 1982.

As an architect expert in the history of pattern and ornament from the Baroque to Art Nouveau, and living in Rome, it comes as little surprise that Portoghesi has designed a number of marble tables. *Roma* for Poltronova has a plain white top, while the aptly titled *Firenze* is patterned in white and green with a red inlaid circle in the centre. The latter refers to the long tradition of marble inlay in floors, and on the facades of buildings such as San Miniato.

His tables for Travertino Romano, *Thuban* and *Aldebarhan*, are named after stars, and have rich, stellated and coloured inlay radiating from their centres. Thuban has a square top, inlaid with brown, pink, white and green marble; *Aldebarhan* is circular, with brown, red, yellow and white inlay. Of these, Portoghesi has written that they 'aim to bring back stone, one of architecture's original and unbeatable raw materials, to the everyday scene. The creation of artificial materials over the last few decades has given us the illusion that it is possible to do without that which for centuries has been the repertoire of forms and materials of architectural tradition; but some particular events taking place in our industrial society have renewed the emphasis on the undying qualities of certain traditions.

'The energy crisis, the upsetting of the ecological balance, the destruction of the beauty of the countryside, the need to build a civilisation of peace, to replace the civilisation of imbalance and conflict, all those problems that can be labelled together as "postmodern" have forcefully suggested that we should consider not a return to the past but the necessity of conserving and protecting our heritage from the past – in order among other things to serve as a permanent example to us . . . Marble furnishings were a characteristic of ancient Rome, and had a great revival in the Renaissance and in the early nineteenth century. The time is right once more for the revival of this local tradition . . . with this aim we wanted to recall, on the table tops, the diametric inlaywork of the floors of ancient times and the creative inspiration that was drawn from them by Borromini in the seventeenth century . . .'[101]

Portoghesi may be making rather a lot of claims through one object but his statement does roll together conservationist Green Party sentiments, as well as those of the Peace movement and others that ultimately go back to Morris and the Arts and Crafts movement. The desire for solidity does reflect the need for an anchor in an ever changing society, and Portoghesi seems to have found his roots in Borromini, and all the marble that constitutes the building of Rome.

Portoghesi has also produced a family of lamps for Travertino Romano. The largest, *Sesquietertia* has a square shade made from four elegant slices of Mexican onyx, through which the light shines; the base and support is made from white marble. Three smaller ones, diminishing in scale, called *Sesquialtera*, are also produced as table lamps, made out of marble and alabaster. For most of his designs, Portoghesi produces elegant, rapid sketches in the manner of old master drawings and of Leonardo da Vinci. One such drawing pens out his curious *Rabiro* writing desk of 1986. This well-made object of wood has two angled, high arched ends, which have characteristic coloured glass infills. This is a very luxurious return to

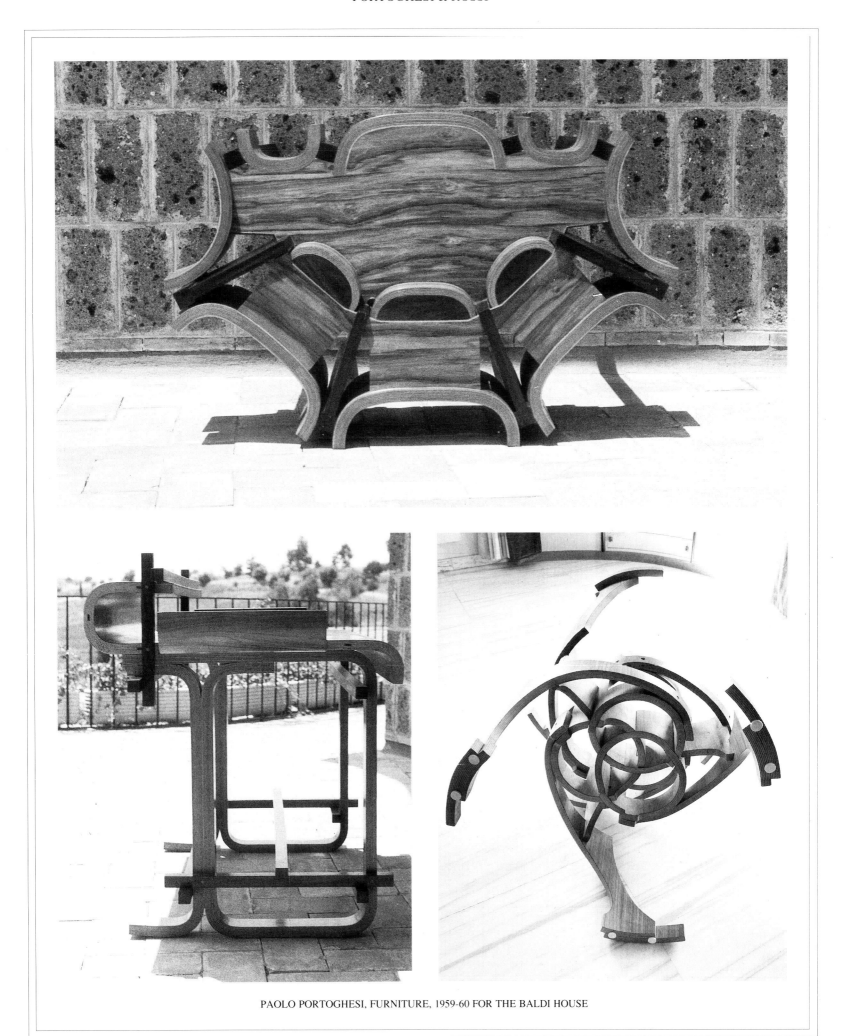

PAOLO PORTOGHESI, FURNITURE, 1959-60 FOR THE BALDI HOUSE

PAOLO PORTOGHESI, *THUBAN* TABLE, 1986 FOR TRAVERTINO ROMANO

high standards of craftsmanship.

Portoghesi has produced excellent designs with equally high craftsmanship for Cleto Munari. One such, a silver set of flatware of 1980, has layered handles that blend the form of a fluted column with the bark of a tree. He has also designed jewellery, for the same entrepreneur, nearly all of which is mimetic of architecture. One, a ring in pure gold, has the shape of a temple with a broken pediment; a second in yellow and white gold, renders a circular Classical building, a little reminiscent of the arches of the Colosseum; the third is a simulacrum of housing typologies and is a ring with three house facades, all topped by sapphires. The houses depicted are of the 'face' house variety, with a 'mouth' door, two 'eyes' for windows, and a 'hat' for the pitched roof. He has also recently designed a gold watch for Munari, which has a broken pediment on the two strap sides of the square face.

Portoghesi has said of his jewellery that 'My pieces are micro-architectures, archetypes of ancient, sacred buildings. I looked at the theme of the house as children do . . . the ancestral house, the house as shelter . . . the house as projection of the body . . . a somehow psychoanalytic view of the house.'[102] Portoghesi, in emphasising the pitched roof, pediment, or aedicule, is drawing upon the rich history of architecture before the flat roofed interruption of the International Style. The fact that so many other Post-Modern architects do the same is indicative of a deep desire to return to base, to find, as Portoghesi does, a larger and longer context for his profession.

Aldo Rossi was born in the same year as Paolo Portoghesi, in 1931. He practises in his native Milan, and like Portoghesi has taught widely, and published, most importantly on urban architecture in his *L'Architettura della Città* (1966). His work is not as clearly Post-Modernist as that of Portoghesi and he has even denied the label. He has written that 'I have been called "Post-Modernist" many times in one way or another, although I have always declared that I am neither a modernist or a postmodernist; I have never taken the position of either. As a matter of fact, the term "Post Modernism" used in the USA might be very difficult to translate into Italian . . . To me, the term "Post-Modern" has nothing to do with any special meaning at all. In the 1960s . . . I was already carrying out a study to overwhelm and criticise the modern movement.'[103]

Aldo Rossi as a designer occupies the middle ground between the Modern Movement and Post-Modernism; he is historicist in searching out the monument and urban forms within the longer history of the city, but these memories of towers, domes and aedicular architecture are stripped down and given a simple Modern surface. Rossi is not an ornamentalist, and differs greatly from Portoghesi in that respect. In fact his work sets up a resonance with French eighteenth-century Rationalist theory, and the work of Jean-François Blondel (1705-1774) or Marc-Antoine Laugier (1713-1769) who broadly encouraged severe, restrained Classicism.

Rossi is well known for his prints and paintings which reveal his interest in assembling his solid forms within a De Chirico-like image. These caprices often render his coffee pots on the same scale as a tower behind them, or show them grouped together.

Rossi's submission to the Alessi *Tea and Coffee Piazza* of 1983 was a silver set, with blue enamel, the lids or domes of each topped by a spherical quartz. These nestled in an open, pedimented case with a 'pitched roof' and a battery clock in the centre of the pediment. The whole ensemble was reminiscent of his design for the Teatro del Mondo, a floating theatre made of wood and steel with applied colour, for Venice in 1979. The coffee pots refer to this theatre and at the same time gently suggest the form of the top of the Campanile in St Mark's Square, and the typology of the bell tower in general. The pedimented form with clock also has a precedent in the facade of Rossi's Scuola di Broni (1979).

Alessi have since then issued several base metal coffee pots designed by Rossi which have a similar form. The first of these, an Espresso coffee maker, was produced in 1984, while the latest, of 1988, has a similar base but a domed lid rather than a conical one. There is also a jug version, of conical form overall. This has been criticised by Otl Aicher as not pouring well, and he has written that 'This jug by Rossi is the juggiest jug of them all, it is the essential jug, the jug-in-itself. But it won't pour . . . to complicate matters, the jug has a centre of gravity that slips into the corner when you lift the jug up, and lifting is made particularly difficult when you tip the jug. But why bother pouring with something so lovely?'[104]

Rossi clearly endeavours to design archetypal form and 'timeless' form. He says as much in his introduction to the Alessi catalogue which announces his watches of 1987: 'we defend the recording of continuity. Thus this familiar watch is, of course, in the majority of cases and for reasons of functionality, round, has Arabic numerals, and contains within itself ever more sophisticated instruments, yet, so to speak, has so far concealed them in a timeless form.'[105] This watch, *Momento*, is stainless steel, and ingeniously the same central case can be used for the wristwatch version as for the pocket watch. It is odd to see a pocket or fob watch after such a long absence, but then, as with Graves' cuff-links, there has been a young fogey revival in old fashioned dressing.

Rossi has also produced excellent furniture for Longoni, of Como in Italy. The first is called the *Cabinet of Elba (AR1)* and was produced in 1982. This is a beach hut-shaped wardrobe with a pedimented, pitched roof. Instead of a clock it has a circular grille in the centre, which presumably allows the clothes inside to breathe. It is available in several finishes including a blue and pink planked effect, the vertical stripes reminding one of deck chairs and similar patterns.

His chair, *AR2*, is more self-effacing, especially in the plain slatted beech version. It is also available in yellow, pink, light blue and black, as is the rest of the range which includes a chest of drawers, kitchen cabinet and display cabinet. The chest of drawers, *AR3*, of 1983, has a welcome deadpan quality, and reverts to the 'Victorian' typology of such furniture, with three long drawers surmounted by two short ones, all with simple wooden knobs. The kitchen cabinet, *AR6*, of 1983, is offered in natural cherry wood or colours, and is simple, using recessed rectangles to provide a gentle sense of interval. Rossi's designs always have a neatness to them, in part because he goes back to well-worn stereotypes such as the ubiquitous nineteenth-century chest of drawers. He uses the same method in his *Rilievo* table of 1986 for Up and Up. This is, like all their products, made of marble, but Rossi's is especially deadpan and based on a very ordinary nineteenth-century table form; the marble legs are turned in a manner that resembles crafted wood turning. It is especially 'quiet' when compared with the rather louder designs in marble for Up and Up by Sottsass or Michele De Lucchi. Aldo Rossi's greatest attribute, as a designer who is aware both of the Modern Movement and of history, is to select quiet, archetypal work from the past as a precedent. He eschews decoration, in the main, for the sake of form; and despite one writer's criticism of one of Rossi's jugs on the ground of its poor ability to pour, this Italian architect has produced some of the most satisfying objects to date. They may indeed become genuine 'classics' of design.

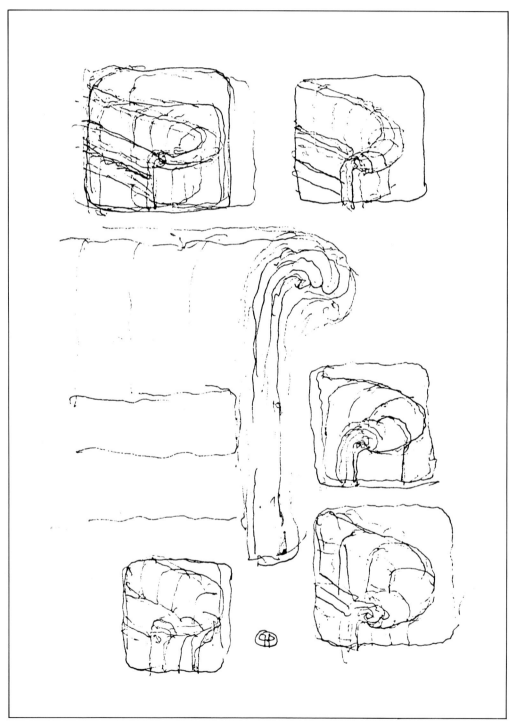

PAOLO PORTOGHESI, STUDIES OF *LIUTO* SOFA, LATE 1970s

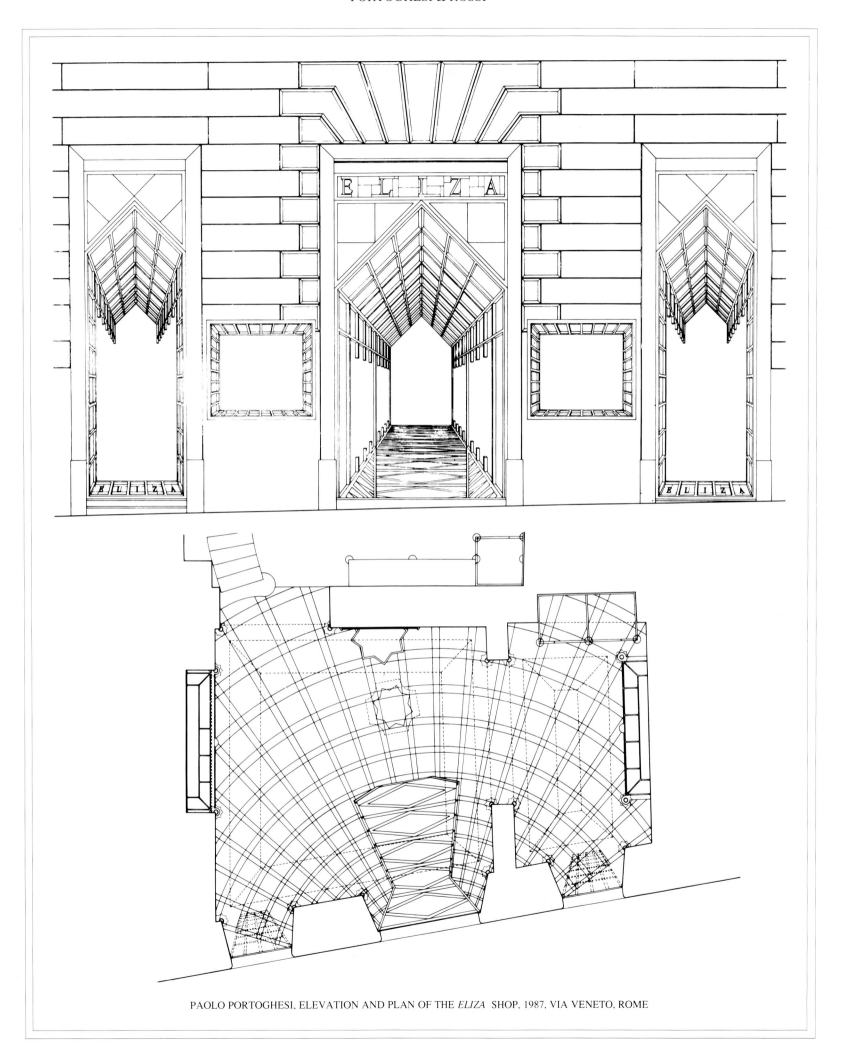

PAOLO PORTOGHESI, ELEVATION AND PLAN OF THE *ELIZA* SHOP, 1987, VIA VENETO, ROME

PAOLO PORTOGHESI, *SESQUIETERTIA* LAMP, 1986 FOR TRAVERTINO ROMANO

THE SYMPATHY OF THINGS
Paolo Portoghesi

PAOLO PORTOGHESI, *ROMA* TABLE, MID-1980s FOR POLTRONOVA

My interest in objects and their forms began, just as I emerged from infancy, in my grandparents' house in Rome, on the Via della Chiese Nuova. While the objects around which my daily life revolved did not capture my imagination, those that I saw on my frequent visits to my grandparents' house held an extraordinary attraction for me. Perhaps this was because the long afternoons that passed while the grown-ups chatted allowed me no other pastime than to interest myself in things that I saw in the various rooms, and other objects that I went in search of, in spite of being forbidden to do so, in the large attic full of trunks and chests, and inhabited – since it was war-time – by prolific chickens and rabbits. It was there, in the half-light that issued from the dormer windows, amidst the roofs of the city, that my lasting recognition was inspired, of objects removed from daily life because they had run their course and were no longer of practical use.

The objects that held the greatest attraction for me were those belonging to a brother of my grandmother, a professor of design and architecture, but above all an amateur in every possible artistic discipline, from painting to music to photography, which he used in the first decades of the century in which he lived, before dying in the very year I was born.

From this imaginary inheritance, the things that most inspired me were the gigantic photographic apparatus, a splendid mahogany box with lots of small bottles containing inks with which to colour the photographs, a typewriter that looked like

a peacock, and a little supple woman in pure Art Nouveau style who held a precious *vide poche* of green glass encased in a spider's web of glass fibres in the manner of the widow Loetz. This little woman, together with two big clocks, one Baroque and one Neo-Classical, and two panels, one Neo-Classical and one Neo-Baroque, positioned one in front of the other in the big drawing room, soon became the only objects with which I entertained a secret rapport, as if they were friends who gave me a great deal of pleasure by always being the same.

The memory of the little Art Nouveau woman may well have been a factor (when I came across very similar objects, leafing through the book by Pevsner on *The Pioneers of the New Movement*) in determining my early passion for that style and in urging me to buy, for very little money and from a small junk dealer, other objects of the same genre – the beginning of a future collection. Those were my school years, the years of my precocious vocation to be an historian and architect. I studied Borromini and Guarini, and followed the rediscovery of Gaudi with great interest, and the re-evaluation of Van de Velde, Horta, Mackintosh. In the mid-1950s, already close to graduating, I became a strong supporter of the so-called Neo-Liberty, a trend that originated from the claim to a certain right: that of redesigning the boundaries of the Modern, including ourselves in the Rational Radicalism, which imposed the *tabula rasa* affirmation of traditions, and also the attempts at the beginning of the century (in the form of Art Nouveau,

Nordic Neo-Classicism, and Expressionism) to find origins for the Modern in historical inheritance and local traditions.

My first house, the Casa Baldi, designed in 1959, was also my first experience as a designer of furniture and objects; I designed tables, two desks, a cupboard, wall mirrors, and also handles and a big vase which were never executed. On the one hand, my passion for Art Nouveau led me onto the road to designing everything, even the slippers of my landlord (who was a director friend); on the other hand I had in mind the paradoxical tale told by Loos in *Words in the* Corpo Minore.

In the objects of the Casa Baldi, as in its architecture, two grammars that are clearly diverse, and also compatible, meet and come together: that of Van Doesberg and Rietweld's Neo-Plasticism, and the curvilinear and plastic grammar that proceeds from the architects of Adriano, through Borromini, Guarini, Neuman, to Horta and Gaudi.

Speaking of the first examples of design, a passage in the memoirs of Horta, dedicated to the Casa Winssinger, built in 1894, might serve as an interpretative key: 'Winssinger had been built with the happiness of a sick wife in mind, whose needs for peace and rest had acted as a kind of 'leitmotif' around which the plan's composition revolved. This resulted in an hotel that was disproportionate in terms of its importance and the native, or let's say the slightly working-class character, of the district.'

Horta expresses a principle of mimesis on this subject between man and his house, which also finds support in the psycho-analytical theory of identification of the e*go* with the home: 'It was at the time when, my thoughts having now synthesised, I proclaimed that the house was not only intended as the image of the occupants' life, but also what should be termed the "portrait".'

Pursuing this idea of a 'warm' rapport between man and objects, in all my experiences as a designer I have never forgotten the danger indicated by Loos, of imprisoning the person among objects that interfere too much with his life, depriving him of the comfort of solitude, and imposing on him, through the forms, a rigid model of behaviour. For this reason, my furniture and objects seek to closely follow tested models to which people have, in a manner of speaking, adapted themselves, and which do not force them to conform to a discipline invented at that moment in time. The modern dream of furniture made ad hoc to fit a certain space from which it can never be separated has never seduced me. As a true collector and lover of antiques, I think that furniture should be designed for an autonomous life, which usually extends much further than the brief season that it will spend in its original spatial situation.

The houses I have designed, above all when remodelling pre-existing spaces, are therefore usually adapted wrappings which see and re-see things that mirror the predilections and idiosyncracies of the owners of the house. The only exception was the Casa Baldi which, being aware of the things that the owner would have amassed in the architectonic wrapping,

and knowing that he did not want a house for himself but rather a show house, I designed it in such a way that everything was so 'complete' that it would not tolerate any additions or inclusions.

The second stage of my designing activities began in the 1970s with the collaboration of a craftsman working in wood, with whom I studied a series of low-priced objects based on the superimposition of layers of shavings cut with curvilinear profiles – a continuation of Art Nouveau themes, with a rapid technology adapted to the changed times. With this system of linear enrichment being far more economical than the plastic enrichment used by curving plywood sheets in the furniture of Casa Baldi, I sought to create a 'sympathy' and a recognisable quality of things that was not too fixed for their use.

This kind of research came close in time to the first pieces designed for industry in the late 1970s: the *Liuto* divans and sofas, a table, and a window which was the fruit of a collaboration with Sergio Camili, an industrial artist who has a very precise role in the story of Italian design.

The 1980s began for me with the operation, proposed by Mendini, of the Tea and Coffee Piazza, with Alessi putting into production twelve table services, entrusted to some protagonists of Post-Modern architecture.

The experience of reading Charles Jencks' book in 1977 had had a liberating influence on me, and the exhibition *The Presence of the Past* at the Venice Biennale had given me the sensation of finally being able to speak out about the discoveries made during my long and solitary voyage of research.

After the Alessi service, the work opportunities in the field of design multiplied, a determining factor being the friendship with Cleto Munari, a collector and producer who, by stimulating and provoking architects into supplying him with designs, enjoyed himself as much as if he were playing a game of cards. For Munari I have designed cutlery, vases, clocks and chandeliers, many of which remained only on paper, developing my present direction by degrees, which consists of designing magical micro-architectures capable of re-awakening in the observer the sensation of *déjà vu*, of the familiar and, at the same time, of the dreamed.

The themes which, with enormous satisfaction, I seek to investigate are the temple, the column, the piazza, the house in the form in which children think of it (with a pointed roof, a door and two windows), the tree, the flower, the shell, the rock crystal and the hand. The materials that I prefer for these objects are the woods most rich in grained and transparent textures – the pear, the olive, the cherry, the maple, and among metals, silver and copper.

My dream is to extend evocative and 'sympathetic' design to practical objects such as cars, televisions and sound apparatus for high-fidelity reproduction. All are still linked to the myth of the *gute Form* and of the mechanical neutrality of the modern object.

In the design of my micro-architecture, decoration has an important role, in particular the band of trapezoids or rhombuses in a row, alternating black and white: a dynamic version of the chess-board of Hoffman and Moser. I use this element, derived from the black and white floors used by Borromini, as a belt to place around my objects to force them to the level of life, as if they were living bodies to be touched.

In order to spread the interest in the new design, which corresponds to Post-Modern architecture, I founded, together with my wife Giovanna, the gallery 'Apollodoro', in Rome near the Piazza di Spagna, which in the field of painting and sculpture promotes an analogous direction uninhibited by the use of languages and techniques and without discrimination between modern and antique.

'Apollodoro' is an elusive space, created by using the instrument of Renaissance perspective with new sensitivity.

The entrance door is the metaphor of the 'Gallery' as an architectonic type and, in this sense is both an element of attraction at a distance, like a Roman gateway, and a speaking element, blessed with its own lateral significance. The objects designed by architects are placed in the bay windows positioned along the walls, as in an ideal museum of the present.

Every now and then someone comes along who, instead of wanting to buy the objects in the bay windows, would like to buy the perspective door. Most are finally content with photographing it, or being photographed from the outside, framed in the last archway of the gallery, which is only about forty centimeters high. Like the objects designed during these years, the door of 'Apollodoro' is a 'machine for playing' which does not exclude it from also being a machine for thinking.

PAOLO PORTOGHESI, *LIUTO* SOFA, LATE 1970s FOR POLTRONOVA

PAOLO PORTOGHESI, STAINED GLASS DOORS, 1978 FOR MARTUCCELLI HOUSE

PAOLO PORTOGHESI, *RABIRO* WRITING DESK, 1986, LAMP, 1981-82 FOR FRATELLI TAVANI AND STAINED GLASS, 1977 FOR MARTUCCELLI HOUSE

PAOLO PORTOGHESI, SILVER BOXES, MID-1980s FOR CLETO MUNARI

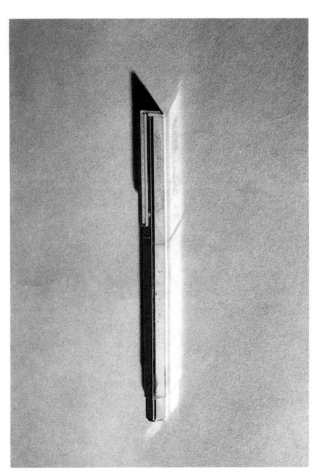

PAOLO PORTOGHESI, GOLD WATCH, 1987, SILVER PICTURE FRAME AND GOLD PEN, LATE 1980s FOR CLETO MUNARI

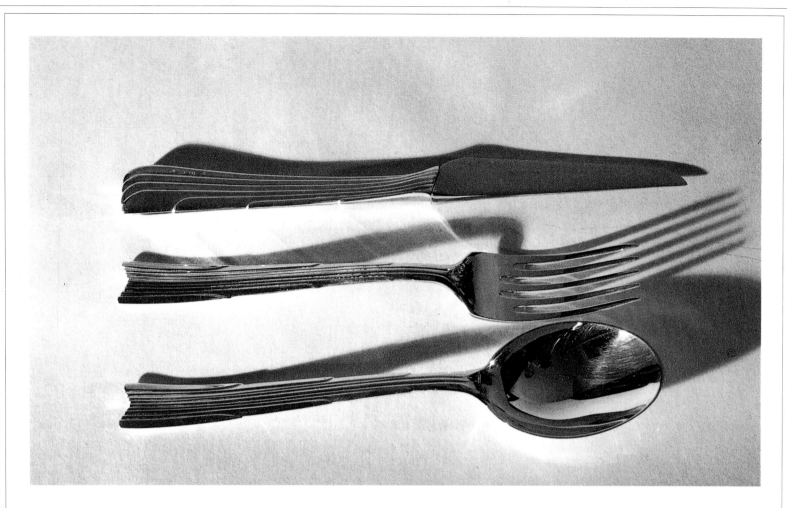

PAOLO PORTOGHESI, SILVER CUTLERY, 1980 FOR CLETO MUNARI

PAOLO PORTOGHESI, SILVER-GILT CUTLERY, 1980 FOR CLETO MUNARI

PAOLO PORTOGHESI, PLATES, 1981 FOR DERUTA

PAOLO PORTOGHESI, BOWLS, 1981 FOR DERUTA

PAOLO PORTOGHESI, CANDLESTICKS, 1980s FOR CLETO MUNARI

PAOLO PORTOGHESI, CANDLESTICK, 1980s FOR CLETO MUNARI

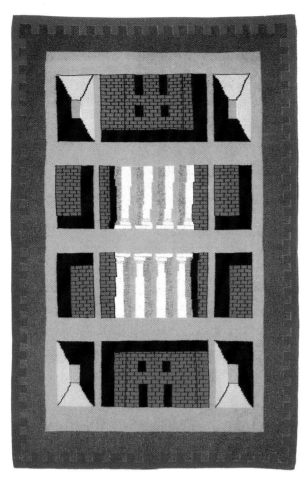
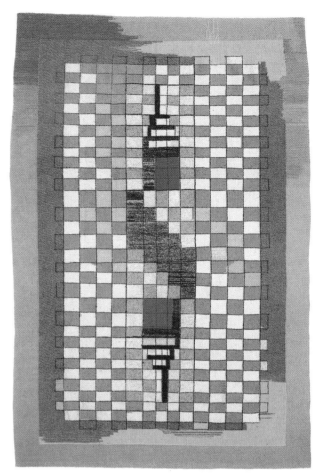

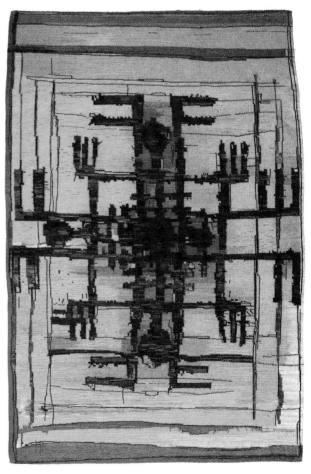

ALDO ROSSI, CARPETS, 1988 FOR A R P STUDIO

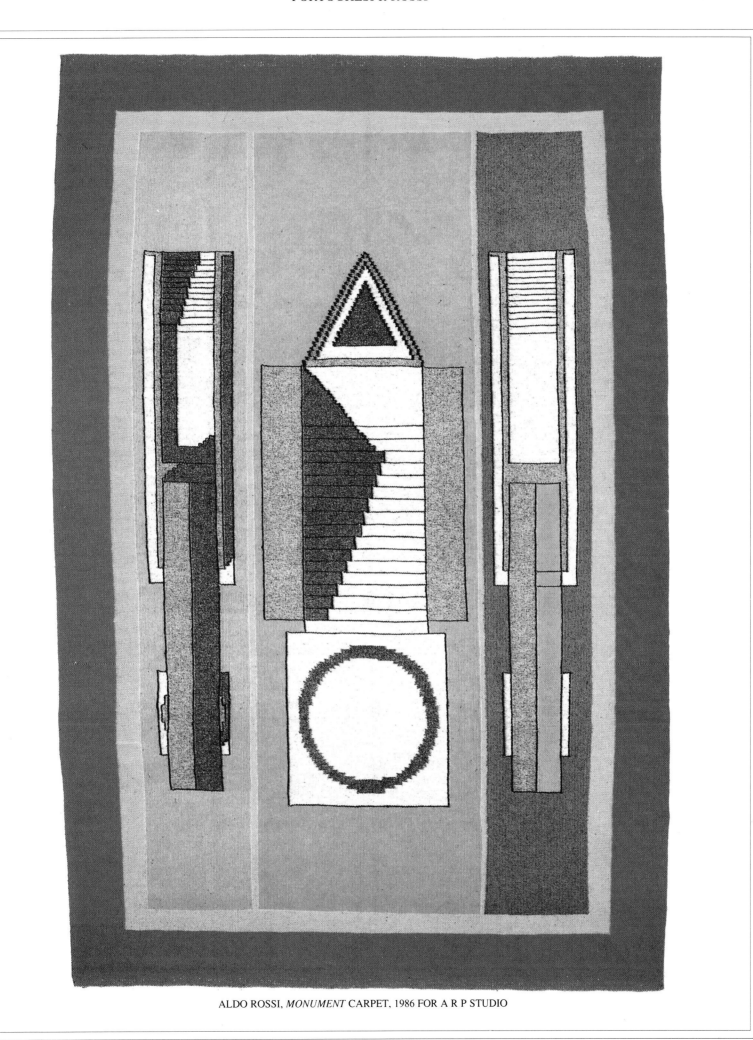

ALDO ROSSI, *MONUMENT* CARPET, 1986 FOR A R P STUDIO

HANS HOLLEIN, *TEA & COFFEE PIAZZA*, 1979-83 FOR ALESSI

CHAPTER VIII

Arata Isozaki & Hans Hollein

HANS HOLLEIN, *FESTIVAL* DINNERWARE, 1985 FOR SWID POWELL

Arata Isozaki's work has something of Aldo Rossi's *media via* approach, and draws upon both the Modern Movement and Post-Modern Classicism. He was born in the same year as Rossi, in 1931, in Oita City, Japan; he was taught by, and then worked with, Kenzo Tange from 1959 until 1963, when he established his own practice in Tokyo. Since that time he has become something of a globe-trotting architect, having built in both Japan and the United States.

Isozaki's work for Memphis and his reference to Michelangelo's Campidoglio pavement in his Tsukuba Civic Centre has already been discussed. His pluralistic approach allows him to draw upon Japanese and Western traditions; at both Tsukuba and the earlier Fujimi Country Club (1973) he appropriated something of the language of Ledoux, especially in the hook-shaped barrel vault of the latter building. His design work often combines oriental and occidental elements and this has been seen in the previously discussed Fuji side tables of 1981, where he has blended the traditional Japanese mirror form with Italianate Memphis colour.

One of Isozaki's first designs, the Post-Pop *Marilyn* chair of 1972 also used the combination of several components. This chair was first made by ICF Spa in Italy in 1972, and then by Sunar; there is a version of 1981 produced by the Tendo Mokko Co Ltd. The chair, in black lacquered wood is Isozaki's homage to Charles Rennie Mackintosh's taxonomy of high-backed chairs, which themselves referred to the ebonised finish, simplicity and verticality of Japanese design. Isozaki thus pays tribute to British design, which had itself drawn from the cult of Japanism at the end of the nineteenth century. This circularity is poignant; a Japanese tribute to a British tribute to Japan. With that element, Isozaki introduces a curve based on Marilyn Monroe's figure, taken from a nude photograph. Not only is this Post-Pop, in common with other tributes to this cult figure, but it also extends the tradition of Japanese erotic art, now inflected towards a stereotype American blonde. Fair haired women (and men) are deemed especially attractive in the new admass culture of Japan.

Arata Isozaki has summed up his process very well by comparing the creation of his *Marilyn* chair (not to be confused with Hollein's couch which has the same name and source of inspiration) with 'a traditional Japanese way of writing poetry, called *honka-dori*. *Honka-dori* is a method of adaptation of an existing poem. (*Honka*, original verse; *dori*, adaptation.) Utilising the given poem as a model, one composes an image, situation and rhetoric to express one's own poem. In such a way it is possible to take advantage of the power and evocative force of the original work. In Japan, *honka-dori* has always been one of the most important methods of writing poetry. In a broader sense, *honka-dori* can be seen as a method of composing a new sentence or new design using quotations of Classical precedent. It is based on the idea that all languages (including visual language) are already contained in a collective text. The

Marilyn chair refers to two sources. One is Mackintosh's high-back chair. Although there are many prototypes of high-back chairs in the world, the *Marilyn* chair's black finish and narrow back which emphasises its vertical line recalls the image of Mackintosh's chair. The other image is the body line of Marilyn Monroe. By combining various curves of her body taken from the famous nude photographs, I had made a special "French curve" for use in my atelier. The curve of the *Marilyn* chair's back is drawn with the "French curve". Thus, the images of these two originals, superimposed, invade each other. This is seen, for example, in the contrastive juxtaposition of the curve of the back and the rectilinear form of the seat . . . it is suggested that the *honka-dori* system should be recognised anew not only as a system of making poems but also as a fundamental principle for designing in a wide sense.'[106] Isozaki's technique of 'superimposition' and 'adaptation of original text' is very much part of the Post-Modern arsenal of design process, and has been seen in use in the work of Venturi. The 'portmanteau-word' may be the equivalent in the English language, and the word 'meld' has already been mentioned in this context. Lewis Carroll, for example, was fond of such humorous invention, rather famously for words such as 'mimsy', a combination of 'miserable' and 'flimsy'. Isozaki pays homage to an oriental tradition of adaptation of whole texts, rather than individual words, and in doing so develops the 'both . . . and' plea expressed by Venturi in the latter's *Complexity and Contradiction in Architecture*.

Isozaki's *Marilyn* accorded well with the Japanese tradition of ebonised furniture, and it was somewhat surprising to see his involvement with colour after that time. He was commissioned to design tables for Colorcore, for display at the *Contemporary Landscape* exhibition held at the Museums of Modern Art in Kyoto and Tokyo in 1985 and 1986. The first, *Zebra Panda A*, was a side-table of stratified Colorcore, of rectangular form, resting on a single, central rough-hewn rock. The second, *Zebra Panda B*, was a bench-table of rectangular Colorcore, this time bowed underneath, resting on two rough-hewn rocks at either end.

These two tables developed Isozaki's interest in colour and layered effects, which he has used subsequently in his door handle for FSB and his jewellery for Cleto Munari. The *Marilyn* chair had a restrained use of black which has become stereotypical of a Western view of Japanese architecture and design, and as we shall see Isozaki associated jewellery with this non-colour as well until he designed for Munari. As their titles suggest, *Zebra Panda A and B* used stripes of colour selected, as Isozaki explains, in a random manner. He has written: 'What I attempt in this work is just to show the section of the Colorcore . . . Colours are chosen at random and their arrangement is decided by means of dice. Anyone who complains about the combination of colours should protest against the God who presides over the chance of the thrown dice. The legs of the bench side-table are made of white and black "Panda Stone". This stone, which comprises black and white in stripes

between the rock formation of white Inada granite, came to light at the quarry of Inada granite a couple of years ago. This part was thrown away before, but once the border of these strata was polished there appears a marvellous pattern which is of a kind impossible to attain by mere design. This must be the result of the God who is in charge of chance that dominates nature. What I attempted was only to arrange these two leaving the rest to chance. The Colorcore with an arrangement of the sections inevitably became a design in vertical stripes, and you may call it "Zebra" in spite of its different colour. On the other hand, it may also be called "Panda" because of its black and white pattern. It is quite a curious name, which also may be the work of the God of chance.'[107]

The 'Zebra' effect is achieved through stripes of blue, green, mauve and red, which have been glued together. Isozaki's use of 'chance' sets up a resonance with the work of Arp, already discussed in the context of Gehry's work for Colorcore. The intervention of such a process may well be inspired by Isozaki's wife Aiko Miyawaki, an artist who was aware of Duchamp, Kiesler, and Dada as well as the Neo-Dada of the early 1960s. Indeed, there was a Tokyo-based group called Neo-Dada Organizer formed in 1960 by Genpei Akasegawa, who was also influenced by Surrealism, Ushio Shinohara, and others.

Isozaki's combination in *Zebra Panda A and B* of natural and synthetic forms, and his use of dice to incorporate chance, has produced a hybrid design, a cross-breed aptly named 'Zebra Panda'. The very title mates an oriental animal, the Panda, with a broadly occidental creature, the Zebra. The new hybrid created is, of course, somewhat strange but, as with so much Post-Modern design, a hitherto unseen mongrel is the result. The natural rock reminds one of the longer tradition of pebbles and stones in gardens which form part of the Japanese poetic of nature; the candy stripes and bright colour indicate Western, popular culture. Part natural, part synthetic, part Western, part oriental, the result is a welcome combination of cultures.

In 1984, Swid Powell produced Isozaki's *Streams* plate, which reinforces rather than transcends Japanese tradition. It is strongly Japanese in its echo of the wave pattern as presented in nineteenth-century coloured woodcuts, such as Hokusai's 'Great Wave' from the latter's *Thirty-Six Views of Mount Fuji* (1823-31). Beyond its oriental rhythm, its black and gold colour establishes a dialogue with traditional decorative arts, such as the use of black and gold lacquer, and bronze or iron and gold in metalwork, sword fittings and armour.

If this latter is a quasi-oriental object, the same cannot be said for Isozaki's series of door fittings of 1986 for FSB in Germany. Isozaki has observed that 'Almost all our homes in Japan are fitted with sliding doors. Doors with latches and handles are seldom to be found . . .'[108] Isozaki furnished three designs: a circular door knob, a lever, and a door grip of bar form in aluminium covered with layered wood, coloured orange, brown, buff and yellow. The result is highly 'tactile' and should be contrasted with the cerebral door fitting de-

ARATA ISOZAKI, *MARILYN* TABLE AND CHAIRS FOR ICF, AND LATER FOR SUNAR, 1972/1983

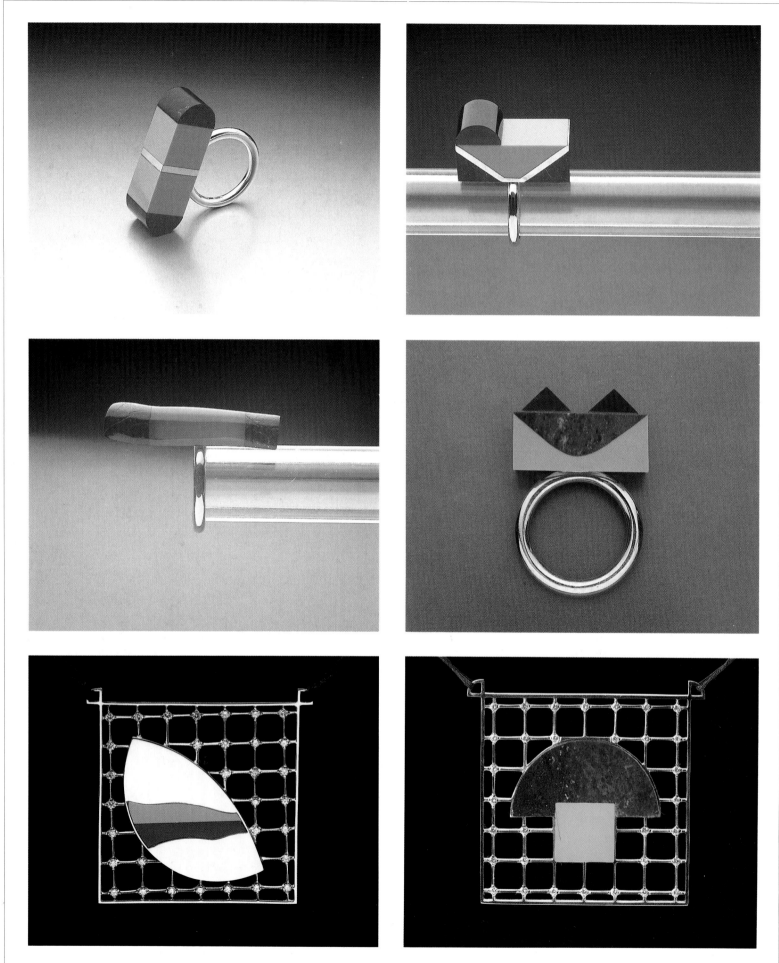

ARATA ISOZAKI, JEWELLERY, 1986 FOR CLETO MUNARI

signed by Eisenman which has been discussed earlier. Isozaki has suggested that 'the door handle is a refuge for eyes and hands and should serve their needs . . . During my deliberations, I kept in mind the fact that we guide our hands with our eyes when we approach a door . . . I then tried to imagine what would especially please the Japanese eye, and settled for wood. We cut various natural woods into layers and then randomly pieced them together. We stained woods different colours and fitted them together in the same way. Given that colour is generally used in a very restrained way in our country, the multi-coloured wooden grips are very striking to the Japanese eye. Having found something for the eye, I then had to discover something special for the hand. Handles are usually round, but that struck me as being a non-committal shape so I cut sharply angular sides into the rounded surface. You feel the edges when you take hold of the handle, and this sharpens your senses . . .'[109]

Isozaki uses a similar layering, this time of coloured semi-precious stones, for his Cleto Munari jewellery, produced in 1986, the same year as the FSB doorhandles. One Munari ring has a hook-shaped form reminiscent of the Fujimi Country Club roof, composed of long and short bisected cylinders of turquoise, lapis-lazuli and red agate; the construction must have been highly complicated. Another ring is formed of lapis-lazuli and turquoise internally jig-sawed with a curve and counter curve assembled to complete a two-tone rectangle, surmounted by two small coral pyramids. Isozaki's watch for Munari is, on the other hand, a square form – the twelve o'clock position indicated by a tiny rectangular sapphire. The other hours are delineated by tiny circular diamonds, and three, six and nine o'clock by rectangular diamonds. As with his architecture, Isozaki extends the Modern reliance on the rectangular solid to embrace the pre-Modern and subsequently Post-Modern solids of pyramid, cylinder and bisected cylinder, and hemisphere. As with his earlier use of colour, Isozaki is conscious of the 'black' inflection in Japanese design, and has remarked that 'My wife always wears black and likes very primitive jewellery, just silver and brass.'[110]

Such a restraint in the colour of clothing is also probably conditioned by the grey, and black and white tonality of Issey Miyake's fashion designs. Thus Isozaki's experiment with colour is adventurous, despite all that is known about the superiority of the colour woodblock print in nineteenth-century Japan. He has, in a sense, had to rediscover colour. Isozaki also stresses the tectonic quality of his work and has stated to Barbara Radice that he 'used vaults, cubes, pyramids, sometimes cylinders. They are really architectural volumes. My jewels are architectural models.'[111] Isozaki's use of geometrical solids sets up resonance with Neo-Classical precedents and his own architectural 'quotation' of Ledoux or Palladio. His work is not 'micro-architectural' and, unlike the jewellery of Graves or Portoghesi for Munari, it is not mimetic of housing or building typology. Instead, Isozaki digs deep into the mine of architectural form, to rediscover its Platonic essence.

Hans Hollein was born in Vienna in 1934 and studied at the Akademie der Bildenden Künste in his native city before going to the Illinois Institute of Technology and the University of California, Berkeley, between 1958 and 1960. After working in various offices abroad, he set up his own practice in Vienna in 1964.

Hollein has taken an active interest in all the visual arts from drawing, graphics, collage, performance, sculpture and design, to architecture. His work resonates with the awareness of Vienna in 1900 and after: the architecture of Otto Wagner and Adolf Loos, the erotic drawing and colour of Gustav Klimt and Egon Schiele, and the sexually open writing of Arthur Schnitzler all inform Hollein's approach as a total artist. Hollein has attempted to reconstruct Freud's couch and accompanying chair, and this object is a recurring motif in some of his designs.

Hollein has absorbed the lessons of Adolf Loos in his architecture, and perhaps also some of his élitism; he has admitted that 'architecture is an affair of the élite', a statement which coincides with the emergence of neoconservativism in the 1980s. The luxurious marble facade for the Schullin Jewellery Shop I in Vienna, 1975, echoes the marble shop fronts executed by Adolf Loos, especially in the Kärntnerstrasse in the same city in the first decade of this century. Hollein even quoted Loos directly in his facade for the 'Strada Novissima', the Post-Modern fantasy street display directed for the 1980 Venice Biennale by Paolo Portoghesi; one of the columns was a copy of Loos' unrealised Doric Chicago Tribune column of 1922. The irony here is that Loos prophesied in 1923 that 'the great Greek Doric column will be built. If not in Chicago then in another city. If not for the Chicago Tribune, then for someone else. If not by me, then by another architect.' Again, in his Austrian Travel Bureau in Vienna of 1976-8, Hollein has quoted the glass roof of Otto Wagner's famous Viennese Post Office Savings Bank of 1906; inside, a fluted column is broken halfway up to reveal a shiny metallic core. Hollein thus combines Neo-Classicism and modern technology, in a way that is highly appropriate for a travel bureau which aims to suggest escape to another world through modern technology. In the same building, the cashiers' counters are protected by a Rolls Royce radiator-like grille – a witty tribute to the Neo-Classical radiator of the famous car with further nuances of money and luxury. The building also contains exotic palm-tree columns in shiny metal, referring to a similar set of cast-iron columns used by John Nash in the kitchen of the Royal Pavilion in Brighton of 1815-22. Further 'quotation' includes a metallic kiosk or pavilion much indebted to the architecture of Sir Edwin Lutyens at New Delhi.

Beyond architecture, Hollein's interest in design has also produced excellent results. His preoccupation with metallic surfaces extends to gold, silver and jewellery, and he has been a prolific designer of furniture, ceramics, and glass.

Uncannily, he shares with Ian Hamilton Finlay a fascination for Neo-Classicism and aircraft carriers. In 1964 Hollein produced a quasi-Surreal photomontage of *An aircraft carrier in the Austrian wheatfields*; the image seems even more bizarre when one remembers that Austria is totally landlocked. In 1983 Hollein repeated the aircraft carrier image for Alessi, and his silver set for the competition nestles neatly in position on its carrier-deck-shaped tray, ready to 'take off' in the user's hands. The vessels are aligned like aircraft. The word-play on 'carrier' is reminiscent of 1970s' conceptual art, especially Simon Cutts' *Aircraft Carrier Bag*, a screenprint on an actual paper bag, of 1972. Ship and Ocean liner metaphors abounded in the Modern Movement, quite consciously in the work of Le Corbusier; Hollein's design may be seen as an extension of it, and although the Alessi set dates from 1983, the idea behind it is still reminiscent of the 1960s.

Hollein's excursions into Neo-Classical and *rappel à l'ordre* Post-Modernism in design began to appear in the early 1980s. In 1981 he designed an exotic acrylic, glass and ostrich-feather dressing table, *Zauberflöte*, for Mobel Industrie Design. The name presumably refers to Mozart's *Die Zauberflöte* (*The Magic Flute*, 1791), and the dressing table is a confection no doubt suitable for the Queen of the Night in the famous opera. The light bulbs round the mirror and the moon-shaped circle set up a resonance with Schinkel's drawing for the *Appearance of the Queen of the Night* (1815), already referred to with regard to Michael Graves; the bulbs suggest stars. Hollein's dressing table is a sensual reworking of Art Deco furniture, and the pink ostrich feathers take this piece of furniture beyond Schinkel, towards a highly charged eroticism. This latter element, along with a fascination with death and mausoleum-like structures, recurs in Hollein's work.

Hollein's *Schwarzenberg* table of 1981 for Memphis is austere when compared with *Zauberflöte* and conveys a tomb-like presence much at odds with the rest of the bright, supersensualist Memphis work. It is in briar wood which, like Graves' work for Memphis, establishes a reference to the use of blond wood in Biedermeier and Art Deco furniture. It is shallow stepped, an inversion of the ziggurat form, and again one is reminded of Loos' interest in a step-pyramid effect of stacking roof lines in his architecture.

Hollein's *Marilyn* sofa of 1981 for Poltronova in Italy contains an *embarras de richesses* of sources. It is made of root-wood with a celadon green and powder pink upholstery, and is aptly described by Poltronova as a 'loveseat'. It is a Neo-Classical couch, a Hollywood casting couch and an Art Deco screen goddess couch all in one. There is a long cultural lineage of such a design. Salvador Dali's gouache of 1935, *The Face of Mae West*, depicted an interior caprice of the actress, the lips delineated as a couch. In 1937 an actual sofa was made to Dali's design, by Jean Michel Franck and others, and one such was owned by Edward James; it was called *Mae West's Lips*, the upholstery coloured red to imitate her lipstick, and pursed accordingly. In the 1960s, Studio 65 had designed a 'Pop' seat for Gufram, coloured red, shaped like lips, and called *Marilyn*; this referred of course to Monroe and was a 1960s update of Dali's 1930s work. Hollein's couch is not Surreal, however,

and simply uses the title Marilyn to convey the sexuality he regularly employs. The complicated metaphors within the design are part of Hollein's Post-Modern approach. His vocabulary draws upon Neo-Classicism, Art Deco, the naming of a couch after a cult figure, Pop and Kitsch in one fell swoop. In being able to do this, and raise a smile, he provides for many visual needs not satisfied by ergonomic or functional furniture.

Hollein's development towards witty and colourful furniture can also be seen in the rather more 'Neo-Classical' veneered *Mitzi* sofa, also for Poltronova, of 1981. Significantly, it too has a girl's name, characteristically Austrian and referential to the same name in a work by Schnitzler. It is available with different upholstery: one has a dramatic black back, red seat and white liquorice allsort-like bolsters; while the second has large pink lily-pads and flowers on a black ground, and pink bolsters. The use of black and blond wood reinforces the reference to Biedermeier so often seen in Post-Modern Classicism. The lily pattern, on the other hand, is reminiscent of Jugendstil textiles of about 1900. An elegant low table has been produced to accompany *Mitzi*. It is also of blond root-wood, and is octagonal in form, with a circular inset of black fabric covered by glass.

Hollein's furniture achieves a sensual and sensuous effect without the high colour employed by, say, Memphis. As early as 1974 Hollein designed the *Ensemble Diagonal* furniture, which is covered with animal skin, for the Austrian firm of Franz Wittmann EG in Etsdorf am Kamp. Hollein's working sketch shows a half-naked girl in black stockings on the chair; he has drawn the naked female form since the late 1950s, and in the early 1970s began Schiele-like studies which, however, associated the position of the woman with the horizontality of landscape.

Hollein, perhaps alone among Post-Modern designers, has ventured into the Germanic concern of 'Green' or ecological furniture. Except for Portoghesi's sentiment regarding durability of furniture, already discussed, or Andrea Branzi's 'Domestic Animals' of 1985, some of which use rough, untreated wooden poles complete with knots and branch-stumps for their backrest, there has been little direct or tangential reference to 'Green' issues. *The Green Bed* was paradoxically commissioned in 1983 by the same firm, Franz Wittmann, which had only a few years previously produced the highly anti-ecological animal-skin furniture by Hollein. This no doubt indicates how much attitudes have changed, especially in Germany. There is now a Green Party in Britain, which wryly comments in the introduction to its 1987 election manifesto that 'many politicians have attempted to provide their own definitions of green politics. All of a sudden "Green" means fashionable. They think they can "capture the Green vote" by developing policies on the rural environment. But there is far more to Green politics than that!'[112]

The Green Bed was nonetheless a serious attempt to use ecologically sound materials, and was a collaborative venture with an engineer from the Vienna Institute of Biological

HANS HOLLEIN, *THE CRYSTAL TOWER*, 1987 FOR DANIEL SWAROVSKI & CO

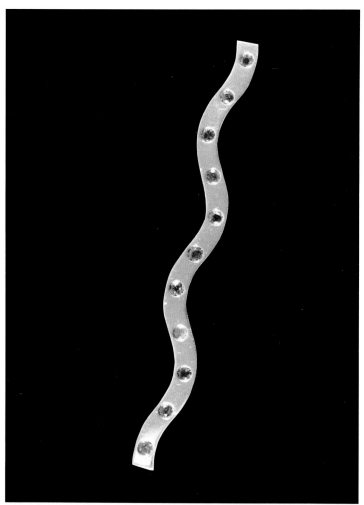
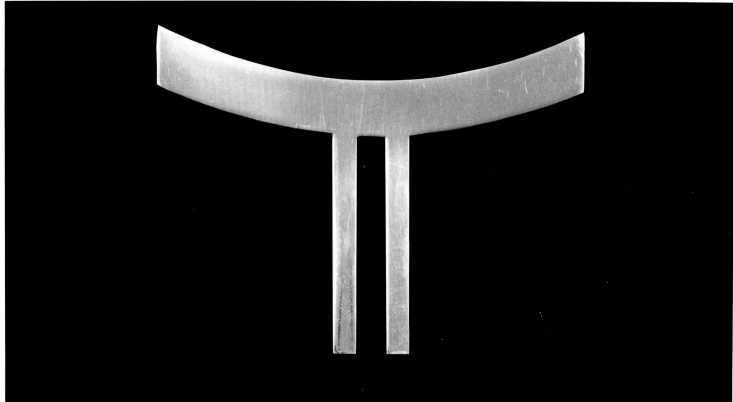

HANS HOLLEIN, JEWELLERY, 1988 FOR A E KOCHERT

Construction. Hollein has said of the beds that they 'use no metal, no artificial glue, no artificial paint; only natural fibres and natural latex, or horsehair. This is because the absence of metal eliminates electric fields while you are sleeping. And it has been proven that laminated composite boards in particular emanate a vapour which is slightly toxic. It you are in bed for six hours each day, you inhale these toxic vapours for much of your lifetime. So we do not have them in this bed.' Hollein has in fact only designed the overall look and the three alternative headboards, which are a textile-covered sunspray, a wooden headboard with a pierced leaf and branch design, and a recti-linear headboard with diagonals of wooden strips that re-sembles a large envelope. One of Hollein's sketched proposals depicted a rustic pole and branch headboard, some years before Andrea Branzi's use of poles already mentioned. In the event, this design by Hollein was not used, but the other three all convey the beauty of wood or the pleasure of the earth through the conventionalised sunrise image.

The intentions of *The Green Bed*, or *Das Grüne Bett*, are expressed by Franz Wittmann when he says 'Green is the colour of hope, the colour of Nature, the colour of relaxation. That is why our new bed is called "the green bed". For us, green means living and continuing to live.' Despite this statement, green as a colour was not used on the bed itself, which relied on the local colour of wood, and a pink sunspray. Hollein did use the colour in one of his Swid Powell ceramic designs, *Festival*, which has a band of green around its inner circumfer-ence, given rhythm by three thin red diagonal lines dispersed with even intervals along the rim. The pulsating effect was taken up again in a ceramic of 1986 for the same firm, aptly called *Kaleidoscope*, with three shades of grey bars in three different thicknesses, setting up a vortex-like optical illusion. Unlike his furniture or some of his metalwork, these ceramics are relatively unrelated to design history, and invent rather than quote.

Many of Hollein's most excellent designs have been for metalwork. In 1980 his circular fruitbowl, square form fruitbowl and candelabrum were made in silver by Rossi & Arcandi, Vicenza for Cleto Munari. The circular fruitbowl, *Tondo,* has a simple bowl supported by undecorated columns that reflect Hollein's interest in the column form, expressed at the 'Strada Novissima' in the same year. This is a 'stripped Classical' design, as is his square fruitbowl; the latter has post and lintel form legs. The candelabrum is reminiscent of a traditional seven candlestick Jewish menorah, with the body filled in to form a semi-circle. In his sketch, Hollein penned out the menorah form, and completed its simplification in the compan-ion drawing which fills in the hitherto separated branches.

Hollein's silver, and his jewellery for Munari, is, as with some of the other Post-Modern work, concerned with architec-tural 'solids'. Thus his plain gold bracelet for Munari is decorated only with small, alternate cylinders and cubes, while a more exotic ring of circular gold is topped with a cube of gold, and four tiny lapis-lazuli columns which support an inverted

pyramid of rose quartz. One of his gold earrings is stepped, reminiscent of the stacked lines in his Memphis *Schwartzen-berg* table. Others are vaguely anthropomorphic, with three dangling 'legs' of gold.

This anthropomorphic quality is a leitmotif which stems from Hollein's rather threatening association of the cross form of the Crucifixion with drawings and photographs of women exercising, or with arms outstretched in a diving position. They have a strong, erotic charge, and evidently Hollein, who is much possessed by sex and death, can combine the two drives in one image. This is demonstrated in his 'Performance Art', notably *Die Turnstunde (The Gymnastics Lesson)*, which was an 'installation' produced in late 1984 for the Stadtisches Museum Abteiberg, Mönchengladbach, the building Hollein designed from 1972 until its completion in 1982. In *Die Turnstunde*, gold painted 'sculptures' are frozen in the position of gymnastics, bending over or with arms outstretched. The attendant catalogue locates Hollein's inspiration as deriving from history, though not listed is the evident intervention of the performance art of Gilbert and George, who used multi-coloured bronze powder on their faces as early as 1969, and in 1970 toured Europe extensively as 'Living' and 'Singing' sculptures. Gilbert and George's use of gold as well as Klimt's at the turn of the century are two sources of inspiration. The catalogue also illustrates Mantegna's *Crucifixion* (1457-9), now in the Louvre, and Hollein's erotic drawings of women bending over or spreadeagled. The most interesting of these, from the point of view of design, depicts from the rear a woman bending over with arms stretched out with, above, a sketch of this form conventionalised into the top section of a circle with two uprights; this was drawn for an exhibition in Stuttgart in 1982. This conventionalised form appears, with variations upon the theme, as an external metalwork detail to the Mönch-engladbach Museum, the facade door surround to the Schullin Jewellery Shop 2 of 1981-2 in the Kohlmarkt, Vienna, in some of the Munari jewellery, and recently in a flat gold brooch designed in 1988 for A E Köchert in Vienna. It is both a reminder of the crucifix and, uncannily, the stylised, erotic, rear view of a woman.

Hollein has written of *Die Turnstunde* that 'The human figure is the vehicle for basic postures which show the symme-try of the body's cultic and ritual communication. From these basic presences and presentations of the female body, eroti-cism and sensuality are built up to sacred dimensions, both in the sculptural figures and in the drawings accompanying the installation.'[113] Hollein, when asked by Barbara Radice to 'explain the language' of his jewellery has also described it in terms of 'erotic ritual' stating that 'My jewellery is related to women.'[114] His metalwork is often exotic, if not always erotic; his watch for Cleto Munari is an excellent *réchauffé* of Art Deco typology, with the added ingredient of fluting and tiny steps at the strap ends which remind one of elements of Greek architecture. His gold and ruby palm tree produced as a jewel for A E Köchert in 1988 is on the other hand inspired by his own use of Nash-like palm columns in his already discussed Viennese buildings.

Hollein's use of gold is a *rappel à l'ordre* to a hierarchical colour eschewed during the Modern Movement's domination. He very early on admitted that 'Architecture is not the satisfaction of the needs of the mediocre, is not an environment for the petty happiness of the masses . . . architecture is an affair of the élite,'[115] and evidently his design has the same inflection towards élite, expensive objects. Hollein does not pretend to be concerned with everyday design, even though on occasions he has produced work such as his sunglasses which aim at the affordable end of the market. This 'affair of the élite' accords rather too well with the neoconservatism of the 1980s, and is one of the reasons why Post-Modernism is open to, and subject to attack by older Modernists. Hollein's work is very definitely not for the masses, and simply establishes a dialogue with the wealthiest sector of society.

Perhaps Hollein has become conscious of this problem, for he has written of his door handle design for FSB of 1986: 'I was attentive to the need to design a mass-consumption product that would suit not just one but several types of door.'[116] The result was three different door handles: the first was brass; the second aluminium; and the third metal with a red plastic grip. The aluminium handle resembles a stork's bill although Hollein has likened it to 'the literal form of a hand', and FSB have suggested that a variation of it 'resembled a lady's shoe.' The brass concave handle has been compared with Freud's couch; this was Hollein's commission in 1969 by the Sigmund Freud Society to turn Freud's house in Bergasse 19, Vienna, into a museum. Hollein attempted a reconstruction of the consulting room with the famous tapestry-covered couch and attendant armchair to its left, but the unavailability of the couch and armchair prevented the completion of the plan. Hollein did in the event produce a plain conventionalised version of the chair and couch, interlocked, for the Milan Triennale in 1984-5. It is true that one of Hollein's FSB designs has a similar concavity, but the comparison is rebutted by him, and he has written that 'Peter Eisenman suggested I had recreated Freud's couch. It's an entertaining allusion, but untrue. I simply wanted to furnish this particular model with the sinuosity befitting a brass fixture.'[117] What is certain is that, at least for FSB, his work is not 'micro-architecture' and he is clearly aware of the distinction between functional design and ornamental decorative art. Some of his most exotic work is purely ornamental, such as his silver and gold tower centrepiece for Cleto Munari of 1985, and *The Crystal Tower* designed for Daniel Swarovski & Co of Zürich in 1987. This latter object is in lead crystal, and topped with characteristic columns and an inverted pyramid.

Hollein is one of the most eclectic of all Post-Modern architect-designers, and he is too interested in all the arts to be either purely historicist or tied down entirely to the traditions of Vienna. It is, perhaps, this inventiveness which makes him stand out from many of the other Post-Modernists, even if on occasions his work is not as easy to understand or approach as, say, that of Portoghesi or Graves. The fact that he is somewhat isolated in Austria separates him from American Post-Modernism and Italian Neo-Modernism, and his iconography is in any case highly personal as well as referential to the longer traditions of art history.

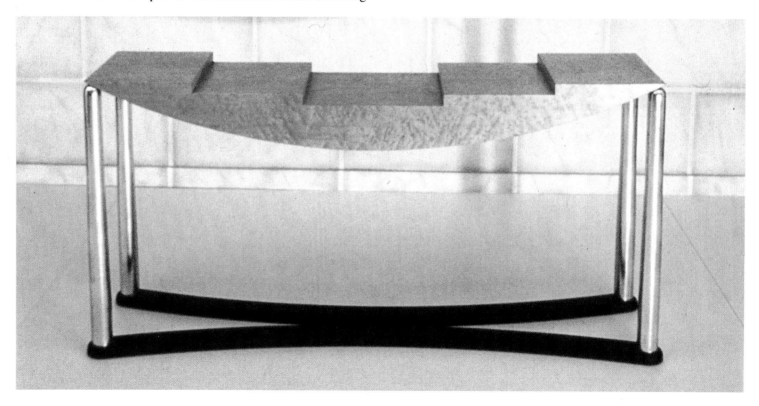

HANS HOLLEIN, *SCHWARZENBERG* TABLE, 1981 FOR MEMPHIS

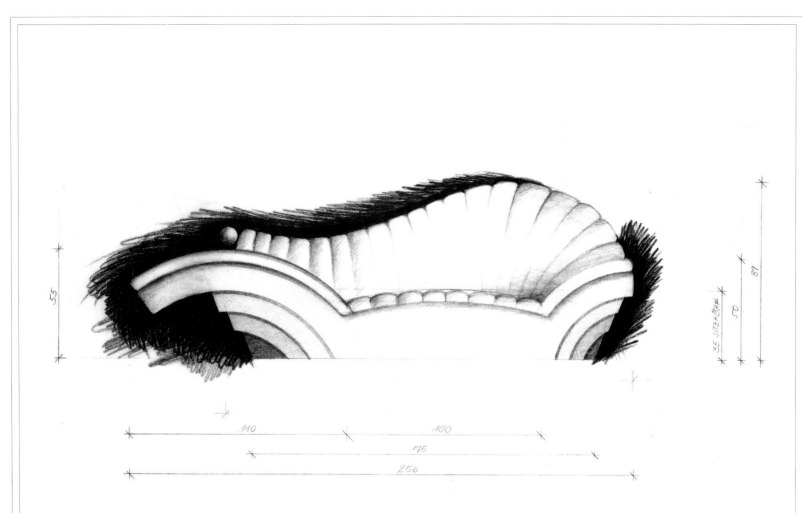

HANS HOLLEIN, STUDY FOR *MARILYN* SOFA, 1981 AND *TONDO* FRUITBOWL, 1980 FOR ROSSI & ARCANDI

HANS HOLLEIN, *MARILYN* SOFA, 1981 FOR POLTRONOVA

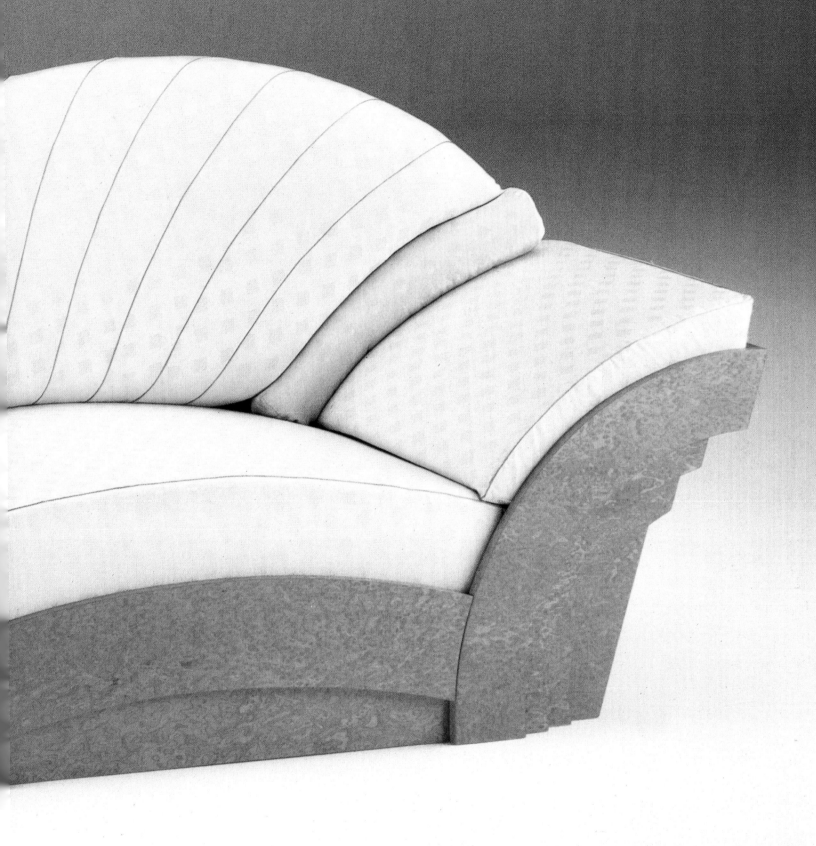

HANS HOLLEIN, *MITZI* SOFA, 1981 FOR POLTRONOVA

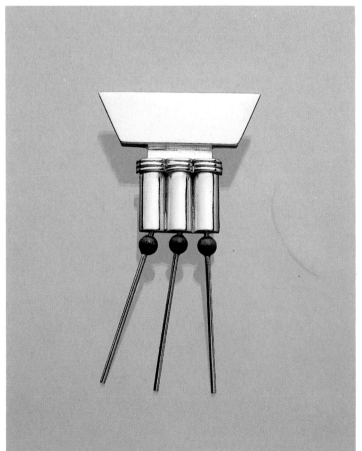

HANS HOLLEIN, JEWELLERY, 1986 FOR CLETO MUNARI

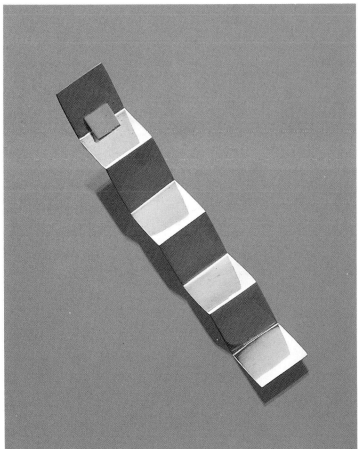
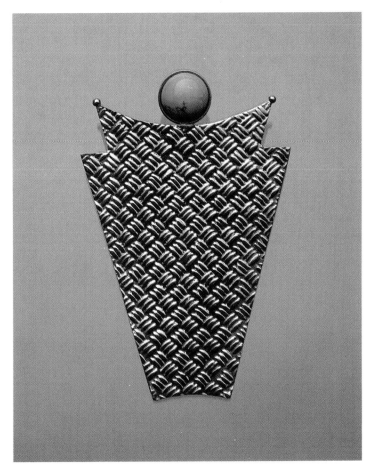

HANS HOLLEIN, JEWELLERY, 1986 FOR CLETO MUNARI

HANS HOLLEIN, *THE GYMNASTICS LESSON*, 1984

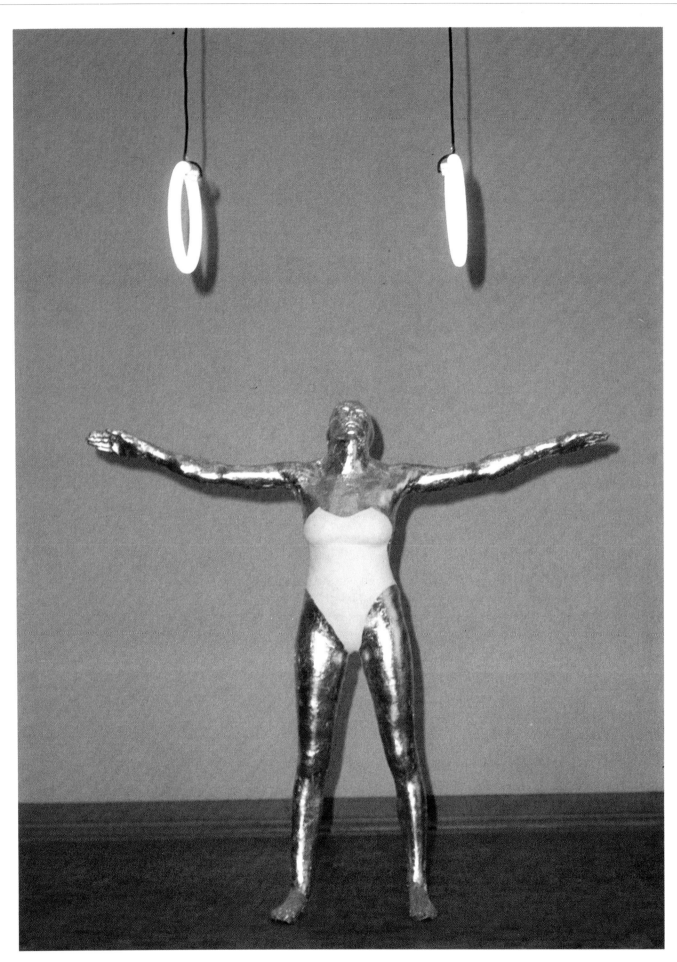

HANS HOLLEIN, *THE GYMNASTICS LESSON*, 1984

ROBERT AND TRIX HAUSSMANN, CANDLESTICK, 1985 FOR SWID POWELL

CHAPTER IX
Secondary Post-Modern Design

ROBERT AND TRIX HAUSSMANN, *STRIPES* PLATE, 1985 FOR SWID POWELL

The work of the major 'primary' Post-Modern architect designers and Neo-Modern groups such as Memphis has had a vast influence on practitioners from smaller or more isolated countries. America and Italy may dominate the language of contemporary design, but Post- and Neo-Modernism can be found in Switzerland, Belgium, Portugal, Spain, West Germany and Great Britain, as well as many other European countries. If design is a language, then it is spoken with an Italian or American accent in Europe as a whole.

Elder statesmen of Post-Modernism include Robert and Trix Haussmann, the Swiss-based husband and wife partnership established in 1967. Robert Haussmann was born in 1931 in Zurich, and his wife in 1933. Their Post-Modern Classical *Colonna* for Studio Alchymia has already been mentioned; they have been experimenting with *trompe-l'oeil* decoration since the late 1970s. They designed a wooden cupboard, *Seven Codes,* in 1978, its mirror painted with a brown and buff illusionistic trick 'fabric' which appears to 'hang' over the top of the front. In 1979-80 the Haussmanns produced a *trompe-l'oeil* installation, *Mira-Marmoreas* for Mira-X, Suhr, Switzerland. In this, a series of textiles and wood boards were decorated to imitate pink marbled rustication, or grey, veined fluting. The fabrics were printed in 1982 by Taunus textile prints at Oberuzel in Germany. The whole installation was photographed by Alfred Hablützel, with the boards and textiles on easels, and the image recalls some aspects of similar illusionism in the work of Magritte.

Optical illusion also informs two plates designed for Swid Powell. *Stripes,* in black and white, has a shimmering Op Art effect, reminding one of the work of Vasarély, while *Broken,* also in black and white, tries to trick the eye into thinking that it conforms to its title. Their *Stars,* with its gold stars on a blue field, sets up a resonance with, on the one hand, the Neo-Classicism of Schinkel, but also, tangentially with the American flag. This latter inflection is more true of their uncoloured glass of the same name for Swid Powell. Pop culture informs their *Mickey* peppermill, with its assertive 'ears' and name drawn from the ubiquitous cartoon mouse. Their candlestick, also for Swid Powell, is a jokey, inverted miniature of the stepped pyramid at Giza. A chair, the *Music Chair* of 1981, has an inverted triangular back rest; the rear of the chair has strings and a central hole to resemble a musical instrument. The whole is made of blond wood, and reminds one of Biedermeier-inspired furniture.

The Haussmanns' work is a microcosm of Post-Modern style, and embraces Pop and Op Art, Mickey Mouse, Neo-Classicism, *trompe-l'oeil* decoration and *faux marbre* ornamentalism. This eclectic, pluralistic approach is characteristic of 1980s' work.

The work of Charles Vandenhove in Belgium represents greater historicism and the *rappel à l'ordre.* He was born in 1927, and studied architecture in Brussels in 1951; he is best known for his renovation of the Hors-Château quarter in the centre of Liège, the city in which he lives. This was executed between 1978 and 1986, and is a careful combination of restoration and invention of pitched roof urban architecture. He has designed a wood table, chairs and a sideboard for Desiron & Lizenof in Liège, all of which exhibit a return to the craftsmanship and form of Arts and Crafts furniture during the first quarter of this century; they were produced in 1986.

This return to the tradition of wood can be seen in the work of Demetri Porphyrios, a British-based academic Classicist; he has produced Classically proportioned light-grey stained oak furniture for Shipping Offices, in the City of London, in 1987. The appropriately-named British architect Robert Adam also uses traditional wood. His *Pembroke* table of 1986 for Alma is not Post-Modern, but is simply Neo-Classical revival. The top is of myrtle with ebony inlay, and the legs are surmounted by decorative bronze heads. The table sets up a resonance with Regency furniture, which is perhaps why one was acquired by the V & A in 1987.

Pluralistic Post-Modernism is evident in the exotic furniture designed by Basil Al-Bayati, who, though born in Baghdad in 1946, works in London. He is steeped in the Islamic architectural tradition, and his *Tower* suite of 1987 is inspired by Persian tomb-towers, Cairo Mosques, minarets, and the balconies of Moghul palaces, to name but a few sources. In the *Wardrobe*, the West meets the Middle East, via the intervention of an Ionic capital. His is fantasy furniture, inflected towards Islamic colour and luxury.

There is much evidence that primary Post-Modernism and Memphis Neo-Modernism are having a stylistic or surface effect on designers, many of whom were only born in the 1940s and 1950s. In general their youth militates against their having had a pure Modern training; in a sense they are not capable of being apostates in the manner of Venturi, Graves or Hollein. These younger, secondary Post- and Neo-Modernists embrace the style without the theory; perhaps, as a result, their work is derivative and sometimes weak. Again, in general, this has resulted in style clichés, such as the reworking of Rossi-like cones, or Gravesian blond wood effects. Spanish and German designers have come somewhat late to the Post-Modern and Memphis feast. Germany, once at the forefront of Bauhaus and Ulm theory, and the last defender of 'good form', has only recently ventured away from Modern design. The presence of James Stirling's Neo-Classically inflected Neue Staatsgalerie in Stuttgart completed in 1984 and O M Ungers' German Architectural Museum of the same date, in Frankfurt, have no doubt been fillips in the direction of Post-Modernism, but the forays into Post-Modern design by Germans or German firms have not been entirely convincing, or without opportunism.

Secondary Post-Modernism is clearly evident in the work of Vendruscolo & Gerard, whose partnership was formed in Venice in 1985. Piero Vendruscolo was born in 1952, in Sacile, Italy, and studied engineering at Bologna University; Franklyn Gerard was born in 1959 in Montclair, New Jersey, and studied

architecture in New York and Venice. Significantly, he worked for Aldo Rossi from 1978 to 1985, and organised the exhibition of the latter's Teatro del Mondo drawings from 1979 for the Venice Biennale. From 1985 Vendruscolo and Gerard launched their *Made in Venice* lamps and clocks, usually with Rossi-like cubes or rectangles of marble, topped with pyramids of Murano glass. These pleasing, micro-architectural forms are typical of younger generation derivative work, and the same has to be said of their marble candlesticks with stepped bases in their *Stones of Venice* range. Everything from the very title of the latter range is quotation but without the strength of the Rationalist conviction of Rossi or even the deep learning of, say, Portoghesi's use of coloured marble. Their approach has been repeated in almost every art college throughout Europe.

Portuguese and Spanish work is also quite secondary, but with a liberating conviction which might be expected in countries only quite recently freed from dictatorship. In Portugal, the regime of Salazar only fell in 1974, four years after the dictator's death, while in Spain democracy was restored only after the death of Franco in 1975.

Tomás Taveira, who was born in the 1940s, is Portugal's leading Post-Modern architect and designer. He practises in his native Lisbon, where his architecture includes the Amoreiras project of housing and offices of 1981. Here he is indebted to the rather chunky vertical columns of some of Ricardo Bofill's architecture, and the blue and terracotta colours of Michael Graves. Taveira has designed furniture and ceramics, entitled *New Transfiguration*, many of which were exhibited in November 1985 at the Galeria Cómicos, Lisbon, and in September and October 1986 at the Amoreiras Shopping Centre. He has produced brightly-coloured ceramics, Memphis-like chairs with 'wings' or in one case 'ears'. This latter chair, *Transfiguration XXI*, has a bright orange and yellow back, two ear-like shapes at the top of the backrest, and asymmetrical treatment of the legs. Others are more anthropomorphic transmogrifications of the form of a man with outstretched arms, wearing a hat, into a chair with 'wings' and a triangular 'head'. Some of his 'funk' ceramics are Shire-like, with bright colours and sharp points; a few are painted in the bright green, red and orange colours of the national flag.

Alessandro Mendini has summed up Taveira's contribution by writing that 'The power of originality and a tendency to the Baroque with which his architectural work is filled is also evident in his furniture design. This is in fact a legitimately expressed quality of nouveau design which can be found throughout the world and is most contemporary. The modelling which he achieves through his own personal experimental style and links, drawing on traditional objects, techniques and forms, is not only pregnant with appeal and a multitude of questions, but is also laced with danger and something rather surrealistic.'[118]

Taveira achieves an interesting blend of tribute to the Baroque tradition of Portugal, and its craft history, and reference to both Post-Modern Classicism in his architecture and

TOMAS TAVEIRA, *TRANSFIGURED SMALL STOVE*, 1985

JO LAUBNER, *ACCENDE* TRAY, 1985 FOR WMF

Italian Neo-Modernism in his design. Though he, too, is a secondary, young Post-Modernist, there is a distinct local flavour in his work. The recent renaissance of Spanish design, particularly in Barcelona, has been spearheaded by Ricardo Bofill, the architect who has so inspired Taveira. Bofill was born in Barcelona in 1939, and founded his practice, Taller de Arquitectura, in his native city in 1960. His earlier work such as Xanadu, Calpe, of 1967, expressed an admiration for Gaudí, in its Romantic piling and asymmetry. Bofill's later buildings such as his Les Arcades du Lac, St Quentin-en-Yvelines, France, 1974-81, exhibit a massive Classicism in concrete.

Bofill is not a designer of objects, however, although other Barcelona-based architects such as Oscar Tusquets have designed extensively. Tusquets was born in Barcelona in 1941, and established his practice, Studio PER, with Lluis Clotet and others in 1964. Tusquets has complained about what he calls the 'Great Circus of the Culture of Architecture' and has stated that 'It isn't easy for Spanish Provincials like us to obtain a role in this troupe.'[119] He was, nevertheless, the only Spaniard asked to design a service for the 1983 Alessi Tea and Coffee Piazza. The result, a tea service issued in 1983 in silver, and in 1984 in electroplate, refers to shell-shapes, and goes back to the ground norm of natural form for inspiration, as well as to Gaudí's curvilinear shapes which inform so much recent work in Barcelona. The biomorphic quality also reminds one of free-flow forms in the paintings of Joan Miró.

Tusquets has designed furniture for the Barcelona firm Casas. His Varius of 1985 has a curvilinear wooden base, with bronze claw-like feet and a glass top; his Alada of 1987 is a variation with a circular glass top. Again the base reminds one of Gaudí's assertive undulations and indentations in his furniture and architecture, but without the latter's asymmetry. Much the same can be said for the Varius chair of 1985, with its eerie, skull-shaped upholstery back and spidery feet. It is a variation upon the theme of the swivel office chair, with the added intervention of Gaudí. Tusquets has recently designed jewellery for Cleto Munari. All refer to hands rather literally, and set up a resonance with Surrealism and the jewellery, sometimes based on detached body-parts, of Dali. Tusquets' necklace of 1983 ends in a pair of clasped hands which rest on the wearer's breasts; the fingers are enamelled blood red, and one 'finger' bears a diamond. A variation is a bracelet, also in gold, in the form of a circular hand, the nails again enamelled red. When asked by Barbara Radice to 'explain the language' of his jewellery, he said that 'As all my recent works, they are definitely figurative and anti-geometric'.[120]

If Tusquets draws upon Spanish traditions of Gaudí and Surrealism, then Pepe Cortès and Javier Mariscal, who often work together, may be said to be nearer a Memphis version of Neo-Modernism. Cortès was born in Barcelona in 1945, and Mariscal in Valencia in 1950. Mariscal is an artist and cartoonist, and became well known for his Hilton metal and glass trolley on wheels for Memphis in 1981. There is a hint of a homage in this to Art Deco typologies of chrome and steel trolleys, particularly the design for the Howell Company in Chicago of 1935 by Josef Hoffmann's son Wolfgang Hoffmann. Mariscal's is brighter, with a yellow handle, and a red front 'bumper' and six small wheels rather than the two larger ones in Hoffmann's design. It was highly successful, selling to 166 customers between 1981 and the end of 1986.

Since that date, Mariscal and Cortès have designed a range of Memphis-inspired lamps for BD Mueblas in Barcelona in 1986. Many have red zig-zag metal attachments which are decorative and suggest electricity; the best, called Arana, is a floor lamp of spidery form, the legs of red zig-zag steel, the body an inverted dome. Gaudí's predilection for insects – or, indeed, Bunuel's and Dali's – lives on in this rather threatening object. Mariscal and Cortès' chair, Trampolin of 1987 for Akaba, is equally strange, with its lipstick-red curved, fabric-covered backrest, seat of carved wood with buttock-shaped indentations, and steel column and base. This somewhat Surreal combination of High-Tech metal and craft wood sets up an internal irony, and juxtaposes two almost conflicting traditions, that of industrial production and carving by hand. Their sofa, MOR Sillon, and the Morsillita sofa and chair for Akaba of the same date have a Memphis-like asymmetry; the backrest of the sofa is a black upholstered 'sausage' which curves to intersect over the seat itself.

Other Spanish-born designers have found success abroad. One such is Javier Bellosillo who, though based in Barcelona, has taught in the United States and designed ceramics for Swid Powell. His dinner service, Figure of 1986, with fractured patterning of orange, yellow, blue and white, suggests a reference to Gaudí's use of broken ceramics in his architecture, especially in the Parque Güell, Barcelona in 1900. His suitably titled Nouveau has a sugar bowl with yellow, blue, red and black decoration and mushroom form which recalls some of Gaudí's strange chimneys, particularly the colourful one at the top of the watchman's house at the Parque Güell of 1911.

New Spanish design is beginning to attract more attention; for example, Liberty in London exhibited the work of many of the aforementioned designers from May until June 1988. Barcelona, in particular, has learned to speak with the Catalonian visual accent again, and not surprisingly, the work of Gaudí inspires most young designers as much as Memphis and 'hot-house' colour clearly does.

The reasons behind the late arrival of German design to Post-Modernism have already been discussed. There is a body of work by German designers and firms produced from the mid-1980s, which also forms part of secondary or derivative Post-Modernism. WMF (Wurttembergische Metallwarenfabrik Aktiengesellschaft) Design Workshop, a firm famous for its mass-produced Jugendstil designs in metal at the turn of the century have produced Post-Modern metalwork by German and Italian designers. Now they have issued candlesticks by Matteo Thun, and work by Vito Noto, Danilo Silvestrin, Jo Laubner and others. Much is unashamedly derivative of the conical emphasis in Aldo Rossi. Danilo Silvestrin was born in

1942 in Bolzano, and has worked in Florence, New York, and now Munich. His WMF silverplated tea set, *Scacco Matto* of 1985, is extraordinarily redolent of Rossi's conical-lidded Alessi metal, topped by a similar sphere. The same must be said for Lugano-born designer Vito Noto's silverplated centrepiece, *Cono* of 1984. At least the German designer Jo Laubner, who works from Frankfurt, inverts his cone in his *Focus* series of plated wine and champagne coolers, and ice bucket, of 1984.

Aldo Rossi's cone appears again in some of the furniture designs of Berghof, Landes and Rang for Draenert Studio in West Germany. Norbert Berghof was born in 1949 as was Wolfgang Rang; Michael Landes was born in 1948. All three attended the School of Architecture at the Technische Hochschule, Darmstadt, and they established their practice in 1981. Their writing bureau of 1985-6 for Draenert is an extraordinary confection of various woods, predominantly maple, with additions of marble, ivory and horn; the left 'tower' is topped by a pyramid, while the right one has a taller, gilded cone. As with all their furniture this bureau, *Franfurter Schrank I*, resounds with blond wood reference to Biedermier and German Neo-Classical furniture, with the added ingredient of a Rossi-like cone, a fashionable pyramid, polychromy in the sense of a rich mixture of materials, and a micro-architectural quality overall. Their armchair, *Frankfurter Stuhl F3* of 1985 to 1986, is also of maple, with marquetry stars, no doubt derived from Michael Graves' work via Schinkel. Another design, a cupboard entitled *Frankfurter Schrank F2* of 1986, has a combination of maple and ebony, and a top section of blond wood on four ebonised columns, complete with ten small bulbs under the top section which is a direct tribute to Graves' *Stanhope* bed for Memphis of 1982, where a similar form is used above the headboard. Such secondary Post-Modern work is visually satisfying, but not exempt from the charge of near plagiarism. Such a charge is highly complicated because primary architects such as Graves and Rossi are themselves derivative, as this is part of the Post-Modern process. The danger here is that Post-Modern work is rapidly becoming a style, with those born in the 1940s and 1950s simply imitating Post-Modern surface without any hard-won theory behind their gestures. In fact, little work produced in Germany, except that by Thun for WMF, has much originality. Thun has been partly discussed, especially for his concept of the 'Baroque Bauhaus'. This oxymoron is serviced in his Morris and Jugendstil-inspired trays for WMF which combine Victorian and Art Nouveau patterning with Neo-Modern metalwork; the same is true of his *Hommage à Madonna* cutlery for WMF of 1985-6. The knife, fork and spoon all have modern forms at their useful ends, while the handles of black plastic have four different 'rings' round them, reminding one of the fashion initiated by American pop singer Madonna for such excesses of jewellery. In crude terms, the handles are 'Baroque' and the bowl of the spoon, tines of the fork and the blade of the knife are 'Bauhaus'–Functional. His work is not mimetic of architecture, of Rossi, Graves, or other Post-Modernists, and is all the

better for it.

Post-Modern design as a whole has attempted a return to symbolism, metaphor, wit and reference. This is all highly welcome in domestic items which are decorative. The new Pluralism is possible in furniture and the decorative arts, but it is much less plausible when it comes to the design of an aeroplane, motor car, tractor or micro-chip. Apart from applied or surface decoration, these objects, regardless of scale, are subject to an evolving technology. Both Neo- and Post-Modernism have a high 'art' content that can be applied to the exterior of industrial design, but have little contribution to make to the workings of artefacts or machinery itself. Post-Modern design may not change technical services one whit, but can perhaps be a selling point of 'style'. Large-scale product design, especially if it moves, like a train or car, is not going to be inspired by symbolism or metaphor more suited to the domestic environment. There are a few examples of Neo- and Post-Modern washing machines, refrigerators, and telephone boxes, and they are worthy of examination as case studies of larger scale design.

Indesit, who for a long time have produced washing machines and refrigerators of the regular, white box variety, have launched a washing machine of usual box form but with applied decoration by Ottavio Missoni. This machine, called *Missi,* was a success on the Italian market before becoming available in Britain from June 1987. *Missi* has a worktop of pink, light green and pastel blue lozenge pattern, while the door is the usual circle, now coloured blue with a pink handle, and the control panel is light green. Ottavio (Tai) Missoni was born in 1921 in Trieste, and is best known for his Milanese knitware shop and fashion design. It is thus hardly surprising that the lozenged top of Missi reminds one of Missoni's patterns.

If the Indesit machine is Italian Neo-Modern, then the Zanussi *Wizard* range of refrigerators of the same year, 1987, is an attempt at Post-Modern form. While the Indesit simply has colour applied to a modern box, Zanussi have produced a new shape. The *Wizard* was designed by Roberto Pezzetta, who was born in Treviso in 1946, and is now in charge of Zanussi's design department. As with so many other young designers born in the 1940s and 1950s discussed in this chapter, he is obviously indebted to Aldo Rossi's work. The form of the *Wizard*, with its squat pyramidal top surmounted by a flag, is rather obviously a homage to Rossi's Teatro del Mondo in Venice. The latter structure has inspired many designers, as we have seen, including the Bureau du Théâtre du Monde by the otherwise ultra-Modern designer Philippe Starck. The *Wizard* also bears a slight resemblance to the Rolls Royce radiator form, especially in the two slatted versions. Although it is an attractive object, the *Wizard* contains something of a formula for Post-Modern surface style; take a Rolls Royce radiator, Rossi's work, put a flag on top and, finally, add marbled or flecked paint. The *Wizard* is available in just such a marbled finish. On a more positive level, the design of kitchen machinery has not changed much since the late 1950s in terms

MATTEO THUN, TRAYS, 1986 FOR WMF *LA GALLERIA*

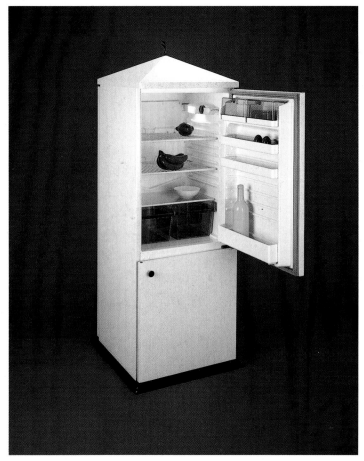

ROBERTO PEZZETTA, *WIZARD* REFRIGERATORS, 1987 FOR ZANUSSI AND OTTAVIO MISSONI, *MISSI* WASHING MACHINE, 1987 FOR INDESIT

of style, and Vance Packard's observation about style obsolescence has been noted earlier. Not since the round-edged designs of the 50s has anything except a straight-edged, usually white refrigerator been available. Zanussi are no doubt aware of 'style obsolescence' and have written in their brochure announcing the *Wizard* that 'Superseded entirely is the traditional concept of the refrigerator as a simple, white box-shape made to match the rest of the kitchen furniture or disappear inside a fitted unit. With *The Wizard's Collection* Zanussi enters the magic realm of Post-Modern style. The role of the refrigerator has evolved from that of a mere performer of a functional task (a household appliance for conserving food) to its new status as the focus of attention in the decorative design of the domestic environment.'[121] The fashionable Rossi-like form and flecked paint used on some versions of the *Wizard* conform to the new ornamentalism which is part of the Pluralism of the 1980s.

Similar flecked paint has been produced by Macpherson since 1963, primarily for industry. They launched a large selection of multi-coloured finishes in their *Portaflek* range in 1988, giving a greater fillip to the domestic use of such paint. With suitably named colours such as *Milano*, *Napoli*, *Melba* and *Butterscotch*, the paint finish resembles the fashionable *faux marbre* of Abet Laminate, Memphis, the work of Robert and Trix Haussmann, and Venturi's marbled *Notebook* ceramic for Swid Powell. Uncannily, the Macpherson catalogue includes a photograph of three Rossi-like cabinets, with pyramidal tops and a flag between them, all painted in different versions of Portaflek. Such an image almost becomes a Post-Modern cliché and one supposes that there is not much more mileage for any further, similar style gestures. The pyramid and the flag have rapidly become as hackneyed in the 1980s as the flat roof and tubular steel appeared to be in the 1930s.

There have been few examples of Post-Modern street furniture, perhaps because symbolism is more befitting to the domestic environment of the interior. The merit of a telephone box design is subject to as much debate as architecture itself, primarily because it is as public. Few can agree on the design of new phone booths, as has been witnessed in Britain in 1988 with the controversy surrounding the removal of most of the excellent red booths. These were based on a design of 1924 by Sir Giles Gilbert Scott; his booth set up a resonance with the work of Sir John Soane, with its roof in part based on the four segmental arches of the breakfast-parlour in the latter's house at 13 Lincoln's Inn Fields of 1812-13. Scott, who was a highly learned architect, became a Life Trustee of the Sir John Soane Museum in 1925, a year after the telephone box design.

Paradoxically, in the Post-Modern 1980s, these aesthetically perfect but somewhat elderly boxes were all replaced, bar a token few, by British Telecom. In their place are glass phone boxes of an indifferent design, which one would have thought more in keeping with 1960s 'good form' than the design style of 1988.

One of the tenets of Thatcherite Conservatism has been to break the mould of restrictive practices and monopoly to encourage competition and choice. The British Government has allowed Mercury Communications to compete with British Telecom, and Mercury has entered the arena with three different designs for alternative telephone boxes for their own system. All have a more positive corporate identity than the British Telecom glass box, and carry the distinctive Mercury logo of an 'M' based roughly on Art Deco precedents.

Three types have been developed. The first, known as *Classical*, was designed in 1988 by the Bloomsbury-based architect John Simpson, who has also projected an alternative, Neo-Classical scheme for the controversial redevelopment of Paternoster Square near Wren's St Paul's Cathedral in London. Simpson's booth for Mercury is of cast aluminium and has Doric columns, and a pedimented roof which has in its centre the Art Deco 'M' logo for the company in a circle flanked by two sphinxes. The second box, known as *Totem* or *Art Deco*, is less assertive, and was designed by London-based design consultants Fitch & Company. The third design is for a doorless wall-mounted booth, and is known as the *Ogee Pylon* or *Conservatory*; the canopy is of ogee form, reminiscent of elements taken from metal and glass neo-Victorian conservatories, which are now so fashionable. This has the Art Deco-inspired 'M' surmounted by appropriate conventionalised wings at its crest. As with the other boxes, it is made from aluminium. The *Ogee Pylon* was designed by Francis Machin and Alan Camp, partners in Machin Architects in London, in consultation with one of Britain's leading Post-Modern architects, Terry Farrell. Farrell, who was born in Manchester in 1938, became well known for his Post-Modern TV-am building in London of 1982-3, for which he also designed lighting fixtures; he also collaborated with Charles Jencks on the design of the latter's own Thematic House in London. The bright aluminium and blue of these boxes is eye-catching, and they have more individuality than the Telecom glass booths. However, they have offended one diehard 'good form' designer, Kenneth Grange, who has said, 'Why can't a modern phone box be modern? They're so crass, so nasty . . . They're all horrific. Why on earth do they have to make such comic-opera versions of post-modern design?'[122]

PIERO VENDRUSCOLO AND FRANKLYN GERARD, ENSEMBLES OF *MADE IN VENICE* LAMPS, 1985

PIERO VENDRUSCOLO AND FRANKLYN GERARD, *REGATA, CODUSSI, TORRE TRAVERTINA* AND *FARO* LAMPS, 1985 FOR *MADE IN VENICE*

MATTEO THUN, STUDY FOR *HOMMAGE A MADONNA*, 1986 FOR WMF, AND PEPPER-POT, APPETIZER HOLDER, TOOTHPICK HOLDER AND
SALT SHAKER, 1982 FOR MEMPHIS

MATTEO THUN, *ESPRIT* TRAY, 1986 FOR WMF *LA GALLERIA*

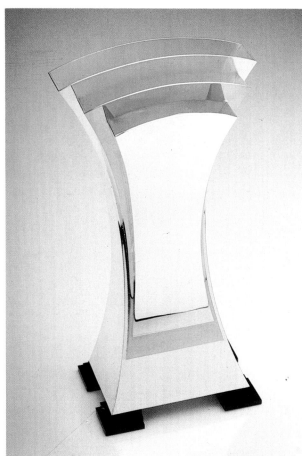

JO LAUBNER, *DOMUS* DRINKS ACCESSORIES, *BABYLON GREETINGS* VASE AND *FOCUS* CHAMPAGNE BUCKET, 1984-85 FOR WMF

JO LAUBNER. *CASTELLO* TRAY AND NAPKIN HOLDERS. 1984-85 FOR WMF *LA GALLERIA*

TERRY FARRELL, TV-AM RECEPTION DESK, 1981-82, ARCHITECT'S OWN OFFICES, 1980-81 AND LIMEHOUSE STUDIOS, 1982-83

TERRY FARRELL, TV-AM HOSPITALITY ROOM AND LOUNGE, 1981-82

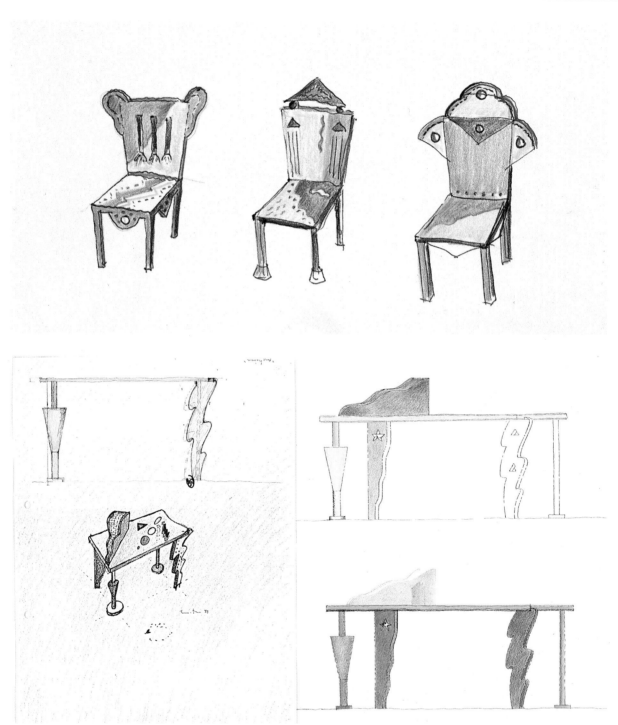

TOMAS TAVEIRA, STUDIES FOR *TRANSFIGURED CHAIRS AND TABLES* , 1985

New Transfiguration

Tomás Taveira has come to be recognised as the Portuguese representative of the now fully fledged Post-Modern movement in architecture. The power of originality and a tendency to the Baroque with which his architectural work is filled is also evident in his furniture design. This is in fact a legitimately expressed quality of *nouveau* design which can be found throughout the world and is most contemporary.

The modelling which he achieves through his own personal experimental style and links, drawing on traditional objects, techniques and forms, is not only pregnant with appeal and a multitude of questions, but is also laced with danger and something rather Surrealistic. This is a kind of means of 'redesigning' which produces all kinds of new visual effects, is a transfiguration of the spirit of Portugal which rests in the earth, and has all kinds of hidden possibilities for the future. I myself consider this 'ceremonial' quality of unimaginable attachment expressive of a future form of man's religious instincts which clearly can be seen in formal dress and a large canopy.

Alessandro Mendini

TOMAS TAVEIRA, *TRANSFIGURED BOOKCASE AND TABLE*, 1985

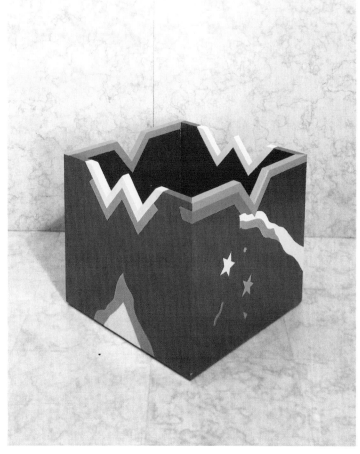

TOMAS TAVEIRA, *SYLVIA* CHAIR, FILING CABINET, BOX AND PITCHER, 1985

TOMAS TAVEIRA, *FORUM* CHAIR, 1985

LUCIEN STEIL, DESIGN FOR A BOOKCASE, 1987

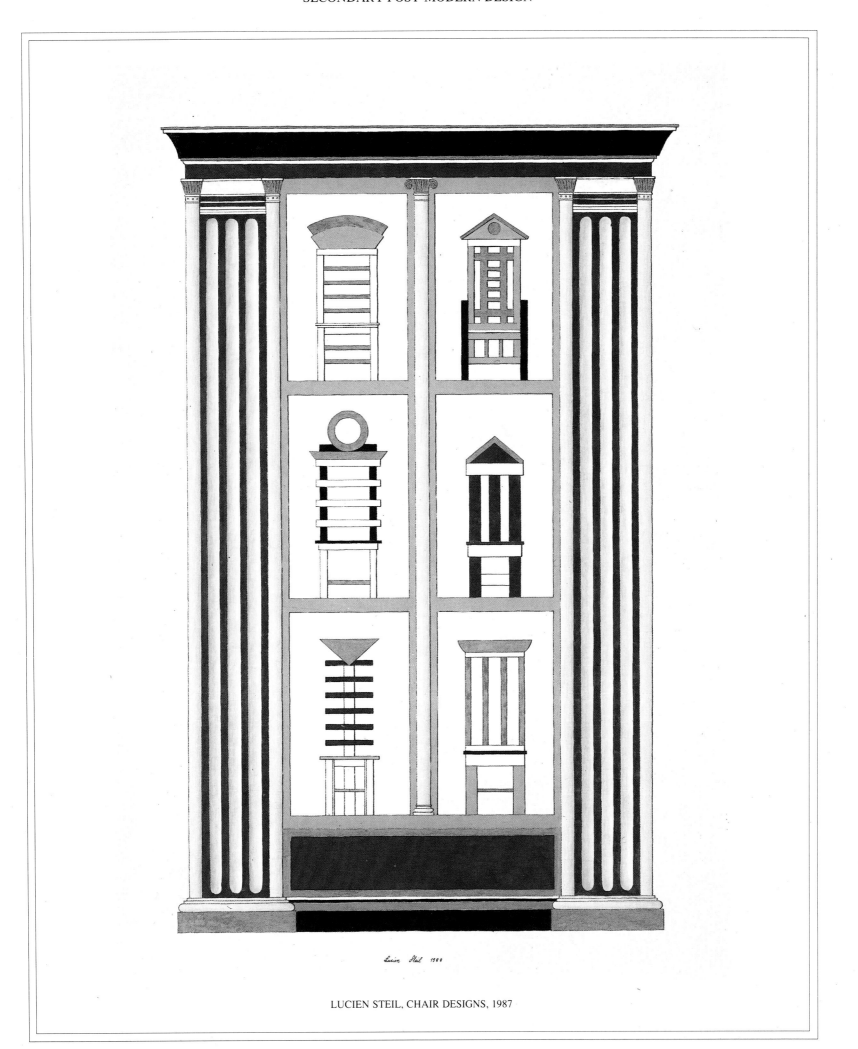

LUCIEN STEIL, CHAIR DESIGNS, 1987

ROBERT ADAM, *PEMBROKE TABLE*, 1986 FOR ALMA

BASIL AL-BAYATI, *THE PALM SUITE* DINING TABLE AND CHAIRS, 1987

ALESSANDRO MENDINI, *TEA & COFFEE PIAZZA*, 1979-83 FOR ALESSI

Conclusion

Mercury Communications require a telephone booth which clearly announces their system; so they need to stress difference. The new booths must resemble neither the red G G Scott ones, nor the Telecom 'dumb' box, but instead must demonstrate a distinctive and positive 'house style'. As so often, stylistic difference reflects an economic imperative, in this case the tenet of Thatcherism: that it is beneficial to break the mould of an entrenched monopoly, and its attendant stranglehold over policy and pricing.

The Modern Movement itself can be seen as having become such a monopoly, its power vested in an oligopoly of an educated, white, middle-class élite, protected by academics, and enshrined in its own literature. By the 1960s Modernism had become repetitive and self-perpetuating and serious charges were levelled against it: that it had become close to the very totalitarianism it once professed to oppose, and Stalinist in its hounding of enemies and competitors such as Expressionism and Art Deco. As with Christianity, Modernism was a salutary force in opposition, but overbearing in triumph when it entered the period of the crusades.

Cultural historians, such as the German Hans Evers, have observed that pluralism and eclecticism are the backcloth of every epoch; when viewed from within that longer historical context, Modernism's purge is just so much railing against the tides. The return to Eclecticism as a cultural norm is not, however, without its accompanying dangers. The resultant orgy has become too gaudy, perhaps an over-reaction to the joys of liberation after all those decades of repression. Post-Modernism has itself become somewhat overbearing. It revels too much in the apparent triumph of capitalism over socialism, and the reign of the haves over the have-nots.

The relearning of history is not an easy process. Frequently, as a result, historical reference only takes place at a surface level, without a thorough examination of content. The more superficial kinds of Post-Modern design are often just nostalgia, dressed up and marketed history. Just as, in the nineteenth century, AWN Pugin and William Morris romanticised the Middle Ages and saw their beauty without the foul stench, so some Post-Modernists look at the Renaissance in a purblind manner, ignoring the religious wars, or squint at a Neo-Classicism censored of the guillotine and The Terror. This sterilised history is a euphoric distortion: the art without the history and the style with the misery subtracted. Only such a partial view may allow for the reverence paid to, and mimesis made of, Victorian housing typologies, without their squalor, lack of sanitation and rigid hierarchies.

Post-Modernism's use of history carries further dangers in that the version of history drawn from is one frequently perceived as masculinist, personality-centred and heavily inscribed by the victors. The Post-Modernists often rely on a construction of the past which serves to accent these inflections, contributing to the continued repression of, for example, women's history, and the traditions of underclass and minorities reinstated by the social historians.

The appropriation of Kitsch and its more sophisticated cousin, Camp, also brings a caveat. Along with the use of third and fourth world motifs, these borrowings are not immune from the charge of cultural imperialism, an accusation increasingly levelled by the 'without hyphen' Postmodernists of resistance against neoconservative Post-Modernism. What may be seen as a sociologically tenable gesture by the designer can be attacked as a form of pillage by the critic. It is too early to offer a confident assessment of the contribution of Post-Modern design as it is still an unfinished chapter, only measurable as a work in progress. On the one hand, Post-Modern design is a luxury, Hollein's 'affair of the élite', and in parallel with so much art, becomes a high-style escapism – a sunrise over a shell-holed landscape. More optimistically, the Pluralism within Post-Modernism may bear witness to a maturing desire for religious and racial, as well as cultural tolerance. Equal opportunity, however difficult to realise, is a healthy aspiration; the risk could only come with the exclusive triumph of the Post-Modern view, in the unchallenged victory of its particular version of freedom and choice. Post-Modern work should, ideally, coexist with all other forms of visual language, colourful or otherwise, in the exploding diversity of Global Villages.

—— * ——

MICHAEL GRAVES, CARPET FOR VORWERK, 1988 WITH FURNITURE BY HANS HOLLEIN

POST-MODERNISM AND CONSUMER DESIGN
Volker Fischer

MARIO VIVALDI, *SOLO* CUTLERY, 1985 FOR WMF *AMBIENTE*

In architecture, Post-Modernism has now been with us for a quarter of a century. What once was hailed as an act of liberation from the dictates of faceless functionalism, a refreshing and imaginative rediscovery of a rich panoply of historical traditions is now in danger of deteriorating into a superficial reworking of existing trends – an aping of current fashions. 'Everywhere you look you find sad evidence of half-baked novelty and hasty shifts of position. A spirit of opportunism is rife.'[1]

Fortunately, developments in furniture and product design are running in the opposite direction, and there is now an increased subtlety in the appearance of everyday objects which comes from a fusion of emotion and stylistic multivalency with historical references. Even firms committed to the classic Modernism and *bel disegno* of the 50s, 60s and 70s, such as Cassina, Zanotta, B&B and Knoll, have been including Post-Modernist forms among their products since about 1975. However Post-Modern interiors still tend to be dominated by one-offs or limited editions – an indication that the prevailing view is that furniture with a high semantic content can only really survive in the market as an *objet d'art*.

While the most visible new influence on product design has been the Post-Modern innovations of groups such as Alchymia and Memphis, other contemporary styles such as High-Tech have also had some effect. More and more utilitarian objects now exhibit an additive approach towards design, rather than the integrated method favoured by functionalism. In products deemed to have a mechanical 'inner life' – such as clocks and radios, pocket calculators, coffee machines, even irons and vacuum cleaners – this additive aesthetic is applied in conjunction with techniques that miniaturise various building forms. On the other hand, in tableware – coffee and tea services, trays, crockery, centrepieces, vases, candlesticks, bowls and cutlery – the only limits to the additive approach appear to be those set by the inherent material properties of the glass, china or metal that the object is made of.

For the first time since the 1920s, there is widespread evidence of a demanding approach to form and style which aims to give a higher profile to the identity of the manufacturers and designers involved whilst raising the aesthetic status of the objects themselves. In Italy they already have a name for these small, specially conceived objects – micro-architecture.[2] It is a very apt term for a kind of product whose design and appearance owes much to architectural thinking, reflecting an interplay of different scales and an alternating logic in its constituent parts.

Given this, it's hardly surprising that the principal achievers in this field have turned out to be architects, from Post-Modernist heroes like Graves, Hollein, Tigerman and Venturi, through the Memphis group's Sottsass and Thun, to Late-Modernists like Meier or Gwathmey and Siegel.

The innovations in tableware design – or 'tabletops', to use the American term – first began around 1980 with a project by Officina Alessi, the avant-garde department of the Italian metalware firm Alessi. Following a suggestion by Alessandro Mendini, eleven internationally famous architects and designers were commissioned to design 'tea and coffee piazzas'. The resulting works – by Venturi, Graves, Tigerman, Jencks, Meier, Rossi, Portoghesi, Mendini, Yamashita, Hollein and Tusquets – were produced in limited editions of 99, each set costing around £11,000, and launched simultaneously across two continents at the Brera in Milan and the Max Protech Gallery in New York. This quasi-endorsement of a product by a cultural institution is in itself a sort of aesthetic upgrading. For the first time in many years the same design principles are being claimed for both architecture and industrial design. Thus the term 'piazza' refers to a spatially defined configuration of coffee pot, tea pot, sugar bowl and milk jug.

Matteo Thun (a founder-member of Memphis and now, with Ettore Sottsass and Andrea Branzi, the most successful Post-Modernist product designer in Italy) has been designing a series of now almost classic ceramic objects since the early 1980s. His 1981 collection for Memphis included cups, vases and tea and coffee pots whose emotive, often spindly-legged forms seemed a cross between Mayan/Egyptian slang and the anthropomorphic figures of lizards, dinosaurs and birds. Over roughly the same period he has been producing lamps, glass objects and cupboards for Italian firms such as Sottsass Associati, Alessio Sari, Barovier & Toso, Bieffeplast, and the German firm Quartett.[3]

Thun belongs to the new network of young 'iconophiles' who believe that different cultural spheres can merge to form a single semiotic continuum. Fashion turns into graphics, graphics into design, design into architecture, and architecture into film. In the process, reality overlaps with the interpretation of reality and soon facts are indistinguishable from opinions and commentaries. The power of the image has suppressed the power of reality, at least in the forming of aesthetic standards. Indeed any distinctions between facts, opinions, symbols and attitudes appear arbitrary and conservative in a post-industrial society which offers such a heterogeneous range of experiences. Designers should accept this 'semantic chaos', says Thun, but they should also try to give it some structure.

Following Ettore Sottsass, but very much in his own independent vein, Thun is attempting to develop a language of product design that is rich in references without being nostalgic. He mixes historical styles, but in strange, inventive ways that give his work a contemporary look. Thun's products stand for a changed perception of what a large firm can – and indeed should – put on the market.

One reason for this change of image is that the markets for the usual mass-produced articles are largely saturated and a firm's share cannot easily be expanded. On the other hand, there is a new market consisting of young consumers who are interested in individualistic design. Firms are recognising that there is money to be made from supplementing – if not

replacing – products with a neutral image with aesthetically upgraded post-industrial products which draw on various languages, traditions and behavioural patterns. In Matteo Thun's words, the industry needs to renew itself 'on the basis of the culture which that industry itself helped create'. For such a process to take place it is necessary to have a period of economic prosperity. In the last twenty years the number of high-income earners in West Germany has, on average, increased 40-fold (in spite of unemployment standing around two million) and, in contrast to the past, the added value created by economic activity is not being saved but spent on 'life-style' objects. According to the sociologist Erich Fromm, there has been a shift since the end of the 1960s from a 'culture of being' to a 'culture of having'. The print media confirm this return to an acquisitive culture with headlines such as 'Hooked on Luxury' or 'The Joys of Consumption'. There is a new social phenomenon: the rise of a consumer élite which is 'gradually taking on the structure of a separate class, united by a cult of the good life and a concern with the outward symbols of prosperity'. The 'approved' symbols of conspicuous good taste now included – as well as clothes, jewellery, homes and travel – designer tableware.

In addition to designing, Matteo Thun has also acted as a corporate identity consultant to a number of rather conservative West German firms over the past few years. Apparently we have him to thank for the restructuring of some of their product ranges.

One interesting case is the old established firm, of WMF (Württemburgische Metallwarenfabrik), probably the world's biggest manufacturer of metal household wares and cutlery. The firm's only previous venture into contemporary avant-garde design had been in 1927, when it set up a 'New Arts and Crafts Department' as a place where artists could experiment with craft-design as an alternative to regular mass production. The war brought an end to the department but now, over the past two or three years, a small number of designers have once again set about changing, or at least extending, the image of WMF. Besides Matteo Thun, they include Jo Laubner, Angelo Cortesi, Mario Vivaldi, Vito Noto, Franz Otto Lipp and Danilo Silvestrin.

1985 marked the appearance of the first of the *La Galleria* range of household artefacts, which now includes wine coolers, ice buckets, trays, vases, candle holders and table centrepieces – every imaginable small object to enhance the living environment. All are made of silver, brass, acrylic or marble. In terms of style they strike a balance between the cool Neo-Modernism of the East Coast of the United States and a Memphis-style narrative symbolism. The tectonics and construction of the objects show clearly in the visual separation of the various parts – plates are supported by small pillars, spheres link pyramids and cubes, rods and cylinders. What strikes the eye is a merging of forms strongly reminiscent of the work of Alchymia and Memphis, which contrasts strongly with the mass-produced, compact style of Modernism and the

MATTEO THUN, TRAYS, 1985 FOR WMF *LA GALLERIA*

TOP TO BOTTOM, L TO R: JO LAUBNER, TRAYS, ANGELO CORTESI, CANDLESTICKS, MATTEO THUN, *HOMMAGE A MADONNA* CUTLERY AND
HELMUT WARNEKE, CUTLERY, 1985 ALL FOR WMF

integrative approach of Functionalism. Nevertheless, each designer uses an individual language of forms. Jo Laubner either adapts Art Deco, designing objects that look like 1930s American skyscrapers, or uses the language of Hollein. Matteo Thun coalesces contrasting epochs, as could be expected from his 1986 aphoristic manifesto, *The Baroque Bauhaus,* which called for not only a new language of myth to replace that of logic, but also a new design dynamic with interchangeable parameters capable of maintaining a dialogue with fashion. In stylistic terms the paradox 'Baroque Bauhaus' means the combination of rich, courtly gilded ornament with the puritanical formal discipline of classic Modernism. Seeing the carefree way Californian and Japanese designers borrow from the mass media, such as the cinema and advertising, Thun urges Europeans to follow suit, and enrich their design with a 'breath of fresh Pacific air'.[5] The work of the other new designers at WMF also reveals a closeness to architectural thinking. Angelo Cortesi relates complete architectural narratives in his objects, whereas Danilo Silvestrin and Vito Noto seem to have found an archaic language similar to that of Aldo Rossi's famous espresso coffee pots. Franz Otto Lipp and Mario Vivaldi, too, are committed to a similar archaic combination of primary forms.

Recently WMF has attempted to expand its production of 'life-style' objects to a larger market. The results – partly because of the necessity for low cost and mass distribution – show clear signs of compromise in their design. The company plans to produce Jo Laubner's neon-coloured *Domus* table service and Matteo Thun's new *La Galleria* trays in runs of 60,000 to 100,000 each. Thun's trays have Memphis-style handles attached to a patterned surface inspired variously by floral Jugendstil, William Morris, Pop Art or High-Tech. Although the colours used are Post-Modern, they are remarkably close to East Asian pastel shades. The restrained pink of the 'Flora' pattern, for example, gives a contemporary stamp to a design that succeeds, through its formal severity, in combining the richness of floral chinoiserie with the reductionist geometry of Josef Hoffmann. Despite making use of reminiscences of the past, Thun frees himself from the metaphors involved, so avoiding lapsing into mere nostalgia and achieving a coincidence of opulence and restraint; in other words, Baroque Bauhaus!

Even WMF's classic cutlery division is proving susceptible to the mechanisms of the new markets and increased design expectations. Mario Vivaldi was the first designer in West Germany to make a Post-Modern decorative cutlery set. The handles of the knives, forks and spoons in his *Solo* series, part of WMF's new *Ambiente* range, are decorated with an inset semi-circle and a line in the direction of the stem. As the semi-circle on the knives is the other way round to that on the forks, the two complement each other on the table and form a complete circle. Apparently it took a long series of tests to find a means of fixing the decoration to the metal. The motif on the cutlery is similar to the Abet laminates used by the Memphis group and its followers. But even without the decoration, this metal cutlery displays a greater formal tension than usual cutlery. The 'anti-classical' basic form, inspired by Hollein, Graves and Isozaki, is most striking in the versions with coloured stems. While some of the other elements in the *Ambiente* range are nothing more than unremarkable variations on the usual conservative spectrum of cutlery design, Matteo Thun's *Hommage à Madonna* really catches the eye. It's a showbiz style, in matt black with gold decorations, alluding to the pop star's early penchant for decorative chains – everything from dog chains to sado-masochistic shackles – in gold, silver, brass and tin. Depending on how you see them, the handles look like either big, fat black cigars or the podgy fingers of a *mafioso* boss, encrusted with opulent rings in different styles. The message is clear: the underworld and the world of showbiz are often not so far apart – something which has been obvious to us all at least since old Blue Eyes' connections became known. It is a cutlery which goes beyond all normal conceptions of what cutlery should be, displaying a mixture of nonchalance and heavy symbolism, a combination of extravagance, cool eroticism and mannered self-confidence.

Thun's glasses in the *Sherry Netherlands* range for Quartett are related stylistically to his early anthropomorphic ceramics and – like the highly praised objects produced by the Czech Borek Sipek for the same firm – they push the techniques of glassblowing to their limits.

Quartett was originally founded as a licensed manufacturer producing goods for the German market, but it has since undertaken the production of its own designs, including some by the owner of the firm himself. Since 1986, it has also been associated in a kind of trust of French, Italian, British and Spanish avant-garde design groups. Design, production, selling, distribution and advertising are tending to become integrated activities in a blurring of boundaries made possible only by the existence of separate sub-markets for the goods. In addition to glass and ceramics, Quartett also makes cupboards and upholstered furniture. Because the large manufacturers have yet to finance any experimental departments of their own, Quartett seems certain to achieve fairly rapid financial success not only in Germany, but abroad as well.

In 1987 Matteo Thun designed a china service called *Fantasia* for Arzberg. It includes a pot which slots into the cup to form an almost geometrical sphere. In 1984 the American firm Swid Powell came onto the scene with a 54-piece collection of china, crystal and silver tableware. Here, too, the owners of the firm had taken the considered step of engaging 'the most glittering stars in the firmament of contemporary architecture'. It is hardly surprising, therefore, that more than 20 percent of the collection has since been selected for the permanent design collection of the Metropolitan Museum of Art in New York. The firm now makes more than 100 products, employing not only important contemporary American architects like Michael Graves, Robert Venturi, Stanley Tigerman, Robert Stern and Gwathmey-Siegel but also non-American, internationally known figures such as Hans Hollein, Arata Isozaki, Ettore Sottsass and the Haussmanns.

Models, symbols and motifs are used extensively in these works, which are in fact micro-architectures expressing the stylistic beliefs that their designers have worked out in their buildings; the architectonic 'hallmarks' give the products an additional 'aura'. The Post-Modern predilection for decoration hasn't prevented some of these objects from being easy to use, but others have so much ornament that they seem stultified, almost like traditional collectors' plates. In addition to these ceramics, Swid Powell also makes silver tableware which draws on the language of architecture, just like the current ranges of WMF and Alessi.

Vittorio Gregotti's tray, the Haussmanns' candlesticks, Richard Meier's table objects and Robert Stern's salt and pepper shakers and candlesticks are examples of a sumptuous tableware which, like Alessi's tea and coffee piazzas, goes back to the rich traditions of 1920s and 30s silver tableware. In addition, Robert Venturi and Stanley Tigerman/Margaret McCurry have designed china services for Swid Powell which are, iconographically, straight small architectures. The pots and bowls in Venturi's service have architectural motifs, and would look almost 'normal' if he hadn't painted them in an alienating, Pop Art style. Tigerman and McCurry, on the other hand, have produced miniature versions of certain traditional architectural forms of the American flatlands, turning the Midwest grain elevator, for example, into an elegant icon through a kind of sarcastic inversion. Their aesthetic strategy is particularly evident in the salt and pepper shakers, which need to be put together to reveal a full motif: the combining of the two surfaces in one single, colourful plane.

An attempt to continue the Wiener Werkstätte tradition is being made by the Viennese painter and sculptress Heide Warlamis, who set up a small manufacturing concern – a kind of family firm – in Austria around three years ago. The firm produces architecturally inspired china objects in limited editions. Its *Secession* bowls and *Skyscraper* and *Metropolitan Tower* vases have very distinctive combinations of external form and appliqué. But while the first two still attempt to make a logical connection between the stepped, sculptural forms of the china objects and the vertical architectural decorations applied to them, the *Metropolitan Tower* combines them in a way that is surreal – even by the standards of the Memphis doctrine of the independence of form and function, material and decoration. The crackled pattern on the first vase might equally well have been designed by Sottsass, Thun or Nathalie du Pasquier, whereas the decoration on the second vase is like the painting of the *Neue Wilden,* or, if you still care to read it architecturally, the projects of Coop Himmelblau. The *Siena* salt and pepper sets and the *Skala* oil and vinegar sets are again variations on these two themes: one set displays a Hoffmannesque black and white reductionist aesthetic, while the other comes across as Pop Art-like, almost a paraphrase of Venturi's little houses for Swid Powell. However, perhaps because of

their techniques of production, the lines of Warlamis' objects are often too 'soft', in an architectural sense, for them to be considered as one-to-one representations of architecture. (It seems that objects in noble metals are better suited to this purpose.)

In contrast, the materials and techniques used in the next series of small objects allow them a full range of architectural expression. The marble table lamps of Franklyn Gerard and Piero Vendruscolo – both pupils of Aldo Rossi – are sharp-edged square or upright rectangular 'houses' resting on four small spherical feet, with window forms cut into all sides. They have an inner core out of which rises a second house form, a translucent, stepped pyramid that allows light to shine through the openings in the outer stone skin as though through lit-up windows. One of the lamps doubles as a clock. The influence of Rossi's and Ungers' reduction of archetypes is obvious, but there is an additional quality deriving from the translucency of thinly cut marble. In this respect, some versions of the lamp are reminiscent of the work of Carlo Scarpa, who has been attempting to reactivate the luminous qualities of marble in memory of medieval traditions of handwork.

Two further table clocks show that differing convictions or strategies of design can also be upheld in this miniaturisation of architecture. George Sowden's *Heisenberg* clock, part of the second Memphis collection, displays the additive aesthetic typical of the group's work as well as an almost childish symbolism of applied decoration and primary colours. The clock has inspired many imitators, who have produced not only freestanding versions for the table but also wallclocks and wristwatches. The almost endless varieties of 'Swatch' watch are typical examples. On the other hand, the totally different philosophy of structural minimalism is evident in Peter Eisenman's clock, which consists of 60 small transparent acrylic glass cubes that can be assembled in a special way to form a new, larger cube. By turning the cube around in your hand you can read off from each spatial axis time's order of magnitude: hours, minutes, seconds. The construction exploits the special light-conducting qualities of acrylic glass and draws its effects from fractures, reflections, optical illusions and focusings. Playing flirtatiously with serious scientific processes, it is a typical expression of the pleasure Eisenman takes in confounding people. Eisenman is an aesthete, but like a latter-day Münchhausen, he would happily have you believe that everything he does has a basis in science.

In 1986 Matteo Thun designed a number of lamps in collaboration with Andrea Lera for Bieffeplast's *Still-light* collection. They produced three tall standard lamps and some small table lamps which all display the High-Tech punched hole aesthetic, although the holes are not round but are precision-cut by a laser into small lozenge shapes. The pattern is thus artificially derived, owing its form not to technology but to aesthetic calculation. Thun elaborates: 'The lights from the scale of night table lamps to . . . the scale of human-size standard lamps are intended as metallic micro-architectures. The shades consist of industrial sheet metal that has been

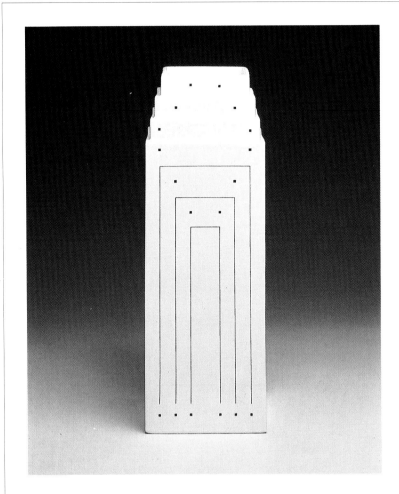

TOP: HEIDE WARLAMIS, *SKYSCRAPER* AND *METROPOLITAN TOWER* VASES, 1984; *ABOVE*: MATTEO THUN AND ANDREA LERA,
BIEFFEPLAST *STILL-LIGHT* COLLECTION, 1986

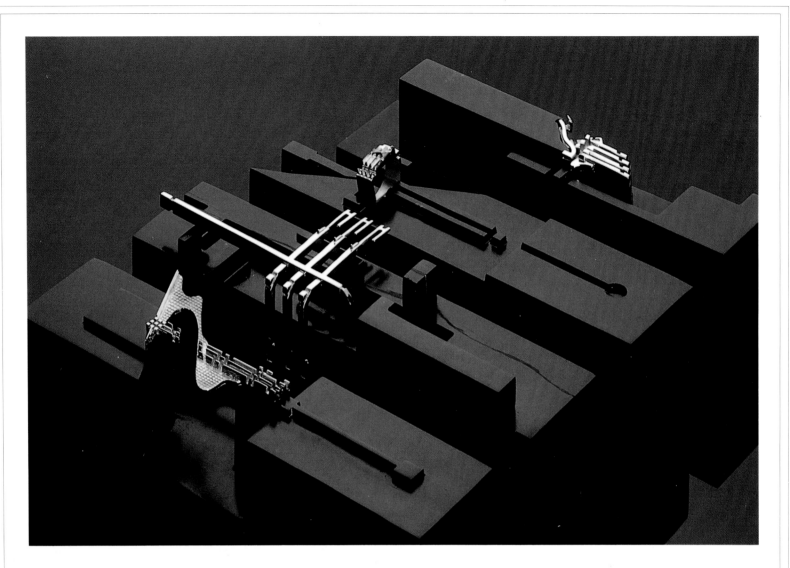

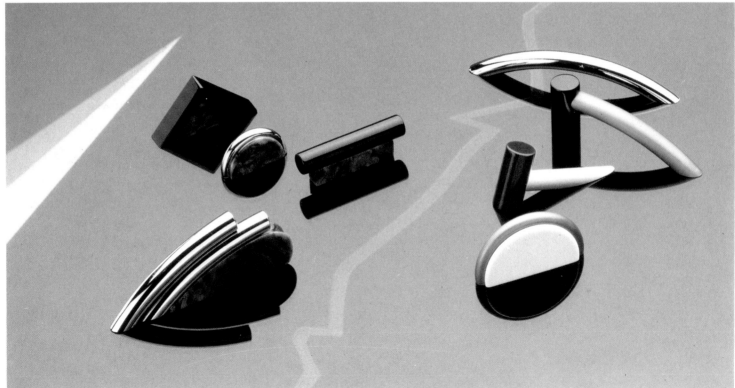

TOP: MASQUE, *FOUR ORDERS IN GOLD AND STONE*, 1987; *ABOVE*: DURON *ART DECO* DOOR HANDLES, 1980s

perforated by a laser. For me, the designer, the *Still-light* collection exhibits a stylistic design dynamic; the dialectic of scale comes from the similarity between the design processes for objects and built architecture. The imagination of the user, on the other hand, is stirred by the make-believe accessibility of the micro-architecture. This gives an emotional charge to the relationship between man and object (little house on stilts object, skyscraper object, light-tower object, etc).[6]

High-Tech references also show through in the small objects by the Munich designer Andreas Weber, which range from vases and bowls to trays, cheese bells and paper files. Weber's works are refinements of the former High-Tech practice of transferring objects relatively rigidly out of the context of primary production into the realm of private use. They evoke the classic Modern language of the 1920s. Their crystal, glass, aluminium or steel surfaces bear no marks of use, contrary to what one might at first expect of a High-Tech object. In fact, they complement perfectly the furniture of Mies van der Rohe and Le Corbusier. What could be described as their strength is at the same time their greatest weakness: the absence of poetic, literary – in a word, emotional – qualities. These qualities are not inevitably absent from minimalist work. Despite their black, puritanical geometries, the trays, pen-holders and plant-stands of the Milan group Zeus, for example, appeal to the emotions much more than Weber's designs.

In micro-architecture, the importance of tableware is matched by that of jewellery. The field has expanded so much – particularly since 1986 when Cleto Munari launched its collection of 80 pieces by leading Post-Modern architects and designers – that it hardly seems possible to give a fair representation of it within the framework of this article. One project should be singled out, however, because it represents the prototypical application of the conceptual and design processes of micro-architecture to jewellery.

In 1987 the New York architectural group Masque (Douglas Frederick and Ann Cederna) realised, with the help of an established goldsmith, a project which they called 'Four Orders in Gold and Stone' in acknowledgement of the old architectural pattern books. Their basic idea was as simple as it was confounding: by reducing or abstracting from historical city plans, the pair developed forms which were manufactured in gold, with the surrounding topography represented as a black onyx base, stepped like the landscape. The plan of Versailles inspired a ring, that of Blenheim a brooch, that of Chantilly (basically, the architectural opposite of Blenheim) an earring set. The final piece was an armband with a very abstract, modular composition that combined the first three orders in a fourth, new order. The system of references and the superimposition of architectural, spatial, structural and visual orders are clearly indebted to Ungers and Eisenman. However, the jewellery seems bound to remain somewhat singular, if for no other reason than its price; at around £5,000 a piece, it's also not likely to be added to the list of items that Yuppies find essential to maintain their self-image.

Many firms in West Germany – including some smaller, previously rather conservative ones – are attempting to share the new design success by inviting internationally known architects and designers to enhance their corporate identity. In 1987, for example, the Wicküler brewery held an architectural workshop to think up new designs for bars with Michael Graves, Matteo Thun, Hans von Klier, Hans-Ullrich Bitsch and Karsten Krebs, while in Spring 1988 the glass manufacturer Vegla (up until then mainly concerned with selling to the automobile market) invited Norman Foster, Philippe Starck, Massimo Vignelli, Hans-Ullrich Bitsch and Karsten Krebs to come up with a new application for glass. This increased awareness of corporate identity extends even to carpet manufacture, where Vorwerk is currently preparing a new collection of patterns by leading contemporary painters, designers and architects. What is evident throughout the whole field of micro-architecture is a more serious, earnest approach towards design. One can only hope that the effect of these initial avant-garde experiments will filter through to everyday design. For if – as the market analysts and the mass media tell us – we in the Western industrialised societies are supposed to define ourselves through what we buy and consume (preferably conspicuously), then why should this not also have an influence on our general experience of everyday life? If stylistic aspirations can even permeate objects of everyday use and the avant-garde can descend from its pedestal of high art and walk freely among the common and hitherto undistinguished artefacts of our otherwise predictable day-to-day existence, then the effect can only be to make that existence more pleasant and more attractive.

However the new spirit of design is to be found not only in the micro-architectures of tableware and objects for the living environment but also in the area of 'no-name' products, in other words objects without a specific brand character or profile, without a publicly named designer or identifiable history. As a rule, objects that are directly connected to a building are anonymous; people just don't go out and search for the 'right' door or window handle, wall socket, light switch, radiator or toilet fitting. Economists also call these things 'low-interest' products. Obviously the rise of mass production and increasing labour costs contributed to this anonymisation of design, but another factor was the shift in attitudes towards style. Throughout the nineteenth century and for a large part of this century – that is, even after the triumph of industrialisation – there was still a rich, individualistic tradition of design in this area. Many Bauhaus and Art Deco artists and architects were involved, not to mention the Arts and Crafts movement, Glasgow School and Wiener Werkstätte. Morris and Mackintosh, Behrens and Gropius, Berlage and Rietveld, Eileen Gray and Charlotte Perriand all designed such objects. After the Second World War, however, individual design in this field was neglected in favour of anonymous mass production. Although the tradition wasn't cut off as abruptly in some countries, such as Italy, Scandinavia and the United States, as it was in West Germany, it suffered a great decline everywhere. Its revival has come only as part of a generally increasing euphoria about design generated by the success of Post-Modernist architecture and post-functionalist design, coupled with a growth in economic prosperity. Market profiles and brand names are now treated like fetishes – think of the Lacoste crocodile, Porsche sunglasses, Gucchi shoes, Adidas trainers. Once again, it seems, internationally known designers are prepared to tackle no-name products.

One middle-of-the-road West German manufacturer took advantage of this situation and invited suggestions from nine top international architects and designers for 'future forms for household fittings'. Although the fees were by no means generous, none of the star designers – Hans Hollein (Vienna), Mario Botta (Ticino), Peter Eisenman (New York), Arata Isozaki, Shoji Hayashi (Tokyo), Alessandro Mendini (Milan), Petr Tucny (Czechoslovakia), Dieter Rams and Hans-Ullrich Bitsch (West Germany) – refused the task. Less than two years later, in March 1986, the designs were presented, and within three months the prototypes had been produced. In September 1986 the firm, FSB (Franz Schneider Brakel), invited all the designers and representatives of the world's specialist press to a symposium. Talks on the literary theme of the 'aesthetics of handles', an informal lunch, workshops with the great men, and visits to the finishing foundry were all presented under the suggestive title of 'FSB Designer Saturday' (the fact that there were similarly named events in New York, London, Brussels, Amsterdam, Paris and Düsseldorf was surely an unintentional coincidence). The results clearly show the phenomenon of aesthetically upgrading a no-name product, in this case the door handle. The last group to pay serious attention to the design of the door handle was the Bauhaus, or perhaps the Ulm School in the 1950s. In the 60s and 70s, the trend was set by the synthetic pipes in primary colours, the ultimate expression of the softline aesthetic, manufactured by Hewi.

The fact that FSB had long ago produced Walter Gropius' famous Faguswerk fitting provided the international grand master of redesign, Alessandro Mendini, with a great excuse to rework it as part of his entry in the competition. In addition, Mendini has revamped the appearance of two other door handles the firm made in the 50s and 60s. Hollein produced miniaturised architectural decorations with elegant precision, one of which can be mounted either horizontally or vertically, and so is called either 'Stork's Beak' or 'Lady's Shoe'. The Düsseldorf professor Hans-Ullrich Bitsch's design, on the other hand, although it refers back to the centuries-old model of the doors of Siena Cathedral, still comes across a bit like an old Hollein design, mixed with a touch of Memphis and Michael Graves. Botta and Eisenman, true to their architectural background, have produced geometric exercises. Botta's rounded-off or curved metal handles are High-Tech products which point directly to the construction process itself, and lend it an aesthetic note. Eisenman allows dimensions to merge into one another, from the door handle to the entire building; for

him, proportion is abstract, and is not to be communicated anthropomorphically, symbolically or iconographically. Both the Japanese designers emphasise the tactile quality of the handles. While Hayashi enthuses about reinforcing the tactile experience of contact with the handle through the use of hard, burnished surfaces or soft 'high-touch' ones, Isozaki appeals to both sight and touch with his colourful laminated wood handles. Isozaki has said that when one touches the door handle on crossing the threshold between rooms, it becomes 'for a moment, part of the body'. Dieter Rams' doorknobs and buttons are as unassumingly elegant as his designs for Braun. They are ergonomically classic products – even though, according to the firm, they are much more complicated to produce than their visual appearance would suggest. The economy of form and function is so extreme that it can be taken both as a symbol and a fiction, a confirmation that Modernism and Functionalism still might wish to achieve an aesthetic transfiguration of their message, a formulation of a 'language of style'. In contrast, Tucny's handles have a certain formal ambiguity, the soft rounding-off of otherwise angular forms resulting in a rather imprecise product language.

In terms of public relations, the 'Zeitgeist in the door handle' venture was a great success, generating the kind of press coverage for FSB a multinational might have achieved with a large advertising budget.[7] It provides evidence of a breakthrough from anonymous no-name mass production to the creation of an awareness of such objects and thus an awareness of the choices available in terms of forms and aesthetic traditions.

There is also an increased awareness of aesthetics in the manufacture of accessories for interior design. Tiles, curtain rods, rugs, fluorescent strip lights, staircase treads and railings exhibit an unprecedented variety of styles and historical references. It seems that even these objects are now considered worthy of an 'aura'. In the design of furniture fittings – a tradition which goes back at least as far as the Wiener Werkstätte – the Union Knopf company in Bielefeld has been particularly successful over the last few years. Its speciality are handles which give a touch of individuality to otherwise anonymous products such as neutral, monochrome storage systems made from synthetic materials. Its range, which is somewhat immodestly called 'A Handle on Creativity', comprises nearly 400 varieties of furniture fittings. Within this specialised market segment, Union Knopf is one of Europe's most successful firms.

The size of its product range comes from combining the different surfaces and materials with variable forms. Thus, for example, the nine basic patterns in the Terrazzo range come in twelve different shapes with an optional metal trim (in a choice of three colours) or man-made base (in two colours) to give a total of more than 100 variables. The Terrazzo range draws its inspiration not only from the Italian tradition of floor-covering from the turn of the century to the interwar period, but also, quite explicitly, from the renewed decorative use of the material by Alchymia and Memphis. On the other hand, the Duron

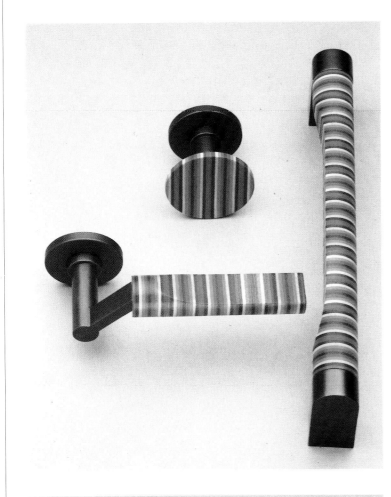
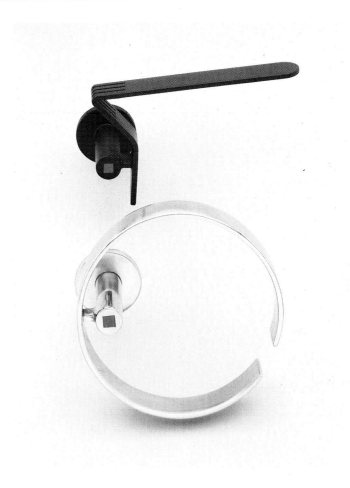

DOOR HANDLES BY ARATA ISOZAKI, MARIO BOTTA, ALESSANDRO MENDINI AND HANS-ULLRICH BITSCH, 1986 FOR FSB

VORWERK CARPETS BY O M UNGERS, MATTEO THUN AND DAVID HOCKNEY, 1988

range, which even includes a furniture knob like a tennis ball, draws on High-Tech images, while two further ranges, *Fifties* and *Art Deco*, are inspired by the current nostalgia for those styles. The *Fifties* range attempts to evoke the mood of the time by using combinations of man-made materials, chrome and aluminium, and employing the same 'skewed' formal vocabulary that produced, say, the kidney table. The *Art Deco* range is all about glamour and Charleston. But here, the same synthetic material, Duro-Horn, is used to imitate wood veneer, marble or even terrazzo. The stylised ornament of the *Art Deco* range is clearly seen by the firm as a counterpoint to the High-Tech look, as expressed, for example, in its own *Duron* series. The firm also makes ranges of fittings that look like marble or brightly coloured, polished glass and have names like *Sea Glass* or *Balloon*. The sales blurb attempts the poetic: 'A walk by the sea. Sand, stones, flotsam, never resting. Amongst it, a fragment of coloured glass. Once sharp-edged and jagged, now round, smooth, velvety. *Sea Glass* – a creation which inspires.'

What is suggested by this wide range of stylistic references is confirmed by a look at how the production process is set up: the firm is geared towards meeting the demands of differentiated, divided market segments. In addition to its own range, it can also produce a prototype of a customer's design in six days: 'You give us a sketch of your idea and our in-house designers will develop your concept up to production stage, remaining in constant touch with you.' The firm has also collaborated with furniture manufacturers such as Rosenthal, Interlübke and Poggenpohl, and even prepared the prototype of the 'Terrazzo' handle Mendini designed for the FSB competition. What is noticeable about its success is that it appears to have been achieved simply through producing a differentiated range of styles. No great fuss has been made of the individual designers.

What has been said of micro-architecture seems also true here: by helping us define our stylistic consciousness and giving us the opportunity, perhaps even forcing us, to become clearer about our own preferences and tastes, these small objects are making cultural connections and lines of tradition accessible to us, and influencing our everyday experiences in a way that high art, being an arrogant preserve, could never do.

Firmly on the floor

The new 'Dialogue' carpet range, developed by eleven contemporary artists and architects working with Vorwerk, is to be seen in the context of a general design reassessment happening at present. In the 80s it is much more readily accepted than in earlier decades of the post-war period that the thoughtful design of mass-produced everyday objects not only optimises their usefulness, but at the same time, and with at least equal justification, enhances the cultural status of such products. This 'ennoblement' – and something similar is happening in contemporary architecture – functions predominantly through 'star' designers, a phenomenon which Deyan Sudjic described as characteristic of the decade in the *International Design Yearbook 1986/87*. Distribution strategies in architecture, design

and, one may add, increasingly in painting, are now becoming more and more 'Americanised', and thus adapted to media interested in a lack of ambiguity and sensation. National or even regional qualities, the context of a design or the technical requirements for its production, are all neglected in favour of a *pars-pro-toto* perception, a stylistic 'password'. By this means, Ungers' experience is reduced to his 'square euphoria', Richard Meier produces apparently ever-new variants on his outline angle deviations, Hollein can be recognised by his absolutely endless creative primary form sections, and Venturi makes an impact only through his ostensibly constantly varying taste for refined combinations of everyday and high art aesthetics. Economically applied, these stylistic 'passwords' become 'corporate identities' embracing entire companies. In our modern post-industrial society certain brand profiles and the image of a firm determine the acceptance and competitiveness of its products on the market to as great an extent as their actual value to the user. Diversifying product range and establishing separate sectional markets associated with this – whose internal interdependence could be likened to the chicken and the egg – are the present-day economic commandments. Products today should and must be more than a mere functional offer to satisfy a need; they should be an indication and proof of a cultural attitude. One may wish to take a critical attitude to developments of this kind, and regret that, as Erich Fromm has pointed out, a 'culture of being' has been replaced by a 'culture of having': more and more outfits, objects, and 'lifestyles' have replaced real convictions and attitudes in people's personal identity banks. However, this culturalisation of consumer goods, of 'banal design' and 'no-name products' may also enrich our everyday environment, indeed to a significant extent. Product strategy would then become cultural strategy in tune with the times – an enrichment of culture which must however remain highly suspect to that basic economic criticism which can only recognise system-stabilising and profit-maximising calculation in any business initiative. However, a few examples of West German production in recent years show that a definite qualitative improvement and associated enrichment of our possibilities of experience with consumer goods is possible and actually comes about precisely because of such allegedly monodimensional marketing strategies.

The essentially middle-class firm FSB from the Weserbergland had great success with a collection of about twenty different door handles by internationally known star designers, predominantly architects. The most striking feature of this is that a firm which for more than twenty-five years had produced anonymous mass-produced goods, usually by unnamed designers, with this comparatively modest project achieved a greater public relations effect than with all its previous policies put together. The equally old-established Wüttemberg metal goods factory WMF recently treated itself to a small experimental field of designs with a whiff of the contemporary, by Matteo Thun, for example. Then there is the example, with more than half an eye on the economic consequences, of the

Italian firm Alessi, which also sells anonymous mass-produced household goods, but also has the exclusive 'Officina Alessi', which for example in 1978 created a stir with its famous 'Tea and Coffee Piazza' series by world-famous contemporary architects and designers. These products were limited editions, however, and cost between ten and thirty thousand pounds per sterling silver item. A regional brewery like Wicküler suddenly establishes a 'workshop' with an international cast and does not shy away from flying megastars like Michael Graves to Wuppertal so that he can design pubs for them. A year ago the Aachen glass manufacturer VEGLA held a glass workshop in the Deutsches Museum in Munich at which internationally famous designers and architects were again asked to find new ways of using scientific glass. It is self-evident that a number of the same people are involved in all these enterprises ; such overlapping is mere chance. And of course here too the star-system mechanism which we have already mentioned plays a part, as one can see at a glance from the press release. 'The names of the eleven artists and architects are internationally known not just by design cognoscenti'.

Our present project is, however, very different from the enterprises mentioned. Here we are dealing not with prototypes, nor with a mere public relations stunt, but with a serious attempt to restore lost expressive power to a product which had become increasingly inconspicuous and neutral as a result of post-war functionalism. Also, for the first time in this category of product, the carpets in this collection are not a limited edition given apparently enhanced value by signatures, but a series product in the middle price range for both domestic and contract use. In contrast with limited area, limited edition carpets designed by artists (which have a long tradition from the Wiener Werkstätte via the Bauhaus to the 'Object-Carpet' series in the seventies), which for all these reasons are then governed by the value-creating mechanisms of the art market, this is a 'wall-to-wall' collection: endless according to tendency, machine produced, limited only by a production width of four metres and the technical restriction of a maximum of seven colours. The price is fixed, regardless of the degree of fame of the artists and architects, at between twenty-five and thirty pounds per square metre. The 'emotional experience value' of the carpet which Vorwerk claims for this collection, and which in the same breath places it in the ennobling tradition of the Bauhaus, applies here in a way which turns traditional interior decorating hierarchies upside down: we don't have a floor which is as neutral as possible fitting in with stylishly placed furniture and lamps, from antiques to High-Tech, but precisely the other way round. The carpeting has high-definition design, and demands furniture which goes with it: the carpet is laid first, and then suitable furniture is chosen.

Economically speaking too, in terms of development costs, this series is unusual and is proof of higher-than-average commitment by the manufacturer which cannot just be explained by a wish to make an impact on the market. In the early stages intensive argument was necessary, simply because the product traditionally has such a boring image, to persuade the artists and architects to take part in the project at all. But then Hockney, for example, became so enthusiastic about this genre of design, which was new to him, that he produced sixteen designs instead of the four requested. Both Lichtenstein and Richter insisted on the development of pure white sections hitherto thought impossible – a demand which necessitated a long and expensive series of experiments. Richter himself finally rejected one of his two designs because for technical production reasons it was not possible to realise the three-dimensional depths of his painted design.

The visual opulence of most of the designs and their high degree of independence reflects moreover that new sensitivity to quality and surface which Matteo Thun has defined with the at first apparently paradoxical notion of 'baroque Bauhaus'. It would be timely to find a product language able to combine the formal severity and Calvinistic discipline of the Bauhaus with the exuberance and luxurious textures of the baroque view of art. Vorwerk suggests with almost incantatory fervour that 'the home becomes more valuable, the number of pieces of furniture in the living room is reduced in favour of higher quality; thus this indubitable development makes it possible to see the floor'; if this is true then to quote Vorwerk again, 'conscious floor design has significance in the structuring of a space'.

As this assessment is completely true, the series opens up new, undreamed-of possibilities. It not only optimises the range of interior design,but is at the same time a further indication of a development in product design which I once described as the 'dominance of the periphery': it is striking that a new space-defining quality is lent to all the linked furnishing systems within a room, starting with wallpaper or ornamental wall design via built-in lighting systems and the design of the floor – whether with suitable carpet, terrazzo refined veneering or prefabricated marble decoration – through to the new refined and luxurious materials available for window design or suitable systems of blinds. It may be the case that this conglomeration in future will define a room almost perfectly in aesthetic terms, and that then the furniture itself, placed in variable arrangements, will effectively turn out to be of only peripheral value.

Last but not least the double strategy of this collection is impressive. On the one hand it is the work of indubitably significant artists and architects, who in their designs also reveal their view of architecture or art and are thus to a certain extent producing a piece of high art rendered banal, which can be admitted on this plane. On the other hand they are designs which, without any prior knowledge of art or art history, give pleasure and are stimulating simply on the level of perception. This is élite banality, democratic art, now realised in a typical no-name product field of all places: a happy combination of 'commissioner's imagination' and 'artist's imagination' which ought to teach us something when carried through so consistently. These carpets speak, they provoke a dialogue between space and furnishings; in a word, they communicate.

Notes

CHAPTER 1

1   *Twentieth Century Houses*, Raymond McGrath, Faber and Faber, London, 1934, p 123.
2   *Towards a New Architecture*, Le Corbusier, trans Frederick Etchells, The Architectural Press, London, 1946, p 85.
3   *The Nineteen Twenties Style*, Yvonne Brunhammer, Paul Hamlyn, London, 1969, p 80.
4   *ibid*, p 127.
5   *The International Style: Architecture since 1922*, Henry-Russell Hitchcock and Philip Johnson, New York, 1932, 2nd Ed 1966, p 14.
6   *Theory and Design in the First Machine Age*, Reyner Banham, The Architectural Press, London, 1960, p 323.
7   'The Heroic Period of Modern Architecture', *Architectural Design*, Dec 1965, p 590.
8   *The Anti-Rationalists – Art Nouveau Architecture and Design*, ed Nikolaus Pevsner and J M Richards, The Architectural Press, London, 1973, p 191.
9   'The New Modernism – Deconstructionist Tendencies in Art', *Art and Design*, Vol 4 No 3/4-1988, p 41.
10 *Art and England*, ed R S Lambert, Pelican Books, Harmondsworth, Middlesex, 1938, p 144 (transcript of a broadcast discussion in Feb 1935 between Eric Newton and Sir Reginald Blomfield).
11 *Taste*, ed Stephen Bayley, The Conran Foundation, London, 1983, p 25.
12 *Homes Sweet Homes*, Osbert Lancaster, John Murray, London, 1939, p 76. (The accompanying illustration shows a pipe-smoking 'Hampstead' intellectual, book in hand, sitting on an Aalto stool. 'New Writing' rests on a Breueresque plywood table. The books on the shelves include *Picasso, Spain? Baukunst* and *Gropius*).
13 *Surrealism and Architecture*, *Architectural Design* Profile, II, London, March 1978, p 142, trans Francis Lionnet from Salvador Dali's *Oui: Méthode Paranoïaque – critique et autres textes*, 1971.
14 *Surrealism and Architecture*, *op cit*, p 141.
15 *Furniture*, Penny Sparke, Bell and Hyman, London 1986, p 68.
16 *Italian Re Evolution* (sic) *– Design in Italian Society in the Eighties*, La Jolla Museum of Contemporary Art, 1982, p 178.
17 *The Hot House – Italian New Wave Design*, Andrea Branzi, Thames and Hudson, London, 1984, p 49.
18 *ibid, loc cit*.
19 *Studies in Art, Architecture and Design, Victorian and After* (Vol Two), Nikolaus Pevsner, Thames and Hudson, London, 1968, p 244. This essay, 'The Return of Historicism', is a last ditch attempt by a 'Modern' to stave off a return to eclecticism. It is, as with nearly all of Pevsner's work, very well written.
20 *ibid*, p 244.
21 *ibid*, p 259
22 *The Waste Makers*, Vance Packard, Penguin Books, Middlesex, 1963, p 119. Packard is more concerned with the sociology of design, however, than with its aesthetics.
23 *Concepts of Modern Design*, ed Tony Richardson and Nikos Stangos, Penguin Books, Harmondsworth, 1974, p 226. Edward Lucie Smith is himself quoting from *Dada: Art and Anti-Art* by Hans Richter, London, 1965.
24 *Pop Art*, Lucy R Lippard, with contributions by Lawrence Alloway, Nicolas Calas and Nancy Marmer, Thames and Hudson, London, 1966, p 36. Alloway's essay was entitled 'The Development of British Pop'.
25 *Camp*, Mark Booth, Quartet Books, London, 1983, p 23.
26 *Notes on Camp*, Partisan Review XXXI 4, 1964, p 278. This is a pioneering work on the subject.
27 *ibid*, p 287.
28 *ibid*, p 292.
29 *Camp*, Mark Booth, *op cit*, p 29. Many of these listed elements resurface in some Post-Modern designs.

CHAPTER II

30 *The Hot House*, *op cit*, pp 51-2.
31 *Charles Jencks*, ed Toshio Nakamura, *Architecture and Urbanism* Extra Edition, Tokyo, 1986, p 15. According to Jencks the 'speculative dialogue' is partly based on Paul Valéry's (1871-1945) *Eupalinos, or the Architect*, (1923).
32 *ibid*, p 15.
33 *ibid*, p 19.
34 *What is Post-Modernism?*, Charles Jencks, Academy Editions, London, 1987, p 14. The short but useful text embraces other disciplines, including painting and sculpture. It excludes design, however.
35 *ibid*, p 7.
36 *Charles Jencks*, ed Toshio Nakamura, *op cit*, p 194.
37 *Contemporary Landscape – From the Horizon of Postmodern Design*, catalogue of an exhibition at the National Museum of Modern Art, Kyoto, September to October 1985, and the National Museum of Modern Art, Tokyo, December to January 1986. This is one of the most important Japanese catalogues on Post-Modern design and architecture to date. Ambasz's quotation appears on p 77.
38 *The Hot House*, *op cit*, pp 4-5.
39 *ibid*, p 4.
40 *ibid*, p 51.
41 *ibid*, p 127.
42 *ibid*, p 127.
43 *Memphis*, Barbara Radice, Thames and Hudson, London, 1985, p 121.
44 *ibid*, p 36.
45 *Glass Art Society Journal*, New York, 1986, p 42, in an interview reprinted courtesy of *Promenade*, November, 1983.
46 *Contemporary Landscape*, *op cit*, p 103. The catalogue, which is also in English, does not always seem to present a totally fluent translation.
47 *ibid*, p 53.
48 *Memphis*, *op cit*, p 88.
49 *Contemporary Landscape*, *op cit*, p 177.
50 *Empire of Signs*, Roland Barthes, trans Richard Howard, Jonathan Cape, London, 1982, pp 108-9. The original *L'Empire des Signes* was published by Editions d'Art Albert Skira SA, Genève, 1970.
51 *Contemporary Landscape*, *op cit*, p 124.
52 *ibid*, p 124.
53 *Memphis*, *op cit*, p 185.
54 *ibid*, p 144.
55 *Contemporary Landscape*, *op cit*, p 106. As with other quotations from this catalogue, the translation is not totally fluent.

CHAPTER III

56 *Postmodern Culture*, ed Hal Foster, Pluto Press, London, 1985, p 3. First published as *The Anti-Aesthetic*, Bay Press, Port Townsend, USA, 1983.

57 *Officina Alessi* catalogue, Crusinallo, Italy, November 1985, p 28. This introduction is taken from *Tea & Coffee Piazza* by Alessandro Mendini, Shakespeare & Company, Milan, 1983, p 6 and following.

58 *ibid*, p 29.

59 From an article on Cleto Munari in *Forme* magazine, Vol 120, Cermenate (Como), Feb 1988, p 50.

60 *ibid*, pp 51-2.

CHAPTER IV

61 *Contemporary Landscape*, op cit, p 126.

62 *Four Designer Clocks, 1966-88*, small catalogue by Alessi, Crusinallo, Italy, 1988, p 14.

63 *Jewelry By Architects*, Barbara Radice, Rizzoli, New York, 1987, p 106. This publication deals entirely with the Cleto Munari jewellery.

64 From a typescript statement by Robert Venturi to the author and Academy Editions, 25th March, 1988.

CHAPTER V

65 *Contemporary Landscape*, op cit, p 73.

66 *Charles Jencks*, ed. Toshio Nakamura, op cit, p 165.

67 *ibid*, p 165.

68 *Jewelry By Architects*, Barbara Radice, op cit, p 30.

69 *Four Designer Clocks*, 1966-88, op cit, p 5.

70 *Contemporary Landscape*, op cit, p 58.

71 From a typescript statement by Robert Stern to the author and Academy Editions of 26 February 1988. His statement includes ideas initially presented in his introduction to *The International Design Yearbook*, Abbeville Press, New York, 1985, pp 8-12.

72 From a typescript statement by Robert Stern to the author and Academy Editions, no date, describing the *Dinner at Eight* carpet.

73 From a typescript statement by Robert Stern to the author and Academy Editions, no date, describing the *Majestic* dinner plate.

74 From a typescript statement by Robert Stern to the author and Academy Editions, no date, describing his work for Swid Powell.

75 From a typescript statement by Robert Stern, 26 February 1988, *op cit*.

76 *Contemporary Landscape*, op cit, p 85.

77 *Contemporary Landscape*, op cit, p 151.

78 From a typescript statement by Stanley Tigerman to the author and Academy Editions, no date, describing his jewellery designs for Cleto Munari.

79 *Jewelry by Architects*, Barbara Radice, op cit, p 94.

80 From a typescript statement by Stanley Tigerman to the author and Academy Editions, February 1988.

CHAPTER VI

81 *Deconstructivist Architecture*, Museum of Modern Art, New York, 1988, pp 10-11.

82 *Artists and Architects Collaboration*, Barbara Diamonstein, Whitney Library of Design, New York, 1981, p 167.

83 From an article on Gehry in *Architecture and Urbanism (A&U)* Magazine, Tokyo, January 1986, p 61.

84 *Contemporary Landscape*, op cit, p 57.

85 *Dada: Art and Anti-Art*, Hans Richter, Thames and Hudson, London, 1965, pp 24-25.

86 *Architecture Today*, Charles Jencks, Academy Editions, London, 1988, Chapter 14, p 251.

87 *ibid*, loc cit.

88 *Contemporary Landscape*, op cit, p 57.

89 *ibid*, loc cit.

90 *Jewelry by Architects*, Barbara Radice, op cit, p 22.

91 From the catalogue *Contemporary Ideas for Light in Jewish Ritual*, Israel Museum, Jerusalem, 1986, p 62.

92 *ibid*, loc cit.

93 From *Door Handles – Workshop in Brakel* with essays by Otl Aicher, Jurgen Werner Braun and Siegfried Gronert, Franz Schnieder Brakel, Brakel, West Germany, 1987, p 27. This important catalogue includes a transcript of a design discussion held at FSB on 20 September 1986 between many of the participating architects.

94 *ibid*, loc cit.

95 *ibid*, p 46. Eisenman's statement is all the more powerful because it was delivered in the presence of Mendini, Hollein and Rams.

96 *ibid*, p 63.

97 *ibid*, p 63.

98 *Jewelry by Architects*, Barbara Radice, op cit, p 22.

99 *ibid*, p 22.

CHAPTER VII

100 *Paolo Portoghesi*, ed Francesco Moschini, Rizzoli, New York, 1980, p 16. One assumes he means the lantern, rather than 'lighthouse' (*sic*) of St Ivo at the Sapienza by Francesco Borromini, 1642-1660. The Temple of Venus at Baalbek (ancient Heliopolis) is a small temple of AD 273; the Mies plan is that for the Barcelona Pavilion of 1929.

101 From a two page brochure on the *Aldebarhan* table, issued by divisione Arte e Architettura della Società del Travertino Romano, Rome, no date.

102 *Jewelry by Architects*, Barbara Radice, op cit, p 64.

103 *Contemporary Landscape*, op cit, p 98.

104 *Door Handles – Workshop in Brakel*, op cit, p 66 in an article by Otl Aicher entitled 'The useless utensil'.

105 From a brochure *Officina Alessi Watches – 'Momento'*, Crusinallo, 1987, p I.

CHAPTER VIII

106 *From the spoon to the town through the work of 100 designers*, Exhibition catalogue, Electa Editrice, Milan, 1983, p 93.

107 *Contemporary Landscape*, op cit, p 69.

108 *Door Handles – Workshop in Brakel*, op cit, p 33.

109 *ibid*, loc cit.

110 *Jewelry by Architects*, Barbara Radice, op cit, p 46.

111 *ibid*, loc cit.

112 *The Green Party General Election Manifesto*, GMP Publishers Ltd, London, 1987, p I.

113 *Die Turnstunde – Eine Rauminstallation von Hans Hollein*, Städtisches Museum Abteiberg, Mönchengladbach, 23rd September to 18th November 1984, p 5.

114 *Jewelry by Architects*, Barbara Radice, op cit, p 34.

115 *Modern Movements in Architecture*, Charles Jencks, Penguin Books, Harmondsworth, Middlesex, 1986, p 55. The statement is quoted from Hans Hollein, in *Arts and Architecture*, California, 1963, p 14.

116 *Door Handles – Workshop in Brakel*, op cit, p 31.

117 *ibid*, loc cit.

118 *Tomás Taveira New Transfiguration catalogue*, Galeria Cómicos, Lisbon, Portugal, 1985, p 3.

CHAPTER IX

119 *Contemporary Landscape*, op cit, p 122. Tusquets first made the statement in *Contemporary Architects*, Macmillan Press Ltd, London, 1980, p 825.

120 *Jewelry by Architects*, Barbara Radice, op cit, p 102.

121 *The Wizard's Collection*, four page colour brochure, c 1987, issued by Zanussi.

122 *The Sunday Times*, London, 24 July 1988, p A3, from an article by Hugh Pearman and Philip Beresford entitled 'New boxes? You've got the

wrong number, sir'.

POST-MODERNISM & CONSUMER DESIGN: VOLKER FISCHER

1   Heinrich Klotz, Foreword to *Bauen Heute: Architektur der Gegenwart in der Bundesrepublik Deutschland*, Stuttgart, 1985, p IX.
2   See Officina Alessi, *The Tea and Coffee Piazza*, Crusinallo 1983. The term 'micro-architecture' was coined by Alessandro Mendini.
3   See Volker Fischer, 'Highrise Application: Der Architekt als Visagist der Metropolen' in *The Heavy Dress: Die Oberfläche als Manifest*. Catalogue to a Matteo Thun exhibition, Vienna, 1986.
4   See the article entitled 'Droge Luxus: Die Deutschen im Kaufrausch' in *Der Spiegel*, No 48, 1986, pp 230-41; also 'Outfit, Kleidung, Accessories, Duftwasser', *Spiegel* Dokumentation, Hamburg, 1986. This article examines the present patterns of consumption of West Germans on the basis of a representative survey of 5,000 people. The survey revealed that two-thirds of West Germans have a net monthly income of over £930, and that over a million of them have a yearly income of more than £62,000. *Stern* magazine calls these people the 'consumer élite': see 'Lust auf Genuß: Schlemmen, Reisen, Kaufen' in *Stern*, No 49, 1986, pp 20-29. When compared with the mid 1960s, the increase in purchasing power becomes particularly clear. In 1968, for example, only around 6,000 white-collar workers had an income of over £31,000 whereas nowadays the number is over 250,000. During the same period the number of those earning between £16,000 and £31,000 a year rose from 38,000 to almost 3 million (figures taken from the *Der Spiegel* article quoted above).
5   See Matteo Thun, *Barockes Bauhaus: Aphorismen zu einem Manifest*, published on the occasion of a WMF product presentation at the Museum for Decorative Arts, Frankfurt, 1986.
6   Matteo Thun, quoted from Volker Albus *et al*, *Gefühlscollagen: Wohnen von Sinnen*, Cologne, 1986, p 27.
7   See Siegfried Grönert, 'Design Weltstars in Brakel' in *Die Zeit*, 26th September 1986; as well as 'Die Form des Banalen' in *Frankfurter Allgemeine Zeitung*, 8th October 1986; 'Türlinken: Zeitgeist im Griff' in *Hauser*, November 1986; 'Klinkenputz' in *Form*, November 1986; 'Banales als Thermometer der Kultur' in *Design*, December 1986; and 'Klinke im Designer-Griff', *Stern*, April 1987.

This is a revised, extended version of an article which first appeared in *Art & Design* No 3/4 – 1987 'The Post-Modern Object'. The author has also written on the same themes in *Design Heute: Maßstäbe, Formgebung zwischen Design und Kunststück*, published in 1988 in Frankfurt and Munich.

PHOTOGRAPHIC ACKNOWLEDGEMENTS

Peter Aaron, Esto Photographers Inc, p 64; Aldo Ballo, Studio Azzurro, Jacket Front, p 10; Richard Bryant, p 195; Richard Cheatle, p 6; Mauro Davoli and Marco Buzzoni, pp 29, 30; Paolo Gandola, p 33; Hedrich-Blessing, pp 65, 67, 68, 78, 178; Karant and Associates Inc, p 3; Paschall/Taylor, pp 2, 126, 129, 146, 147, 148, 150, 151, 153, 154; Erich Pedevilla, pp 238, 239; Folco Quilici, p 197; Jo Reid, p 256; Georg Riha, p 227; Oscar Savio, p 199; Tony Gilbert Studios, pp 72, 73. All other illustrations courtesy of the designers and/or manufacturers.

SELECTED BIBLIOGRAPHY

AMBASZ, EMILIO. *The International Design Yearbook 1986/7.* Thames and Hudson, London, 1986.

BANHAM, REYNER. *Theory and Design in the First Machine Age.* Architectural Press, London, 1960.

BOOTH, MARK. *Camp.* Quartet Books, London, 1983.

BRANZI, ANDREA. *The Hot-House.* Thames and Hudson, London, 1985.

CAPELLA, JULI AND LARREA, QUIM. *Designed by Architects in the 1980s.* Mitchell, London, 1988.

COLLINS, MICHAEL. *Towards Post-Modernism.* British Museum Publications, London, 1987.

DETHIER, JEAN (ed). *Images et Imaginaires d'Architecture.* Centre Georges Pompidou, Paris, 1984.

DIAMONSTEIN, BARBARA. *Artists and Architects Collaboration.* Whitney Library of Design, New York, 1981.

DORFLES, GILLO (ed). *Kitsch: The World of Bad Taste.* Studio Vista, London, 1969.

FISCHER, VOLKER (ed). *Design Heute: Maßstäbe, Formgebung zwischen Design und Kunststück.* Prestel-Verlag, Munich, 1988.

FOSTER, HAL (ed). *Postmodern Culture.* Pluto Press, London, 1985.

HIESINGER, KATHRYN B AND MARCUS, GEORGE H. *Design since 1945.* Thames and Hudson, London, 1983.

HITCHCOCK, HENRY-RUSSELL AND JOHNSON, PHILIP C. *The International Style: Architecture since 1922.* Norton, New York, 1966.

HORN, RICHARD. *Memphis.* Running Press, Philadelphia, 1985.

ISOZAKI, ARATA (ed). *The International Design Yearbook 1988/9.* Thames and Hudson, London, 1988.

JENCKS, CHARLES. *Post-Modern Classicism.* Academy Editions, London, 1980.

———. *The Language of Post-Modern Architecture.* Academy Editions, London, 1984.

———. *Modern Movements in Architecture.* Penguin Books, Harmondsworth, 1986.

———. *What is Post-Modernism?* Academy Editions, London, 1986.

———. *Architecture Today.* Academy Editions, London, 1988.

JENSEN, ROBERT AND CONWAY, PATRICIA. *Ornamentalism.* Allen Lane, London, 1982.

JOHNSON, PHILIP C AND WIGLEY, MARK. *Deconstructivist Architecture.* Museum of Modern Art, New York, 1988.

KOHMOTO, SHINJI. *Contemporary Landscape – From the Horizon of Postmodern Design.* National Museum of Modern Art, Kyoto, 1985.

KRON, JOAN AND SLESIN, SUZANNE. *High Tech: The Industrial Style and Source Book for the Home.* Allen Lane, London, 1978.

LYOTARD, JEAN-FRANÇOIS (ed with Thierry Chaput). *Les Immatériaux.* Centre Georges Pompidou, Paris, 1985.

———. *The Post-modern Condition.* Manchester University Press, Manchester, 1986.

MOSHINI, FRANCESCO (ed). *Paolo Portoghesi.* Rizzoli, New York, 1980.

NAKAMURA, TOSHIO (ed). *Charles Jencks.* Architecture & Urbanism, Tokyo, 1986.

NORRIS, CHRISTOPHER. *Deconstruction: Theory and Practice.* Methuen, London, 1982.

PEVSNER, NIKOLAUS. *Studies in Art, Architecture and Design.* Thames and Hudson, London, 1968.

——— AND RICHARDS, J M (eds). *The Anti-Rationalists – Art Nouveau Architecture and Design.* Architectural Press, London, 1973.

PORTOGHESI, PAOLO. *After Modern Architecture.* Rizzoli, New York, 1982.

RADICE, BARBARA. *Memphis.* Thames and Hudson, London, 1985.

———. *Jewelry by Architects.* Rizzoli, New York, 1987.

SAMBONET, GUIA. *Alchimia.* Umberto Allemandi, Turin, 1986.

SPARKE, PENNY. *Ettore Sottsass Jnr.* Design Council, London, 1981.

———. *Furniture.* Bell and Hyman, London, 1986.

STARCK, PHILIPPE (ed). *The International Design Yearbook 1987/8.* Thames and Hudson, London, 1987.

STERN, ROBERT A M (ed). *The International Design Yearbook 1985/6.* Thames and Hudson, London, 1985.

THACKERA, JOHN (ed). *Design After Modernism.* Thames and Hudson, London, 1988.

VENTURI, ROBERT. *Complexity and Contradiction in Architecture.* Museum of Modern Art, New York, 1966.

WOLFE, TOM. *From Bauhaus to our house.* Jonathan Cape, London, 1982.

INDEX

of Designers and Manufacturers

Figures in italics refer to illustrations

ABET: 35, 80, 198, 249, 273.
ACME: 131, *161, 177.*
ADAM, ROBERT: 242, *264.*
AIDA, TAKEFUMI: *4.*
AKABA: 245.
AL-BAYATI, BASIL: 242, *265, 288.*
ALCHYMIA: *29, 30,* 32, *33,* 35, 36, 69, 241, 270, 278.
ALESSI: *JACKET FRONT, JACKET BACK, 10,* 12, *13,* 79, *82-83, 84-85, 86-87, 88-89, 90-91, 92-93, 94-95,* 108, *109, 118, 119,* 124, 127, 128, 131, 135, *153, 174, 175,* 184, *196,* 198, 201, 206, *220,* 226, 245, 246, 270, 274, 282.
ALESSIO SARI: 35, 42, 270.
ALIAS: 74, *75, 76, 77.*
ALMA: 242, *264.*
ARC INTERNATIONAL: *114, 115, 117.*
ARC 74: *46, 50.*
ARP STUDIO: *218, 219.*
ARQUITECTONICA: 35, 39, 80, 186.
ARTEMIDE: *23,* 32, 35.
ARZBERG: 273.

B&B: 269.
BAROVIER & TOSO: 270.
BD MUEBLAS: 245.
BEDIN, MARTINE: *49.*
BEEBY, THOMAS: *3,* 141.
BELLOSILLO, JAVIER: 245.
BERGHOF, NORBERT: 246.
BIEFFEPLAST: 270, 274, *275.*
BITSCH, HANS-ULLRICH: 277, 278, *279.*
BODUM: 39.
BOFFIL, RICARDO: 66, 245.
BOTTA, MARIO: *23,* 74, *75, 76, 77,* 80, 141, 183, 278, *279.*
BRANZI, ANDREA: 18, 31, 32, 35, 36, *59,* 226, 229, 270.
BRITISH TELECOM: 249, 267.

CASAS: 245.
CASSINA: 32, 269.
CASTIGLIONI, ACHILLE: 79.
CERAMICHE FLAVIA: 35, 47.
CHIASSON, PAUL: *78.*
CIBIC, ALDO: 35.
CLETO MUNARI: *60, 62, 63,* 80, 108, 128, 131, 135, *160, 176,* 183, 184, *189,* 201, 206, *210, 211, 212, 213,* 222, *224,* 225, 229, 230, *236, 237,* 245, 277.
CORTES, PEPE: 245.
CORTESI, ANGELO: 270, *272,* 273.

DANIEL SWAROVSKI & CO: *227,* 230.

DE LUCCHI, MICHELE: *12, 14,* 32, 35, 36, *43,* 80, 202.
DESIRON & LIZENOF: 242.
DRAENERT STUDIO: 246.
DU PASQUIER, NATHALIE: 35, 36, 39, 42, *50, 51, 52, 53,* 274.
DURON: *276.*

EDRA: *195.*
EISENMAN, PETER: 74, 80, 103, 124, 136, 179, *182,* 183, 184, *188, 189,* 225, 230, 274, 277, 278.
ELIO PALMISANO: 39.
ESPRIT: 39.

FARRELL, TERRY: *5,* 66, 123, 249, *256, 257.*
FAUCHEUX, BRIAN: *67.*
FITCH & COMPANY: 249.
FORMICA: *1, 3, 64, 65, 67, 68, 70, 71, 72, 73, 78, 79, 81,* 123, 132, 135, *170, 178, 181,* 222.
FOSTER, NORMAN: 74, 140, 277.
FRANZ WITTMAN EG: 226, 229.
FRATELLI TAVANI: 198, *209.*
FSB: 80, *182,* 183, 222, 230, 278, *279,* 281.
FURNITURE OF THE TWENTIETH CENTURY: *27,* 131.

GEHRY, FRANK: 74, 79, *178,* 180, 183, 184, 222.
GLASER, MILTON: *68.*
GRAVES, MICHAEL: *JACKET FRONT, 2, 17,* 35, 47, *62, 63,* 66, 74, 80, *86-87,* 103, 123, 124, *126,* 127, 128, *129,* 131, 132, 136, *146, 147, 148, 149, 150, 151, 152, 153, 154, 155,* 184, 186, 201, 225, 226, 230, 242, 246, *268,* 269, 270, 273, 277, 278, 282.
GWATHMEY, CHARLES AND ROBERT SIEGEL: 74, 80, 103, *120,* 124, *179,* 184, 186, 269, 273.

HADID, ZAHA: 74, 179, 184, 189, *192, 194, 195.*
HAMANO: *177.*
HAUSSMANN, ROBERT AND TRIX: 32, 35, 69, 80, *120,* 128, 186, *240, 241,* 241, 249, 274.
HEJDUK, JOHN: 124, 140, 184.
HERMAN MILLER: *169.*
HOCKNEY, DAVID: *280,* 282.
HOLLEIN, HANS: 27, 28, 32, 35, 47, *62, 63,* 66, 69, 79, 80, 127, 131, 141, 183, 184, 186, *220, 221,* 221, 225, 226, *227, 228,* 229, 230, *230, 231, 232-233, 234-235, 236, 237, 238, 239,* 242, 267, 269, 270, 273, 274, 278, 281.

ICF SPA: 221, *223.*
INDESIT: 246, *248.*
INTERLUBKE: 281.
IOSA-GHINI, MASSIMO: *59.*
IRVINE, JAMES: *49.*

ISOZAKI, ARATA: *11,* 27, 28, 31, 35, 47, *62, 63,* 66, 69, 79, 80, 107, 108, 131, 186, 197, 221, 222, *223, 224,* 225, 273, 274, 278, *279.*
ISRAEL MUSEUM: *188.*

JAHN, HELMUT: 79.
JENCKS, CHARLES: *6, 10,* 12, 21, 25, 27, 28, 31, 32, 66, 79, 80, *82-83,* 103, 110, *122, 123,* 123, 124, *125, 136, 137, 138, 139,* 139, *141, 142, 143, 144, 145,* 180, 206, 249, 270.
JIRICNA, EVA: *71.*

KNOLL INTERNATIONAL: *19,* 79, *102,* 104, *105, 106,* 107, *110, 111, 112, 113, 116,* 123, 127, 135, *166, 167,* 269.
KOCHERT, AE: *228,* 229.
KREBS, KARSTEN: 277.
KRIER, LEON: 35, 66.
KURAMATA, SHIRO: 28, 35, 42, 47, 74.

LANDES, MICHAEL: 246.
LASKIN, REBEKAH: *73.*
LAUBNER, JO: 240, *244,* 245, *254, 255,* 270, *272,* 273.
LERA, ANDREA: 274, *275.*
LICHTENSTEIN, ROY: 25, 36, 282.
LIPP, FRANZ OTTO: 270, 273.
LONGONI: 201.

MACHIN ARCHITECTS: 249.
MADE IN VENICE: *250, 251.*
MARCOT, ALAIN: *71.*
MARISCAL, XAVIER: 35, 245.
MASQUE: *276,* 277.
MATYSIK, HELMUT: *190, 191.*
MEIER, RICHARD: 74, 79, 80, *90-91,* 103, 124, 184, *185,* 186, *186, 187,* 269, 270, 274, 281.
MEMPHIS: *JACKET FLAP, 12, 12, 14, 20,* 25, 31, 35, 36, *37,* 39, *40, 41,* 42, *43, 44, 46,* 47, *48, 49, 50, 51, 52, 53, 56, 57, 58, 59, 61,* 79, 80, 107, 108, 127, 141, 186, 221, 226, 229, 241, 242, 245, 246, 249, *252,* 269, 270, 273, 274, 278.
MENDINI, ALESSANDRO: *15,* 28, 32, 35, 79, 80, 183, 206, 242, 258, *266,* 270, 278, *279,* 281.
MERCURY COMMUNICATIONS: 249, 267.
MISSONI, OTTAVIO: 246, *248.*
MOBEL INDUSTRIE DESIGN: 226.
MOORE, CHARLES: 66, 79, *81,* 103, 123, 131, 132, *133,* 135, *162, 163, 164, 165.*

NAVONA, PAOLA: 32.
NOTO, VITO: 245, 246, 270, 273.

PAYNE, LEE: *67.*

PEZZETTA, ROBERTO: 74, 246, *248*.

PIER-LUIGI GHIANDA: *45, 50, 51*.

POGGENPOHL: 281.

POLTRONOVA: 31, *34*, 198, *202, 207*, 226, *231, 232-233, 234-235*.

PORCELLANE SAN MARCO: 35, 42.

PORPHYRIOS, DEMETRI: 242.

PORTOGHESI, PAOLO: 32, *34*, 35, 66, 79, *92-93*, 107, 108, 197, *197*, 198, *199, 200*, 201, *202, 203, 204, 205, 207, 208, 209, 210, 211, 212, 213, 214, 215, 216, 217*, 225, 226, 230, 242, 270.

PUPPA, DANIELA: 32.

QUARTETT: 270, 273.

RAGGI, FRANCO: 32.

RAMSHAW, WENDY: *72*, 80.

RANG, WOLFGANG: 246.

ROSENTHAL: 281.

ROSSI, ALDO: *JACKET BACK*, 32, 66, 74, 79, *196*, 197, 201, 202, *218, 219*, 221, 242, 245, 246, 249, 270, 273, 274.

ROSSI & ARCANDI: 35, 229, *231*.

RYERSON, MITCH: *70*.

SAPPER, RICHARD: *13*.

SAWAYA & MORONI: 123, 124, 127, 140.

SCARPA, CARLO: 274.

SHIRE, PETER: *20*, 35, 36, *38*, 39, *54, 55*, 80, 242.

SILVESTRIN, DANILO: 245, 270, 273.

SIMPSON, JOHN: 249.

SIPEK, BORIS: 273.

SITE: *64*, 79.

SOTTSASS, ETTORE: *JACKET FLAP*, *26, 27*, 32, 35, 36, *37*, 39, 42, 47, *56, 60, 61, 62, 63*, 66, 69, 74, 79, 80, 131, 186, *188*, 202, 269, 270, 274.

SOWDEN, GEORGE: 35, 39, *44, 45, 46, 57*, 80, 186, 274.

STARCK, PHILIPPE: 74, 246, 277.

STEIL, LUCIEN: *262, 263*.

STENDIG: *162*.

STERN, ROBERT: 66, 79, 80, 103, 123, *130*, 131, 132, 135, 156, *156, 157, 158, 159, 160, 161*, 186, 273, 274.

STUDIO RAINBOW: 35.

SUNAR: 2, 127, *146, 147*, 221, *223*.

SWID POWELL: *26, 37*, 80, *103*, 108, *109, 120, 121, 126*, 128, 131, 132, *134*, 135, *158, 159, 172, 173, 179*, 183, *185*, 186, *186, 187*, 221, 222, 229, *240*, 241, *241*, 245, 249, 273, 274.

TAUNUS: 241.

TAVEIRA, TOMAS: 242, *243*, 245, 258, *258, 259, 260, 261*.

TECNO: 74.

TENDO: *190*.

THUN, MATTEO: 35, 42, *48, 49*, 74, 197, 245, 246, *247, 252, 253*, 269, 270, *271, 272*, 273, 274, *275*, 277, *280*, 281, 282.

TIGERMAN, STANLEY: 66, 79, 80, *88-89*, 103, 123, 131, 132, *134*, 135, 136, 166, *166, 167, 168, 169, 170, 171, 172, 173, 174, 175, 176, 177*, 186, 269, 270, 273, 274.

TOSO VETRI: 35.

TRAVERTINO ROMANO: *197*, 198, *200, 204*.

TUCNY, PETR: 278.

TURLER (OF ZURICH): *15*.

TUSQUETS, OSCAR: 79, 245, 270.

UMEDA, MASANORI: 35, 47.

UNGERS, OSWALD MATHIAS: *24*, 66, 74, *96, 97, 98, 99, 100, 101*, 242, 274, 277, *280*, 281.

UNION KNOPF: 278.

UP AND UP: 35, 202.

VANDENHOVE, CHARLES: 241.

VEGLA: 277, 282.

VENDRUSCOLO, PIERO AND FRANKLYN GERARD: 242, *250, 251*, 274.

VENTURI, ROBERT: 11, *19*, 25, 27, 28, 31, 32, 35, 65, 66, 79, 80, *84-85, 102*, 103, *103*, 104, *105, 106*, 107, 108, *109*, 110, *110, 111, 112, 113, 114, 115, 116, 117, 118, 119, 120, 121*, 123, 127, 131, 132, 141, 222, 242, 249, 269, 270, 273, 274, 281.

VIGNELLI, MASSIMO AND LELLA: 68, 277.

VIVALDI, MARIO: *269*, 270, 273.

VON KLIER, HANS: 277.

VORWERK: *11*, 128, *154, 280*, 268, 277, 281, 282.

V'SOSKE: 128, *155*.

WARLAMIS, HEIDE: 274, *275* .

WARNEKE, HELMUT: *272*.

WATKINS, DAVID: *73*.

WEBER, ANDREAS: 277.

WILSON, PETER: *190*.

WMF: *244*, 245, 246, *247, 252, 253, 254, 255*, 269, 270, *271, 272*, 273, 274.

WRIGLEY, RICK: *1*.

YAMASHITA, KAZUMASA: 79, *94-95*, 270.

YAMIGINA: *17*.

ZANINI, MARCO: 35, 36, *49, 58*.

ZANOTTA: 269.

ZANUSSI: 74, 246, *248*, 249.

ZEUS: 277.

BASIL AL-BAYATI, *THE TOWER SUITE*, 1987 WARDROBE